Bendhu
and its
builders

Andrew Cowser

ULSTER ARCHITECTURAL
HERITAGE SOCIETY

THIS BOOK IS DEDICATED to the memory of Richard Mac Cullagh, the second custodian and bard of Bendhu, *that wind walled citadel defying Atlantic storms.*

And to my parents, Sybil Clarke and John Cowser, who first brought me to Ballintoy.

First published 2009 by the Ulster Architectural Heritage Society, 66 Donegall Pass, Belfast BT7 1BU

COPYRIGHT
Text © UAHS & Andrew Cowser
Photographs & images © as credited

All rights reserved. No part of this publication may be reproduced, stored in a retrieval system, or transmitted in any form or by any means, electronic, mechanical, photocopying, recording or otherwise, without prior permission in writing of the copyright owners and the publishers.

EDITORS   Karen Latimer &
          Terence Reeves-Smyth
DESIGN   Fishbone Studio Ltd
PRINT   W&G Baird Ltd

PAPERBACK
ISBN 978-0-900457-71-5

A CIP catalogue record for this book is available from the British Library.

COVER PHOTOGRAPH
Aerial view of Bendhu in 1949.
Photo by Anthony CW Merrick

FRONTISPIECE PHOTOGRAPH
Bendhu viewed from Bendoo cove in 2009.
Photo by William Galbraith

Contents

PREFACE	VI
INTRODUCTION	X

NEWTON PENPRASE — 001

1	Redruth	002
2	Belfast & the Art College	014
3	Grasmere Gardens	026
4	An interest in the north Antrim coast	038

THE FIRST 40 YEARS — 049

5	A new site, a new design	050
6	A living work of art	070
7	Recognition & final years	088

THE BATON HANDED ON — 101

8	Richard Mac Cullagh	102
9	Michael & Lorna Ferguson	120
10	Bendhu extended	136

BENDHU IN COLOUR — 149

APPRAISAL — 165

11	Bendhu in its time	166
12	Design elements considered	180
13	End piece	200

APPENDICES — 209

1	Chronology	210
2	Review of artworks	212
3	Transactions with local authority	222

BIBLIOGRAPHY	232
PICTURE CREDITS	236
INDEX	238

Preface

I seem always to have known about Bendhu. My first visit to the barely habitable concrete building, truly a work-of-art in progress, was in the early-1960s. That left a lasting impression, as have subsequent visits to the house in its completed and extended form. For me, visiting Bendhu was my first real experience of engaging with a building, where the structure and its materiality directly communicate something profound: organic yet man-made, unfinished yet very solid, the individual creation of a highly developed artistic personality – Newton Penprase (1888-1978).

Other buildings, both well known and anonymous, in many different places, later enthused me, but Bendhu was the first of these encounters.

Among the pleasant things about researching this book has been the people it has been my good fortune to meet. Bendhu seems to have a special place in the hearts and minds of those who know the building, have worked on its construction, have owned it, or belong to the wider circle of people who are familiar with Bendhu. There is now a great deal of good will towards the building but that was not always the case.

To the present and past owners of Bendhu I would like to express my thanks and admiration – thanks in letting me share the history and progress of Bendhu with them, and high regard for the tenacity with which they, the custodians of the house, and their families have worked in all weathers and conditions, to build and complete the building of Bendhu. My thanks go to:

the family of Newton Penprase (*who spell their surname with a 'z'*) the late Richard Penpraze, and to David and Yvonne Penpraze, for providing information in response to extended query lists, making archive material available, copying memorabilia and answering endless questions.

the late Richard Mac Cullagh and his son Richard MacCullagh (*here, too, there is a difference in the surname used by family members*), and further thanks to daughter Nuala Wade, for much helpful information.

Michael and Lorna Ferguson, for their hospitality and friendship, enthusiasm and encouragement, and generous response to requests for information, visits, and photographs of the building.

I would like to express my thanks to the main funders of the book: the Esme Mitchell Trust, the Marc Fitch Fund, the AE Harvey Charitable Trust, Edward & Primrose Wilson, and the Ulster Architectural Heritage Society (UAHS), and to the private individuals whose donations were critical in making publishing possible.

Particular thanks go to Karen Latimer, who, on behalf of the UAHS, has managed this publishing venture, and acted as principal editor – without her energy, enthusiasm, experience and unfailing support the book would not have happened.

Thanks also to Terence Reeves-Smyth, chair of the UAHS Publications Sub-Committee, whose role as co-editor has been highly supportive.

I would also like to express my appreciation to the following people and organisations:

Sam Bell and his team at Fishbone, who have designed the layout of this book;

Tony Merrick, photographer;

Kim Cooper and her predecessors Terry Knight and Joanna Laing, of the Cornish Studies Library in Redruth, Cornwall;

Professor James Stevens Curl, for reading drafts and generally advising;

Professor Brian Campbell;

Anne Davey Orr, for proof reading, publishing advice and friendship;

David Evans, for deliberation on aesthetic precedent;

Martyn Anglesea, Keeper of Fine Art at the Ulster Museum, for several illuminating discussions, and making available study works on paper from the collection;

Nicola Gordon Bowe for information on the stained-glass artist Wilhelmina Geddes, and discussions on the stained-glass at Bendhu;

staff, students and colleagues of the School of Architecture, Queen's University, Belfast; and to Ivan Ewart and Martyn Boyd at Media Services; Dan Holden at the APIS library at Queen's; Ruth McDowell for transcripts; and to Dee Agnew for secretarial assistance;

Nicholas Allen for comparative plans of the building, notably new computer drawings of Bendhu representing different stages in its history;

The late Sir Charles Brett *(who changed his opinion about Bendhu over the years)* for advice received;

Mike Catto of the University of Ulster, for his always-interesting input on the history and staffing of the College of Art in Belfast;

Robert McKinstry and Joe Fitzgerald, each of whom lent valuable photographic material of Bendhu, from the early- to mid-1960s;

PREFACE VII

Friends in London and Belfast who have supported the project in various ways: Ralph Turner, David Reekie, Sarah Gilson, Eamonn Reid, Shirley Ainger, John MacArthur, and the late David Belchak.

While I have enjoyed much assistance from friends and colleagues in writing this account, I myself am entirely responsible for the content, and for any errors or omissions.

On the matter of dating buildings mentioned in the text, if there is only one date given this is generally the completion date, or near completion date. Where there are two dates, the first denotes the design date or start of the commission, and the second its completion date.

Various terms relating to the word 'modern' are used in the text in connection with 20th century architecture, and these are used with the following meaning:

MODERN - the new, contemporary, of the present (*especially the 20th century*),

embracing present-day ideas and theory, life and technology;

MODERN ARCHITECTURE - architecture that is Modern, contemporary, of its time; typically that developed by the architectural masters of the 20th century; rejecting historical styles; embracing new forms and technology;

MODERN MOVEMENT, AND MODERNISM - a corpus of work that is Modern across many art forms, including architecture;

MODERNE - in architecture, a hybrid style of the 1920s-1930s, partly Modern, but overlaid with other movements that may include Art Deco, inter-war Classicism, and Streamlining;

My uncle, the architect Ben Cowser (1897-1981), has a walk-on part in these proceedings. He designed a house for Newton and his wife Mildred in the 1920s in the Antrim Road area of Belfast, described later. And it was my uncle who, by family tradition, introduced Newton to the North Antrim coast, leading to his interest and later involvement with Ballintoy.

As indicated, the spelling of Newton's surname varies amongst different family members. On occasion Newton Penprase and his father both spelt their surname with a 'z' (*as in Penpraze*). Newton and Mildred signed their wedding vows as Penpraze, resulting in Mildred using that mode of address throughout her life, handed on to their son Richard Penpraze and grandson David. But in everyday life, including his forty-two years at Belfast College of Art, Newton used the appellation Penprase, with an 's'. He was also widely known as 'Pen' by friends and family, colleagues and students – a term of respect and affection that is used in the accounts that follow.

Newton Penprase has been the subject of many stories over the years. A typical tale recounts Penprase with a group of students from the College of Art, walking around Smithfield Market in Belfast. Suddenly Pen noticed a bus going to Ballycastle (*a two hour journey*), and without further ado, and with no prior warning of his intention to travel, rushed to the bus stop and hopped on, to the astonishment of his students.

On another Friday afternoon, he surprised passengers on board the same bus by embarking in Belfast carrying a full bag of cement for the weekend's work. A further tale recounts Pen with another group of students at Bendhu, all of them staying at the house. In the evening Pen suggested they go up to the village for a drink. The students were a little shamefaced about this because Pen was looking pretty scruffy, dressed in old working trousers worn away at the knees. Ever resourceful, Pen took off the trousers and re-dressed, this time with the same trousers worn back to front. At least his bare knees were no longer visible! The students were still a little embarrassed on entering the bar, but to their relief and admiration Pen was welcomed by a number of regulars.

Introduction

This is the story of the building of Bendhu, the unusual house, some would say weird, others wonderful – overlooking the harbour at Ballintoy on the northern Irish coast. It is an odyssey that has lasted for 75 years carried out by three resourceful explorers, all three tenacious and inventive.

The north Antrim coastline is famous for its dramatic scenery, and the village of Ballintoy is typical of other small communities, located in a sheltered vale on the Antrim plateau above the cliffs. The prominent early-19th century parish church of Ballintoy sits in splendid isolation some distance from the village, and marks the start of a winding road leading down to the harbour. Bendhu is the unlikely building – for many years a bare concrete structure – perhaps a war-time structure or, as revealed on closer inspection, a Modernist house, that comes into view towards the end of the harbour descent.

Bendhu was built from the imagination of Newton Penprase, a Cornishman of great energy and spirit, who at the age of forty-seven started construction, changing the design as work proceeded and new opportunities arose, defying Atlantic gales and occasionally the hostility of local people and the authorities. Of unique design, the house defies architectural classification – John Hewitt in his book *Art in Ulster* likened Bendhu to a "Turkish fort assaulted by a cubist task-force". Little surprise then that Bendhu's design, never mind its very existence, has, from the outset, attracted controversy.

The building's present-day exterior of pristine white – characteristic of Modernist houses of the 1930s, the decade in which construction started – differs from what is believed to be the original concept, a house made in concrete with the finished appearance of concrete. For many years the incomplete stained concrete structure polarised public opinion, from friendly curiosity to a degree of ridicule. To this were added ongoing difficulties with the authorities regarding building consents and conforming to byelaws. Sir Charles Brett, in his book *Buildings of County Antrim*, commented that the distressed concrete appearance of Bendhu over such a long period may have single-handedly done more to prevent the acceptance of modern architecture in the north of Ireland than any other single building.

For forty years Newton Penprase was the sole builder of Bendhu, apart from occasional help from local builders. After his passing, the house was held in trust by his family for a short period, and then offered for sale on the open market. Richard Mac Cullagh bought Bendhu in 1979, and was custodian for fifteen years. Describing himself as a Connacht man, he was, like Pen, an artist and educator. Despite significant repairs and alterations carried out during his tenure, Bendhu remained unfinished when Richard sold the building in 1994. The present owners, husband-and-wife team Michael and Lorna Ferguson, deserve the credit for completing the building of Bendhu. Michael Ferguson is by profession a house builder and developer, but has had a lifelong interest in Modern Architecture – an ideal combination of talents with which to tackle Bendhu. He and his wife Lorna have – with expertise, skill, and tenacity – repaired, completed, and extended Bendhu, and brought the building up to current standards of comfort and amenity.

So the story of Bendhu rightly includes these later custodians – remarkable individuals who fell in love with the building and the locale of Ballintoy harbour. Despite many practical difficulties, Mac Cullagh and the Fergusons found the project inspiring, and accepted the challenge of working with Newton Penprase's creation.

I have already declared a personal interest in Bendhu, going back to the early 1960s, when I first visited Bendhu with my mother and father. In those days the house was commonly referred to as Pen's Folly. We made the visit on a glorious sunny day, and Newton and his wife Mildred made us afternoon tea, seated on the external steps on the west side of the house. I remember thinking that I had never seen anything like Bendhu before; I was fascinated by the sculptural quality of the concrete, its materiality from being cast in a mould, and by the panels of stained-glass let into the structure. My mother mentioned casually that I was studying art at school, whereupon Mildred, a former student of Pen's at Belfast School of Art, said wistfully "Ah ... Art", holding a long pause while looking out to sea, "taking the abstract from nature and putting it down on paper." That profound definition stayed with me for many years.

But why should Bendhu attract our interest now, seventy-five years since the first foundations were laid? It is certainly a building that captures the imagination, intriguing young and old alike, and attracting new friends and supporters in the twenty-first century. The building has now been featured on national television several times, and been of interest to groups such as the Twentieth Century Society, who, in their visit in 2007 declared Bendhu to be a highlight of their architectural tour. This book seeks to extend that dialogue, by discussing Bendhu and its builders in the context of Modern Architecture, locally and abroad, in the 20th century.

Newton Penprase

REDRUTH

BELFAST & THE
ART COLLEGE

GRASMERE
GARDENS

AN INTEREST IN
THE NORTH
ANTRIM COAST

1 Redruth

The Cornish town of Redruth is situated in the eastern part of a once prosperous mining district, midway between Truro and St Ives. Until the beginning of the 18th century it was a small market village but with the advent of copper extraction the town expanded to become one of the leading mining centres in Cornwall. It was here that Newton Herbert Penprase was born on 23 March 1888, one of five children born to Richard and Susan Penprase.[1]

His father was a decorative painter[2] well known for his work in local churches. In 1891 the family, six in all – three sons, an aunt, the parents (it was before the birth of two sisters) – lived at No 7 Blight's Row in Redruth.[3]

The name Redruth comes from its Cornish roots (rhyd = ford or shallow river, ruth = red) and refers to the iron oxide seeping out of mineral workings, colouring the local streams and rivers. With the neighbourhood town of Camborne, Redruth was the centre of a tin and copper mining industry of national importance, at one time the largest and richest metal mining area in Britain. The industry was in serious decline by Newton's childhood, although a maze of chimney stacks and engine houses still dotted the Cornish landscape of the turn of the century.

The railway age came to Redruth in the late 1830s, joining up with the West Cornwall Railway that, twenty years on, linked Redruth with Penzance and Truro. The system later became part of the Great Western Railway connecting London Paddington to Penzance. The viaduct that bestrides Redruth so dramatically today, built of stone and iron in 1888, replaced Isambard Kingdom Brunel's earlier structure in timber construction.

1.1

1.1
Blight's Row,
Redruth: Newton
Penprase's birthplace

1.2
Newton Penprase,
1905, aged 17

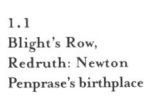

1.2

Redruth sits in close physical proximity to the granite hills of Carn Brea, which has the remains of one of the oldest human settlements in Cornwall. The 46-acre Neolithic hill fort was an important prehistoric gathering place. By the Middle Ages mining for metals was established, and by the 18th and early-19th centuries, some of the deepest and most intensive mining in Cornwall took place in the Carn Brea foothills. Even today climbing the steep ascent is a dramatic experience, offering panoramic views from the summit to St Michael's Mount in the west, and Devonshire in the east. On the plateau, giant granite boulders dwarf the human scale, as does the 90ft-high granite monolith erected by public subscription to the local landowner, Lord de Dunstanville, which stands overlooking the land and mine workings he once owned. Additionally a small 'castle', a one-time hunting lodge (much altered over the centuries) has survived; this will reappear later in the Bendhu story.

A recent account of Redruth and the surrounding area describes the importance of the mining industry:

It was the deep mining of copper [that] raised Redruth's status to ... capital of the largest and richest metal mining area in Britain. At the peak of production in the 1850s, two-thirds of the world's copper came from Cornwall ... Tin mining had employed relatively few people, but copper mining was labour intensive. The population of Redruth and the nearby villages greatly increased.[4]

1.3

Working conditions were dangerous, and despite fortunes made by owners conditions in the mines were grim:

Accidents were frequent, and there were many deaths. Life was cheap. The average lifespan of the miners was under forty. Women worked on the surface handling the ore as bal-maidens,[5] and children started work as young as eight. Most mining families were desperately poor ... Riots against wage-cuts, working conditions and redundancies were common, drunkenness, brawling and vice endemic. In this atmosphere, similar to that of the Klondike frontier towns, the mining communities were a fertile recruiting ground for early Methodists and Chartist groups.[6]

The long decline, brought about by international competition, began in the 1860s. Twenty years later, two-thirds of Cornish miners had

1.3
Carn Brea castle

1.4
Portrait of a miner, by Newton Penprase, undated

1.5
Newton Penprase's parents: Richard Henry Penprase & Susan Ann Dunstan

OVERLEAF
Geevor mine at Pendeen, closed in the 1990s, now a mining heritage centre run by Cornwall Council

emigrated to mining centres in the Americas, Australasia and South Africa. Against this environment of hardship, Newton Penprase spent his formative years in Redruth, but the young man seemed happy enough developing his own interests and skills.

In his early teens Newton Penprase enrolled at the Redruth School of Mines,[7] not to train in mining or engineering, but to attend the "Art side attached to the School under the able conduct of Mr H.C.Wallis".[8] Wallis, as art master, was to be an important influence on the young man, and it was probably his encouragement that prompted Newton to submit examples of his work to the 1902 Exhibition of the Royal Cornwall Polytechnic Society in Falmouth. Under the heading *Work submitted by the Redruth School of Art*, Penprase is credited with six items including a *Group of Models* and *Shaded Ornament*, the latter highly commended. The catalogue lists him as being twelve years of age, an early recognition of talent, and probably indicating that these works had been produced before he attended the School of Mines. At the same event in 1906, Penprase again exhibited – this time under the heading *Amateur Oil* – two paintings entitled *Wheel*, and *Tresidder's Farm*.[9]

We may speculate as to whether Penprase had any training in building construction at the School of Mines. The School premises on Clinton Road were shared by both the mining and art courses, and pupils would have been aware of the other subjects being taught. His two brothers, Richard John Penprase who was two years older and William Hogarth Penprase who was three years younger, both trained in mining before emigrating to the USA to seek work in the New World. Contemporary records show the curriculum of the Redruth School of Mining included subjects such as assaying,[10] mine and land surveying, geology, mineralogy, mine engineering, mathematics, mechanics, steam physics, and building construction.[11] If the practical techniques involved in these subjects were accessible to students on the art side of the School, they would conceivably have been useful to Newton in his future building ventures.

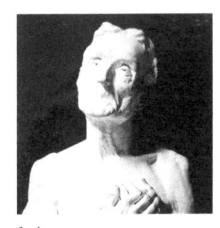

1.4

1.5

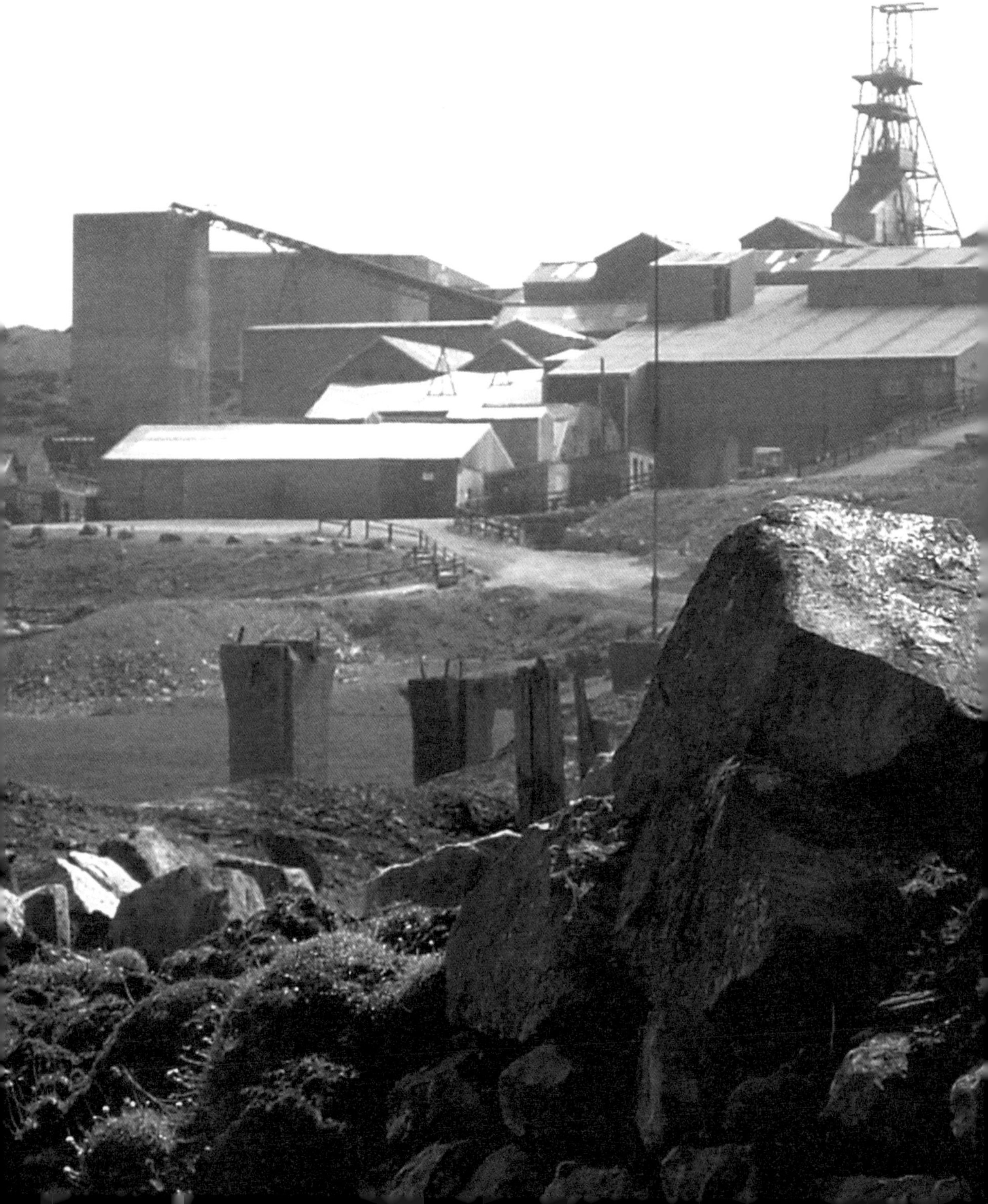

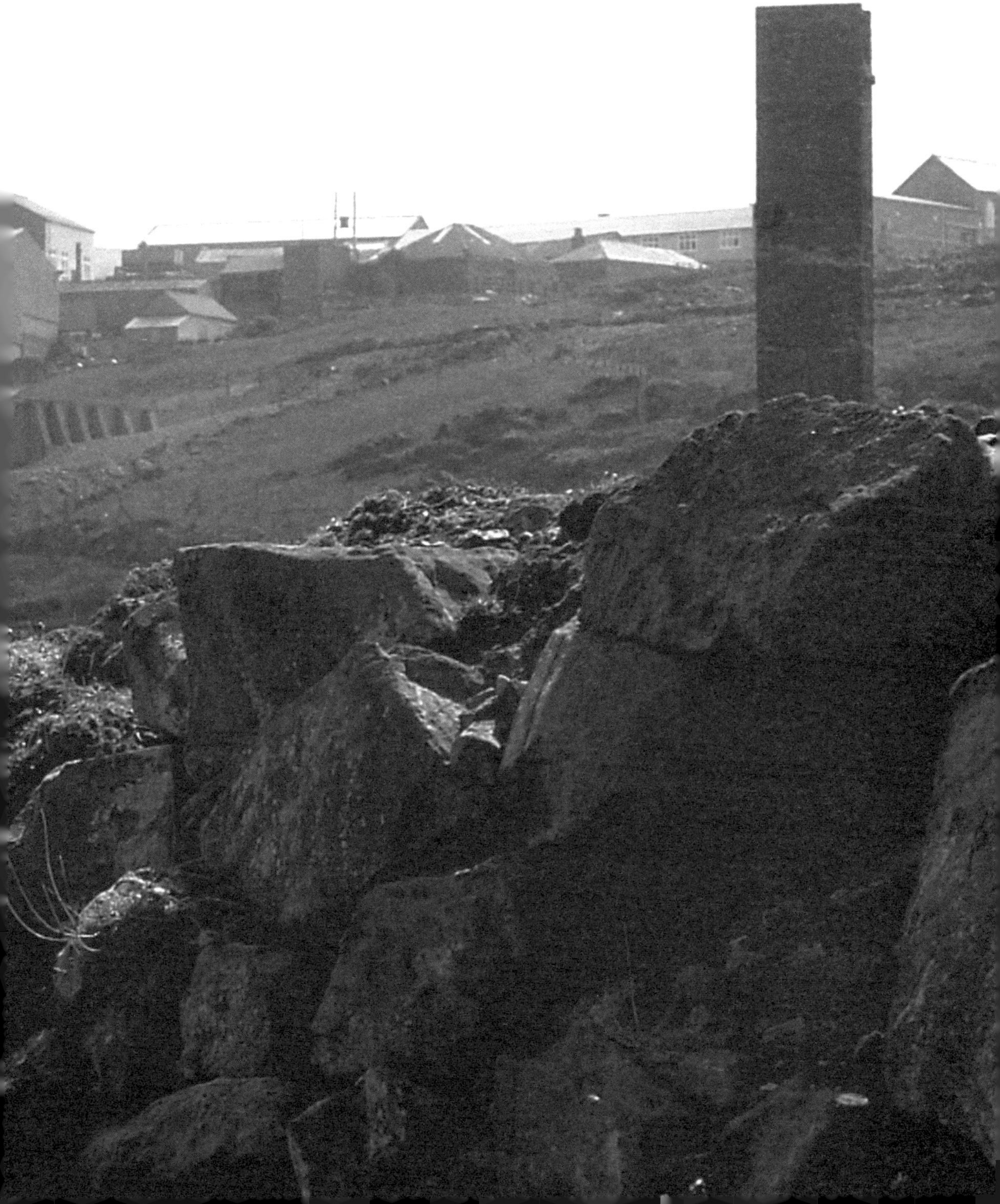

A photograph of Newton Penprase's sculpture *Portrait of a Miner*[12] survives from this time. Modelled from life, it depicts a weather-beaten face and upper body reflecting the tough life underground, showing both sensitivity and a degree of pathos for the subject.

A major influence on Newton was his father, Richard Henry Penprase. He was of stocky build like his son, about 5ft 3in tall, and something of a character. He was proficient in taxidermy, and was an accomplished tap-dancer and musician reputed to play a mean fiddle.[13] He was also an accomplished artist and watercolourist.[14] Penprase senior was prominent in the Plymouth Brethren community in Redruth, a side of life over which he and Newton reportedly fell out, and possibly one of the reasons for Newton leaving Cornwall.

In his youth Newton accompanied his father to the churches where he worked as painter and decorator. The story is told about one occasion when his father was obliged to mix paints that were to be an exact match of the existing colour of the church ceiling. Without ceremony, his father lay down on his back in the centre of the nave, and for half an hour without a word intently studied the ceiling colours; later that day he had mixed paint that was an exact match of the colours required, having combined the pigments from observation and memory. Apocryphal though this tale may be, it indicates that Newton's father had, quite possibly, exceptional talent as artist and colourist.

While his father was working, Newton devoted his time to sketching. He was especially good at making drawings of church decoration, including the wood carving of pulpits and choir-stalls, church-plate and silverware. The highly finished presentation drawings that survive indicate that he must have made preliminary sketches, and taken measurements and notes within the churches, of the fitments and objects that caught his attention. This preparatory information was then translated into true-to-

1.6–1.7
Disused engine-
house in 2006,
Cornwall

1.8–1.9
Mid-19th century
views of Redruth,
town and
mining-works

1.9

scale drawings and coloured renderings, drawn up later in the art classroom of the School of Mines, or at home. The finished presentation boards are typically 61cm x 81cm, and are highly accomplished in the standard of draughtsmanship, accuracy of survey, and near photographic quality in rendering three-dimensional objects.

Three of these panels were entered for the National Competition of the Board of Education at South Kensington in 1904, when Newton was 15 years of age. They depict the oak pulpit and wood-carving from St Martin's Church, Camborne, and are executed in ink and colour wash on light-cream coloured board, annotated "from actual measurement", the school stamp confirming Newton Penprase as artist, age 15. These three panels were awarded a National Book Prize by the Board of Education at South Kensington. In the following year, 1905, Penprase consolidated his achievement by winning further prizes in the same competition – another National Book prize, and the prestigious Gold Medal, one of only nine awarded that year to art school students throughout the British Isles.

The Gold Medal was awarded for two drawings showing a selection of antique silverware from Cornish Churches. Drawn in ink and colourwash, with white highlights on grey board, the drawings are signed and dated Newton Penprase 1905, age 16. The silverware illustrated includes chalices, a tazza[15] and an apostle spoon, all drawn at full scale, with some twice-full-size details from St Stithians, St Weldon, St Mabe, Perran-an-Worthall, Abbey Lelant, St Ives, and Penryn – all Cornish churches. The examiner's report records that "a Gold Medal is awarded to Newton Penprase of Redruth School of Art, for a well-chosen set of studies of historic silverwork in Cornwall. The work is well presented both as regards its execution and the necessary explanatory details and sections. The examiners are glad to note that all the examples shown appear to have been studied from objects existing in the locality".[16]

In the following year, 1906, Penprase consolidated his achievement by winning the Silver Medal of the Royal Cornwall Polytechnic Society for the same sheets of drawings.[17]

The prime mover in encouraging Penprase to enter work for these awards and competitions was his art master Mr H.C.Wallis. It was Wallis, as sponsor for his pupil, who made the hand-written declaration (on each prize-winning sheet) that "the drawings had been undertaken by the student under his sole and personal supervision".[18]

The four other drawings that received a Book Prize in 1905 are arguably the finest, with their astonishing three-dimensional clarity, depicting oak-carving from another set of Cornish churches: Leven, Zennor, Gwinear, Lelant, Perranzabuloe, Madron, St Ives, and St Andrews. The Victoria & Albert Museum purchased all nine drawings by Penprase as examples of prize-winning student work for the years in question, as was their custom at this time.[19]

Winning the Gold Medal and having his work purchased by a national museum in London must have boosted Newton Penprase's confidence. Early talent and recognition augured well for his career ahead, but here, alas, there is a break in

1.10

1.11

1.10
One of two drawings of church silverware, by Newton Penprase, for which the Gold Medal was awarded in 1905

1.11–1.12
Details from drawings of church silverware, by Newton Penprase

1.13
Capital of a column "designed and executed in Marble"

our story. How he spent his time, and where, for the next few years is a mystery.

If Penprase left the School of Art in Redruth in 1905 or 1906, he would have been 17 or 18 years of age. What he did in the intervening five or six years, before arriving in Ireland in the autumn of 1911, is largely unknown. Usually a formative time in a young person's life there are few clues as to how Newton spent these years. Mining in Cornwall was in steep decline, and his brothers had emigrated to the USA. He may have continued working with his father in the decoration and refurbishment of churches, but this is supposition.

1.12

1.13

There is some evidence that Penprase continued sculpting and drawing in the years between 1906 and 1911, and for part of this time at least was in Redruth. He was the recipient of a further Book Prize won in the National Competition of 1910, for *Modelled designs based on a flowering plant*,[20] and in the list of awards Penprase is recorded as still being a student at the Redruth School of Art (School No 163 in the Competition). Modelled designs seems to indicate sculpture or three-dimensional relief work of some sort. This is compatible with a photograph depicting the capital of a column "designed and executed in Marble", the photograph signed Newton H Penprase. The marble capital is, architecturally, a hybrid design of no recognisable style, based neither on the acanthus leaf of the Corinthian order, nor on any other obvious precedent. The marble carving, of which only the photograph survives, was 33cm high, and

1.14 1.15 1.16 1.17

1.14–1.17
Details from drawings depicting wood carving in Cornish churches, by Newton Penprase

labelled and dated "part of a set for which a book prize was awarded 1910".[21] This indicates that Penprase was still at the School of Mines in some capacity, as student, assistant teacher or assistant master, at least in the immediate period before coming to Ireland.

In his later years, on one occasion, Newton maintained that he had trained as an architect in his youth, but had not enjoyed office work and had therefore abandoned the notion of architecture as a career.[22] If this were true his apprenticeship to an architect's office would have taken place sometime in the years 1905-1911. The extent of any formal training in architecture, if any, is discussed in more detail in later chapters.

There has been speculation in Penprase's family that he came to London during this period and was enrolled at the Slade School of Art, but enquiries at University College London and the Slade have drawn a blank; there is no record of his enrolment. Neither are there any drawings, paintings, or artworks depicting life in London, or reference to the city in his private papers, that might indicate time spent in the capital. In any event, Newton Penprase arrived in Belfast in the autumn of 1911.

ENDNOTES

1. Richard Henry Penprase (1859-1956) married Susan Ann Dunstan in 1885.

2. Recorded in the 1891 Census, Public Record Office, Ref: RG12/1847. The Census lists Richard H(enry) Penprase, age 32, as a Decorative Painter.

3. Idem, 1891 Census. The 1911 Census lists Newton and his parents residing at 9 Blights Row, Redruth.

4. www.cornwall-online.co.uk/kerrier/redruth.htm (Accessed 6 February 2009).

5. Bal Maidens - the word Bal being ancient Cornish for mining place; in the mid-1800s there were approximately 6000 Bal Maidens working in Cornish mining – see www.balmaiden.co.uk (Accessed 6 February 2009).

6. www.cornwall-online.co.uk/kerrier/redruth.htm (Accessed 6 February 2009).

7. The School of Mines was originally called the School of Science and Art, the name incised in stone above the School entrance fronting Clinton Road, Redruth.

8. Peter (1904).

9. This time with the correct spelling of his name, Newton H. Penprase.

10. Assaying – analysing the purity of an ore or precious metal.

11. Peter op.cit.

12. Compare with terracotta bust *Tired-out*, Appendix 2.

13. Source: David Penpraze.

14. Surviving examples include watercolours of St Michael's Mount, Penzance, and Carn Brea, Redruth.

15. Tazza – an ornamental vessel, that has a shallow bowl, mounted on a pedestal.

16. Board of Education (1905).

17. *Cornubrian* newspaper, 15 Sept 1906, p 4, col 3.

18. Annotation to the drawings listed in the next note.

19. V&A Printroom reference nos. for the nine drawings purchased by the Museum:

    D1711-13/1904: 3 drawings of pulpit, plans and elevation (bookmark C.C.9a).

    D552-3/1905: 2 drawings of silverwork (bookmark M.115).

    D554-7/1905: 4 drawings of wood carving (bookmark W.18).

    The V&A received from Newton Penprase 'Measured drawings of a carved oak pulpit' on 10th October 1904; and 'Drawings of antique' on 20th November 1905.

20. Board of Education (1910).

21. The style of the label is similar to other labels attached to the drawings held by the Victoria & Albert Museum.

22. Larmour (1973).

2 Belfast & the Art College

Penprase took up his teaching appointment as Assistant Art Master at the Belfast School of Art on 1 October 1911. He was 23 years of age, and he remained at the School, which was part of the Municipal Technical Institute, for the next 42 years until his retirement in 1953. Within the often insecure world of art, Penprase had secured himself an enviably stable career, which was salaried at the princely starting rate of £120 per annum.

As discussed in the previous chapter, what he had been doing in the immediate years before coming to Belfast is speculation. The art historian and author Mike Catto has outlined some possibilities:

Penprase once told James Warwick[1] that he "travelled and studied the Old Masters". At that period, many people working in Art colleges would have had no formal qualifications. Many colleges did not offer full-time study, and even when they did, the hangover from the South Kensington centralised system of teaching across UK schools put students through Subjects, not Courses. As late as the 1940s, the College of Art in Belfast, in line with many regional colleges gave students Certificates of Proficiency [Drawing from Life, Drawing from the Antique, 3D Modeling, etc] for each subject at each level. Cumulatively, these slips of paper, often known as Class Tickets added up to proficiency and were, along with the all-important portfolio, the key to further study or employment ... So, Pen probably got his job on the strength of his Class Tickets and a bloody good folio of work ... particularly drawing. In 1911 [at the Belfast School of Art] ... full time [male] staff were formally known as Teachers or Masters, not as Lecturers. Nearly all the Teaching Assistants were female ... As for subjects, they all taught everything, and

2.1

2.1
Municipal Technical
College, Belfast:
exterior view

at all levels ... I do mean EVERYTHING *... I spoke once to a student from the late 1930s who, unsurprisingly, remembered that Mr Penprase taught his own weird, wonderful and totally subjective version of Art and Architectural History.*[2]

The Municipal Technical Institute, occupied the new building designed by Belfast architect Samuel Stevenson. It had opened in 1907, a couple of years after the completion of another Edwardian tour de force, the Belfast City Hall. The 'Tech', as it became known, was constructed in a monumental Classical style on the north-east corner of College Square, occupying half the front lawn of the building next door, the Royal Belfast Academical Institution (or 'Inst'). The school had for many years housed the nascent School of Art in its north wing, but by the turn of the century was in financial difficulties and obliged to raise capital. Hiding a good part of John Soane's 'Inst' façade, the overwhelming scale of the 'Tech' in relation to its surroundings has always been controversial.[3] It was to this recently completed behemoth housing the Municipal Technical Institute that the young Newton Penprase came to work.

An additional storey had been added to the 'Tech' during construction, with large studios built on the north side of the building. The Art School occupied this floor and the one below, in twenty-six rooms. The accommodation was reported to be either too hot or too cold for most of the year, the result of lofty ceilings, poor insulation, vast windows and a rudimentary heating system, but the studio spaces did have excellent daylighting and a generous allocation of space. The School of Art housed plaster-casts of Classical sculpture, some of enormous size. These stood sentinel in the corridors of the School till the mid-1960s, when the Belfast College of Art, as it had been renamed, moved to York Street, soon to become part of the University of Ulster.[4]

2.2

Mike Catto has documented the life and times of the Belfast College of Art,[5] discussing the curriculum and the many roles that a limited number of teachers had to fulfil. Throughout its history the College of Art has produced "far more practitioners of design and the applied arts than it has painters and sculptors".[6] The biggest number of students attended evening classes, and by the mid-20th century the range of subjects included:

Drawing and Painting; Printed Fabrics; Woven Fabrics; Silver and Jewellery; Pottery and Terra Cotta; Stone and Wood Carving; Dress Making and Embroidery; Stained Glass; Etching and Wood Engraving; Painting and Decorating; Lettering; Writing and Illumination; Printing and Book Production; Commercial Design; Furniture ... Teachers were expected to do 54 hours contact teaching per week, for 36 weeks in the year. On top of this they organise[d] trips and exhibitions, put on plays and pageants and ran weekend and vacation sketching courses.[7]

2.2
Plaster casts of Classical sculpture, Art Department 1910

2.3
Municipal Technical College, Belfast: North facing studios

OVERLEAF
Staff of the Belfast College of Art. Standing: Edward Mansfield, John Luke, Seamus Stoupe, Edward Marr, William Murray. Seated: James Dibble, Fred Allen, Ivor Beaumont, unknown, Newton Penprase

Though Catto is here discussing the range of subjects studied in the early 1950s, the long working hours had not substantially changed since the beginning of the 20th century. There were admittedly fewer students in the earlier period, but also proportionally fewer teachers and assistants; Penprase's own correspondence suggests that the demands were just as onerous in the 1920s and 1930s.

John Hewitt records Pen's lifelong fascination with how things are made and the techniques of making – skills that would stand him in good stead at Bendhu: "[Penprase] remained for forty-two years [at the College of Art] enlarging the range of crafts he already possessed: wood-turning, metal casting, designing a vertical loom when he had mastered the technique of damask weaving; [he was] a superlative instructor in the science of perspective".[8]

Rowel Friers (1920-1998), best known for his career as a cartoonist, was another former student with fond memories of Penprase. He found that Pen's great quality was "in encouraging us to draw well – on our instincts. He told me not to rough out sketches but start in detail and keep the desired end in the mind's eye".[9] Friers describes the atmosphere in the College of Art during the 1940s, and provides a pen-portrait of student life on a typical day:

2.3

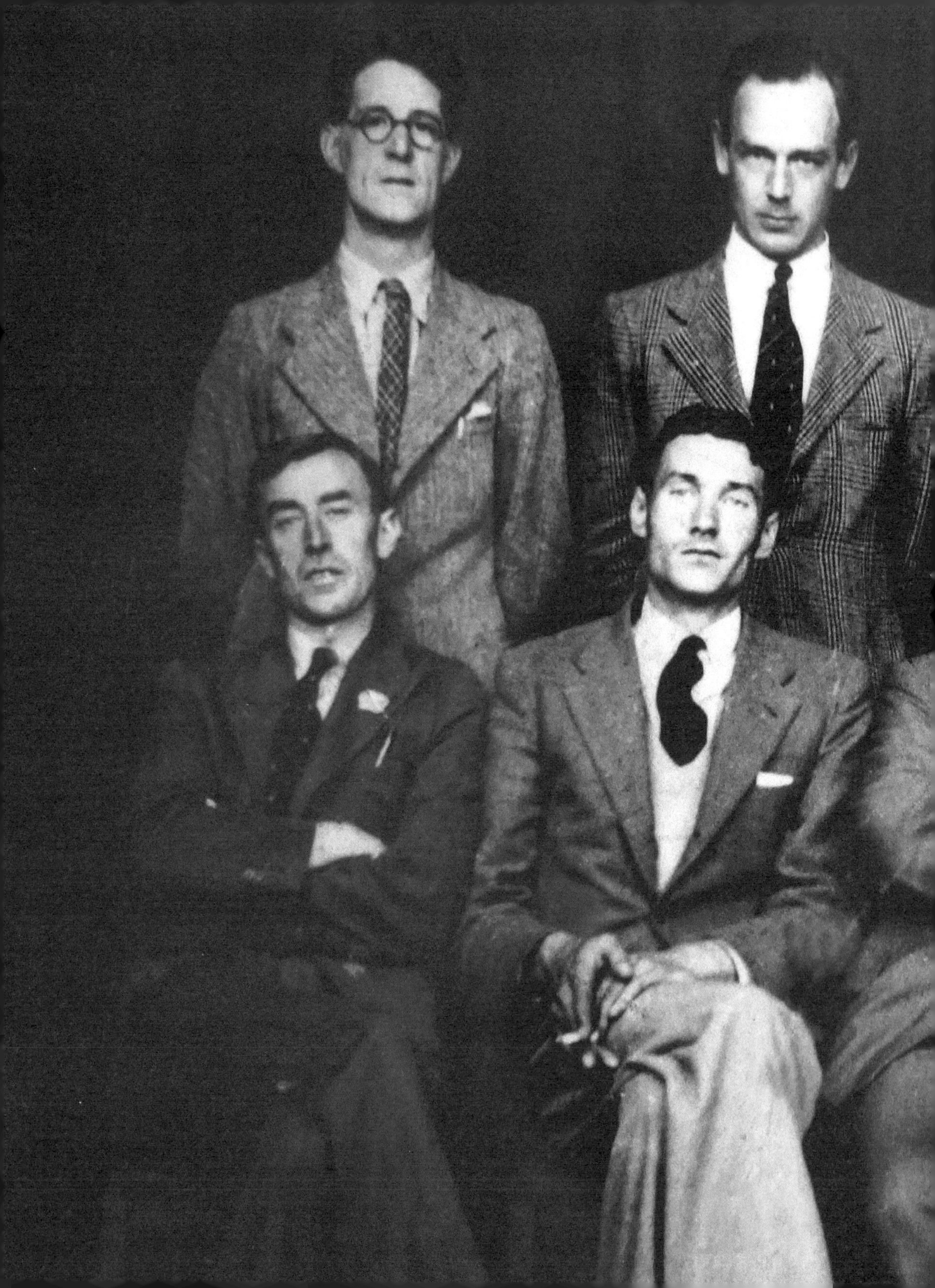

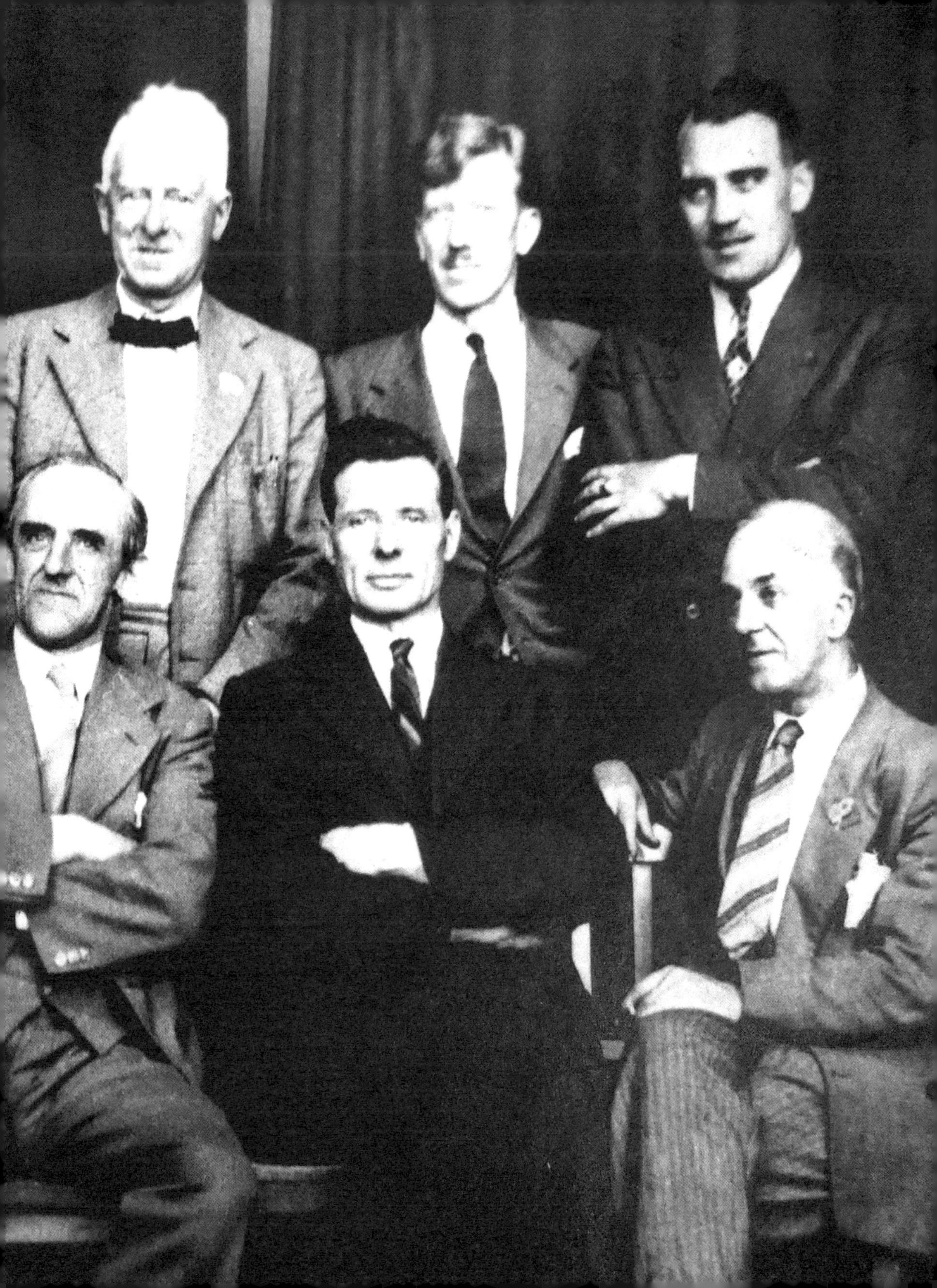

As you entered the hallowed portals, to the right was an aperture in the wall from whence an inquisitive face [of the janitor] would peer. This was where you purchased your requirements for the day ahead – large sheets of cartridge paper for a penny, pencils, rubbers, anything you needed, at prices which, when you look back, seem untrue. Having collected the essentials ... the fittest of us would race up the stone stairway to the top floor. The less fit ... would head for the lift. There were often mad impulses to race the lift to the top, a feat which was accomplished quite regularly without any losses, other than that of breath.[10]

Rowel Friers gives credit to Newton Penprase as an exceptional teacher:

The natural forms class, where you drew or painted plants, flowers, birds and animals, consisted of two students – Raymond [Piper] and myself. The lecturer was Newton Penprase, and we had the great good fortune to have the full benefit of his outstanding abilities as a teacher. It was he who made us aware of the range of colour you could get with a pencil alone, colour created by sensitivity of touch, a delicate line drawn with minimum pressure for where the light was hitting your object, then the pressure increasing for the areas in shade. A flower would be drawn in line only, yet it could have dimension, light and shade. Pen had that knack of making you think with the pencil, so much so that your fingers became as deft as those of a flute player. To draw a bird or an animal, he would not permit you to rough the subject out beforehand. 'No, boy,' he would say, 'study the form, keep it locked in your mind. Then start from its eye, tail or wherever you please, drawing it hair-by-hair, or feather-by-feather. You have a sure line, so draw without hesitation, keeping the whole shape in mind, and though you may, in the first few attempts, go a little awry, you will master it in no time, I assure you ...' At that time it seemed all wrong, because we had roughed everything out in other classes. However, he proved to be right, and for both Piper and myself he created a confidence in approach that has proved invaluable.[11]

The headmaster of the School of Art was Ivor Beaumont,[12] who loomed large in Penprase's life over the years:

Ivor Beaumont was a small man with bushy eyebrows which met in a perpetual frown over his nose ... He had the sharp

2.4

2.5

eyes of an owl, and his beaked nose, which shaded a tight mouth and a slightly jutted, but rounded chin, made him resemble even more closely that bird of the night ... His temper was not on a long fuse.[13]

Newton Penprase himself is characterised by Friers:

... equally small, and what hair he had looked like a grey laurel wreath ... He too had bushy eyebrows, shading sharp blue, but kindly, eyes. He hummed to himself as he skimmed along the corridors. Although he usually appeared to be of a most happy disposition, he could erupt like a volcano without warning. Fortunately, it never happened with his students, but quite often with his sparring partner, Mr Beaumont. An antipathy existed between the two that often resulted in battles royal.[14]

Penprase had many disputes with Beaumont, who had joined the staff in 1919, the disputes often to do with the unequal teaching loads required of Penprase, Beaumont being adept at off-loading additional duties, as indeed his role as headmaster might require. Friers recalls:

Loud, even hair-raising, noises would issue from the headmaster's office, echoing and re-echoing round the hard marble-floored corridors. Students and lecturers would get offside and feign deafness. When the protagonists eventually put in appearances at their various classes, the scenes of battle, although obvious, would go unnoticed by everyone. Familiarity had bred consent.[15]

The annual Arts Ball of Belfast College of Art was held every January.[16] Teachers and students transformed the Great Hall of the College with decorations and

2.4–2.5
Cartoons of 'the Life Class', & Ivor Beaumont,
by Rowel Friers

constructions, and the student revellers were similarly transformed in fancy dress on the night of the dance. In 1931 the theme for the Arts Ball was The Ocean Bed, or Davey Jones' Locker under the Sea. The Belfast News-Letter reporting that "too much praise could scarcely be accorded to Mr Penprase, who, as usual, was largely responsible for the arrangements …"[17] and goes on to describe the 'Tech' transformed with paintings of mermaids, sea serpents, unusual varieties of fish, and a ship wreck. The following year, 1932, the theme was Ghosts and the Supernatural. Held on Saturday 23 January, this particular Arts Ball seems to have had less input by Penprase, but nonetheless was the occasion of a major altercation between himself and Ivor Beaumont. Beaumont had approved the transformation of the Central Hall (by staff and students) with representations of ghosts, spooks, wraiths, and witches, but curiously the decorations included a life-size caricature of a well-known member of staff, easily identified as Newton Penprase. Penprase maintained that he had been insulted, not by the caricature in itself, but by his depiction as sham justice, as witness the out-of-balance scales held in the left hand. Symbolically, honourable justice would have shown balanced scales in the right hand. Moreover, the head of the figure was "probably not painted by a student" – the clear implication, though not stated, that it had been directed by, if not painted by, Ivor Beaumont. Beaumont contested that any insult had been intended, but did not deny supervising the student decorations. Penprase saw his opponent on the morning of the event, and at the end of a heated debate struck Ivor Beaumont. Far from being the aggressive act that it might appear, Newton claimed that what he had done was in self-defence, the headmaster having pushed him towards the door of his office to make him leave; Beaumont had then raised his hand as if to strike, and Penprase had, intuitively, struck first. Penprase refused to apologise in the days that followed, and was stood down by the "Gentlemen of the Committee of Technology".[18] To keep his job he was required to write a formal note of apology to Beaumont, which he did with outward good grace, in a letter dated 10 February 1932. The following day a letter from the Principal reinstated Penprase in post.

For both young and established artists in Ulster there were limited opportunities for exhibiting art in a public gallery in the first

2.6
Cartoon of Newton
Penprase,
by Rowel Friers

"MORNING DEAR"!
2.6

half of the 20th century. Belfast was the natural focus, as the largest city, though the local press periodically lamented the lack of gallery space for displaying painting and sculpture, comparing the provision for the visual arts unfavourably with venues available for performing music, literature, and drama. The Belfast Art Society was founded in 1890 and grew out of artists' rambling clubs, popular in the latter part of the 19th century, typically running weekend visits to places of scenic beauty such as the Mournes and the Glens of Antrim. The Society was open to both professional artists and amateurs, encouraging painting and sketching *en plein air*. It continued until 1930, a year after the new Belfast Museum and Gallery opened at Stranmillis. Thereafter the Society was reformed as the Ulster Academy of Arts, existing in this format from 1930 to 1950, when it was granted its present-day charter, the Royal Ulster Academy of Arts (RUA).

Central to all these manifestations, whether as Society or Academy, was the annual exhibition of members' work, sometimes supplemented by an additional winter or spring exhibition, with the dual benefit of exhibiting artists' work before their peers, and to the public – to whom it was usually, but not always, offered for sale.[19]

In February 1915, four years after arriving in Belfast, Newton Penprase was elected a member of the Belfast Art Society. Pen resigned two years later in May 1917 for unknown reasons, perhaps due to responsibilities at the School of Art, or the fact that he had married the year before and had new commitments with the birth of a son. The continuing ravages of the First World War must have thrown a shadow over everyday life. The ethos of the Belfast Art Society is difficult to gauge from this distance but the period that followed – the 1920s – was presided over by individuals who were pillars of the establishment, including Sir John Lavery, the Lords Londonderry and Charlemont, and the Duchess of Abercorn; the Belfast Art Society in the first decades of the century may just have felt too patrician for Penprase, by temperament an outsider.

As if life was not full enough with a busy career and family commitments, Pen took up a new interest in the 1920s – a building venture that started in Belfast but ultimately led to the north Antrim coast.

ENDNOTES

1. Headmaster of the Belfast College of Art 1952-1972.

2. Correspondence with the author.

3. 'Inst' was not the only casualty of the arrival of the Municipal Technical Institute – the latter so dwarfed the early 19th century terraces surrounding College Square, blocking daylight and views of greenery, that the majority of doctors and residents were prompted to move, many to the area south of the city surrounding Queen's College, an area favoured by the professional classes.

4. The plaster casts were all destroyed at this time, being considered outmoded and irrelevant to the teaching of art in the mid-20th century – described in correspondence with James Stevens Curl as "an act of idiotic vandalism".

5. Belfast School of Art renamed the Belfast College of Art as a result of re-organisation in 1920; and further re-named the Ulster College of Art and Design in 1970 with the move to York Street; subsequently part of the Ulster Polytechnic, and then a Faculty, now a School, within the University of Ulster, accommodated within new and expanded buildings in York Street opened in 2007.

6. See essay: "A Normal School?" by Mike Catto, published in *Art and Design Matters* by the University of Ulster, 1994.

7. Idem.

8. Hewitt & Catto (1977).

9. Friers (1994).

10. Idem.

11. Idem.

12. Ivor Beaumont, ARCA, LRIBA, FIBD (Lond.) was head of the Belfast School (later College) of Art 1919-1952.

13. Friers op.cit.

14. Idem.

15. Idem.

16. The Arts Ball was held at the end of the Art College year, in the last week of January, until the end of th 1950s. The handing out of diplomas, the nearest equivalent to graduation, took place each year in late January / early February.

17. *Belfast News-Letter*, 26 January 1931, pp 5,8.

18. This was the Technical Instruction Sub-Committee, who met in the City Hall on 4 February; Penprase was instructed to be in attendance "in case the Committee may wish to see you".

19. For an historical account of the RUA, see Anglesea, (1981).

3 Grasmere Gardens

On 20 January 1916 Newton Penprase married Mildred McNeice,[1] a former student of Belfast School of Art. He was twenty-seven, and she twenty-one. Mildred and her family, including two sisters, lived at Glenburn in Bangor, and she and Newton married at the Registrar's Office in Newtownards, Co Down.[2] Newton signed his name on the marriage certificate with a 'z' – as in Penpraze – and consequently this is the surname adopted by Mildred throughout her married life, and passed on to their son and grandson. Pen's reason for changing the spelling may have been nostalgia for his Cornish roots, or a whim of the moment. He was still Penprase at the Art College, in correspondence and everyday life, and continued with that mode of address for the rest of his days.

The McNeices originally came from Dublin, and claimed kinship with the Belfast-born writer Louis MacNeice (1907-1963), but there seems to have been little, if any, contact between them. Mildred and her immediate family were Jehovah Witnesses – a potentially volatile background for Newton, who had repudiated his father's Plymouth Brethren beliefs, and is reported to have been antipathetic to all religions.[3] Mildred developed a lifelong interest in Egyptology, doubtless inspired, as were many others, by the discovery of Tutankhamen's tomb in 1922. The Belfast Psychic Circle was another interest that developed in the years ahead.

In 1917 Newton and Mildred's first child was born, Richard (Dick) Penpraze.[4] He was partially brought up by two spinster aunts, when Mildred was unwell.[5] In 1923 Mildred's father died, leaving her a small inheritance. There was

3.1

3.1
22 Grasmere
Gardens, Belfast

3.2
Ethel Mildred
McNeice

3.2

sufficient money to contemplate building a house for the family, particularly as this was being encouraged at the time with grants available under the Housing Act (Northern Ireland) of 1923. Grant aid was available for new dwellings, the so called 'subsidy houses', usually bungalows, within a stipulated floor area of between 600-950 sq.ft. The purpose of these grants was to encourage house-building in the private sector, provide homes near places of employment, and to stimulate the economy. Mildred and Newton bought a site on the northern fringe of the city in the Fortwilliam area of Antrim Road, at that time the main arterial route heading north out of Belfast. The architect Ben Cowser prepared plans for the house, and a Section 23 grant was duly made; under the provisions of the Act work had to be completed by 1 April 1925, though this date was subsequently relaxed.

On a first visit[6] to Grasmere Gardens my notes record:

That No 22 is the house of an artist can be surmised from the first approach. Set in a street of redbrick two-and three-storey Edwardian terraces and semis, No 22 is free-standing on a corner plot, a medium-sized double-bay bungalow, white-rendered. With its large expanse of roof and expressive entrance porch, the house is loosely Arts and Crafts in style – with a suggestion of Art Nouveau in detail. There is a generous scale to the house, and an almost tropical feel to the garden.

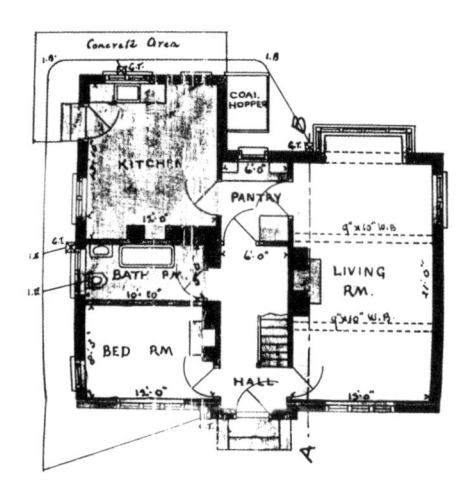

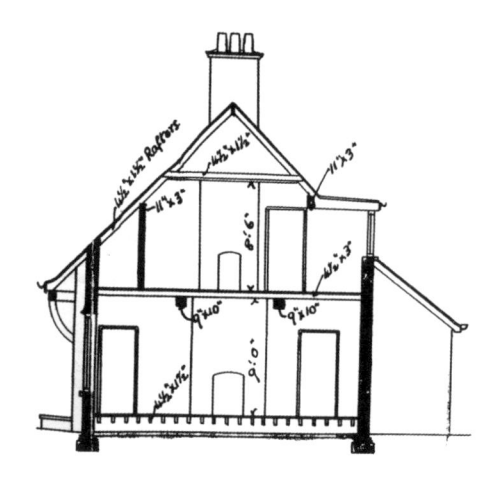

3.3

3.4

The arrangement of the house is typical for a bungalow of the period. The plan has a central entrance hall and staircase leading to two bedrooms constructed within the roof, with downstairs living room occupying one side of the hallway, a further bedroom (used as a study), bathroom, and kitchen on the other side. A double-pitch roof with quarter-hipped gables, and unusual curved brackets supporting the entrance porch, give the house its distinctive character. The fireplace in the living room, still existing, was custom-made and consists of a semi-circular brick arch surround, with a copper-beaten overpanel and mantelshelf above, designed by the architect. Floor traps either side of the hearth were used to store timber and coal for the fire, a provision later repeated at Bendhu. Windows have stained-glass upper panels in the opening lights, a normal feature of such houses, freely interpreted later at

Bendhu. Storage spaces were plentiful on the upper floor, with built-in wardrobes and other storage utilising the eaves space.

While there is no record of Newton Penprase taking part in the actual building of the house, he must surely have followed its construction with interest. But it was Mildred, rather than Pen, who had commissioned the house and presumably paid for the greater part of its cost. The approved building plan is entitled "Cottage Grasmere Gardens for Mrs Penpraze" and signed Mildred Ethel Penpraze, 6 June 1923, approved by the Belfast City Surveyor's office on 28 June. Approvals were still being sought a year later, probably in connection with the grant application: plans for the house were re-submitted and approved in June 1924, signed this time by both Mildred and Newton, certifying that the proposals conformed with the requirements of Section 1 of the Housing Act 1923, Northern Ireland. Newton also counter-signed the drawings a second time, under the words: "through the procrastination of the architect this plan has been neglected". Whether he and Mildred had fallen out completely with their architect, and under what circumstances, is not on record. Construction probably started in 1923, with the approval sought the following year relating only to the release of grant monies, and occupation sometime in 1925. The house is named 'Newlyn',[7] a reference to the Cornish fishing town popular with artists since the 19th century, perhaps another sign of Pen's occasional nostalgia for the county of his birth.

3.3–3.4
Ground floor plan & section, 22 Grasmere Gardens

3.5
Richard (Dick) Penpraze

OVERLEAF
Penprases' house in Belfast at 22 Grasmere Gardens

3.5

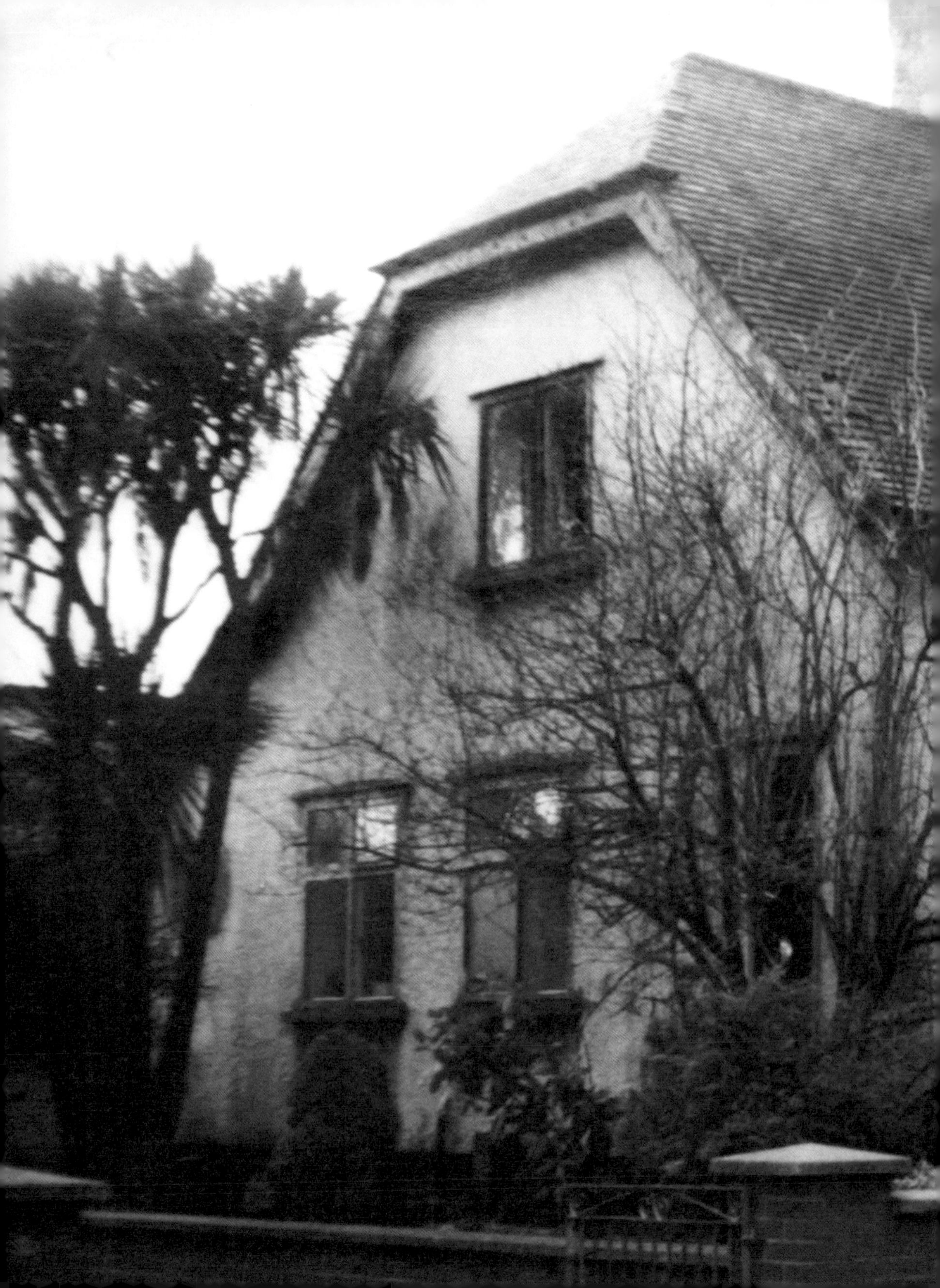

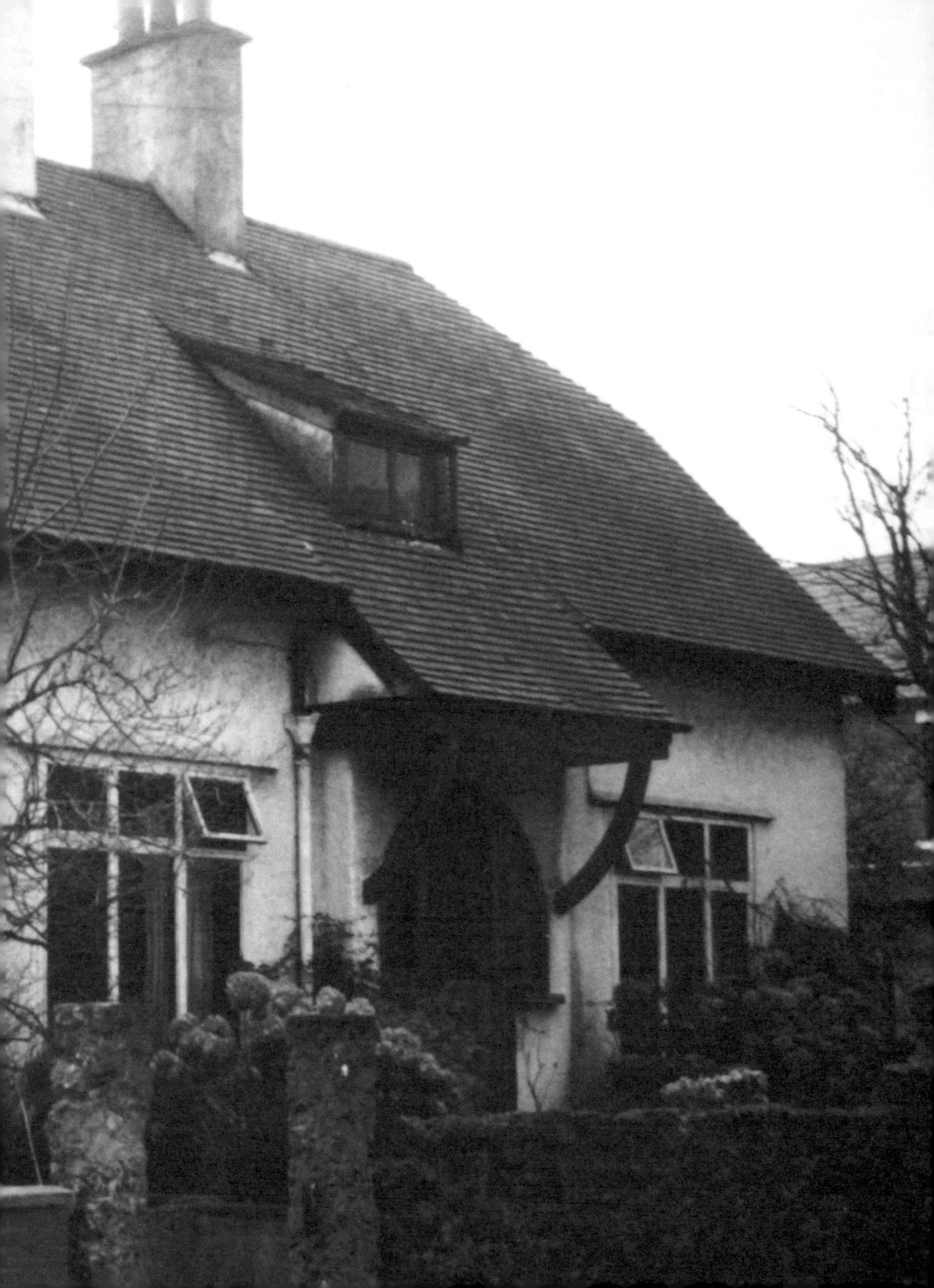

3.6

Newton devoted much of his spare time from the mid-1920s to early 1930s decorating and embellishing the Grasmere Gardens home. The need for furniture led him to make six solidly built dining chairs of quasi-medieval style, carved from mahogany.[8] One of the ground floor rooms, probably the bedroom / study, was decorated with astrological hieroglyphs at cornice level, executed by either Mildred (more probably) or Newton. This decoration no longer exists.

In 1927 a separate garage was added to the house, which in 1930 was extended upwards – with an additional storey for studio room with north-lights, and extra ground floor space for a staircase and ancillaries. This created an independent artist's studio for Pen, a den for his painting and sculpture, separate from the main house. Clearly Newton, rather than Mildred, was the moving force in making the

3.8

3.6
Garden studio,
Grasmere Gardens

3.7
Design A, detail
of a symmetrical
group of figures
surmounting
Cenotaph

3.8
The Cenotaph in
the Remembrance
Garden, Belfast
City Hall

3.7

studio,[9] though whether he took part in its construction is not known. There are Penprase-like details in the design of door and window casements, and in the string-course facing the garden. These indicate a likely involvement by Pen in creating the studio, which may have been a dress-rehearsal for building at Ballintoy a few years later.[10]

While living at 'Newyln', Newton found time to engage in other extra-curricula activities. One of these was taking part in the Belfast Cenotaph competition of 1928, in which he was one of twenty entrants in the event organised by Belfast City Council. The competition was for the design of a sculpture group to complete the topmost part of the Cenotaph, already constructed in the grounds of Belfast City Hall. The competition precedes Pen's building ventures at Ballintoy, and demonstrates his use of Classical symbolism in an architectural setting.

Sir Alfred Brumwell Thomas, the architect for the City Hall which opened in 1906, had added a Garden of Remembrance and Cenotaph to the west of the building in 1925-1927. The Cenotaph was placed at the centre of a semi-circular screen of columns, designed by Thomas in a variant of the Corinthian order, and the construction was in Portland stone. The Cenotaph's form recalls the simplicity and dignity of Lutyens's Whitehall Cenotaph of 1920. The commission was not a good experience for Brumwell Thomas, who worked intermittently

GRASMERE GARDENS 033

on the design of the memorial from 1923 until his resignation in frustration in May 1928. Apart from the recurring differences between the architect and Council on the matter of fees, at issue was the strong desire by many influential persons (who were members of the War Memorial Sub-Committee of Belfast City Council) that there should be some sort of representational sculpture surmounting the Cenotaph.

Various themes were explored, and eventually the idea of a Lion couchant found favour, representing, arguably, strength in repose and the battle over. Despite the efforts of its diligent chairman Sir Frederick Moneypenny, the Sub-Committee was indecisive in choosing a final design. On numerous occasions they asked the architect for fresh ideas and visualisations for the "termination of the Cenotaph", and on almost each occasion Thomas had responded, either by letter from London[11] or by attending the Committee in person, that he had already complied with all the requests from members of Committee, and furnished all necessary sketches and information, sufficient for scaled models (to assist a further assessment) to be made locally. Synergy between the Sub-Committee and the architect was clearly lacking at this time. Meantime the contractor[12] had constructed the Cenotaph to within the topmost section, probably up to the first cornice line, and required instructions for completing the monument.[13]

After Sir Alfred Brumwell Thomas resigned from the enterprise,[14] the Sub-Committee set about holding a design competition for completing the Cenotaph. They invited Mr Arnold Thornely, architect of the new parliament buildings at Stormont, to be the adjudicator. He was favourably disposed to the undertaking, but only under RIBA rules whereby he would act as the sole adjudicator. The Sub-Committee, true to form, wanted the final say in choosing the design and Thornely politely withdrew. Without an adjudicator, the City Council proceeded in November 1928 to offer a prize of £100 for a winning design to complete the Cenotaph, but did not commit itself, necessarily, to award the prize or to implement the winning design. The competition was advertised in the press and

3.9

3.10

3.11

3.9–3.11
Belfast Cenotaph competition, Penprase's Design B for an asymmetrical group of figures, general view and detail

trade journals, the conditions of the competition calling for anonymous submissions. Thirty-two designs were received from the twenty entrants, including four designs from Newton Penprase.[15]

Newton's competition entry, submitted under the *nom de plume* "Innominatum", consisted of four boards each with a different proposal, two of the schemes further illustrated in plaster models that may have been included in the entry. Each competition drawing had a short description explaining the symbolism of the sculptural group proposed, and for Design "A", which depicts a symmetrical group, the commentary reads:

The Sarcophagus surrounded by Earthly & Heavenly Beings – the soldier and sailor – mourning the loss of their comrades. One Angel holds the sword turned downwards – the symbol of peace after war. The second holds the torch the flame ascending, the symbol of renewed Life. The third holds the hourglass representing the passing of Time. The fourth holds the Laurel wreath and Palm branch – Earthly and Heavenly glory respectively.

For Design "B", an asymmetrical composition, the commentary reads:

The sleeping lion without ears and without claws is symbolic of a dead Hero. [He has heard the call and finished the fight]. The lioness with ears alert is the symbol of the Mother Country. The Cubs symbolic

GRASMERE GARDENS   035

of the Colonies. The pillars behind – Unity and Strength – surmounted by the Phoenix representing renewed vigour and resurrection. The flames represent Purity. Placed between the pillars is the Alter of Sacrifice which is decorated with a Ram's head and festooned with the Cultivated Rose, the symbol of Victory over Death. The Urns surmounting the Piers represent Cessation or Dissolution.

Of the thirty-two designs submitted, three were short-listed, including one by Penprase. In the event, the Council vacillating yet again, decided not to go ahead with any of the short-listed proposals, choosing, finally, to dispense with any sculpture or figures for the top of the Cenotaph. By the end of January 1929 they had asked Belfast architects Young and Mackenzie to prepare designs for completing the Cenotaph "with a plain top". In the space of a month new designs and estimates were ready, and work was complete by the end of August. Field Marshall Viscount Allenby officiated at the formal unveiling on Armistice Day 1929.

Penprase seems to have entered into the spirit of the competition happily enough, and been at ease in proposing the sculptural groups illustrated, each with a story-board of symbolic interpretation. The material for the sculpture group was not stipulated, but Design "A" indicates stonework, and Design "B" a casting in bronze. It would have been a major commission had it gone ahead, and the prize money, which in the event was not awarded, was a not inconsiderable sum.

The boldness of his proposals for the Cenotaph competition show that Penprase readily embraced a set-piece architectural setting, but his next building venture would emerge in entirely different surroundings.

3.12
Newton Penprase's driving licence 1927

3.12

ENDNOTES

1. Ethel Mildred McNeice (1894-1975).

2. Mildred's father is described in the Certificate of Marriage as an *agent* – perhaps a land agent for the Glenburn estate. Newton's address is given as 4 Adela Street Belfast (located off the Antrim Road, near Carlisle Circus – within easy walking distance of the Belfast School of Art).

3. Penprase's dislike of contemporary religion was recounted to the author by David Penpraze.

4. William Richard Newton Penpraze (1917-2001). Another child, believed to be a son, was either stillborn or died a few days after birth, some time later.

5. Mildred suffered from severe bouts of depression, sometimes prolonged.

6. The author's first visit was in March / April 1995.

7. 'Newlyn' is carved into the entrance gate, and Penprase used the house name in correspondence.

8. The chairs referred to were exhibited in the Arts Council Exhibition *"All his own Work"* in 1977, (Ex Catalogue).

9. The drawing of the studio submitted to Belfast City Council is dated June 1930, and includes sketches and notes on building materials by Pen.

10. Later their son Richard (Dick) Penpraze together with his wife Marie Goldberg lived in the studio in the early years of their marriage.

11. From his London flat in the Albany, Piccadilly.

12. W J Campbell & Son of Ravenhill Road, Belfast.

13. An account of the proceedings may be traced in Belfast City Council files held at PRONI, reference: LA/7/16BA/2.

14. He was 60 years of age at the time.

15. Amongst the 20 entrants was the sculptress Rosamund Praeger (1867-1954) of Holywood.

4 An interest in the north Antrim coast

In Cornwall one is seldom far from the sea, the landscape ranging from towering cliffs and rocky headlands to gentler coves and beaches warmed by the Gulf Stream. Redruth is 10 miles from Falmouth, 16 from St Ives, and 5 miles by road to the nearest beach and harbour at Portreath. The seaside was thus within striking distance of Penprase's home town. Now based in Belfast, he was, perhaps inevitably, attracted to Ulster's seashore, and specifically to the North Antrim coast, that for grandeur and drama arguably rivals its Celtic counterpart in the toe of England.

Pen's early visits were experienced through camping holidays spent near the wide sweeping beach of White Park Bay.[1] Nearby is the village of Ballintoy, its harbour set amongst giant basalt stacks of dramatic form. Pen by all accounts appreciated the splendour of the setting and its strong affinity with Cornwall, both places having been moulded over millions of years by the forces of geology and the natural environment.

The raised beach at White Park Bay is clearly visible today, and there is evidence of Neolithic settlements in caves along the coast from White Park Bay to Carrick-a-Rede Island and Kinbane Head beyond. On the landward side two dolmens, sited south of the rector's house, Mount Druid, on private land, give further sign of the landscape's ancient history.

4.1

4.1–4.2
White Park Bay &
Ballintoy Port,
Co Antrim

4.2

Ballintoy, in the barony of Cary and on the north coast of Co. Antrim, was part of the huge estate – comprising all four northern baronies in the county – of the MacDonnell family, earls of Antrim. During the first third of the 17th century, Alexander Stewart, the trusted and long-serving (1620 – c.1665) agent to the 1st and 2nd Earls, acquired long leases of extensive lands at Ballintoy and Ballycastle. In the mid-18th century, Stewart's descendant sold this estate, which passed into the possession of Dr Alexander Fullerton, a local man (an ancestor had successfully defended Ballintoy Castle against the rebels in 1641) who had made a fortune as a physician in Jamaica. Of this fortune, £20,000 was spent on the purchase of the Ballintoy estate. Dr Fullerton had no son, and bequeathed his property, at Ballintoy and elsewhere, to his brother's daughter, Catherine. She had married, c.1770, Dawson Downing of Bellaghy and Rovesgift, Co. Londonderry, and their son, George Alexander Dawson, the ultimate heir to the Fullerton estates, assumed the name of Fullerton instead of Downing on succeeding to them in 1794. In 1878, the Ballintoy estate amounted to 5,611 acres.[2]

The Fullerton Arms, still the main hotel today in Ballintoy, reflects the importance of the family as landlords and employers. At the time of Pen's growing interest in building a holiday home on the Antrim coast, the Estate of George Cecil

4.3

Downing Fullerton had recently sold part of the demesne to a local farmer, Daniel McCurdy. This included the purchase of 28 acres between the harbour and main road,[3] which McCurdy in turn divided into several plots to sell to private individuals wanting to build holiday homes. The scale of building for this holiday accommodation was generally modest, some amounting to little more than a corrugated iron shelter, reflecting budgets and aspirations in the early 1930s. It was here that Newton Penprase bought a plot of land on which to build his holiday retreat.

Penprase, with the encouragement of his wife, designed a single-storey house, and in the spring of 1935 began construction. Mildred contributed a budget of approximately £100 for this venture, a sum that was probably

4.3
The Parish Church (1810-13), with Harbour Road to right, and Rathlin Island beyond

4.4
The abandoned foundations of the shoreline building

OVERLEAF
1935 shoreline design for single storey 'bungalow', by Newton Penprase

sufficient to build a small holiday cottage in those days.[4] The foundations were cast direct on rock for a house plan measuring 27 feet by 23 feet overall, the foundations 2 feet wide in concrete. The concrete was reinforced with old railway lines, a practice Pen was to use later at Bendhu.

H.M.Coastguard, Bangor, wrote on 3 July 1935 to Penprase advising him to contact the Board of Trade regarding his earlier correspondence, in which he had sought permission for building a "small break-water wall with the foundations below high-water mark". One may speculate as to whether the breakwater was a separate structure designed to protect the single-storey house from the sea, in which case it might have needed to be a rather large breakwater. Alternatively "a small breakwater" might have been Pen's euphemism for the foundations for the house that he was already building at the time. In any event, this routine enquiry may have led to a greater interest in what Pen was doing on the part of the authorities.

Penprase was soon advised that he was building too near the shoreline, and the position of the building was illegal.[5] This brought into question the whole purpose in buying the land. Pen maintained that he had bought the site in good faith as a building plot, and that there were precedents of other houses built on the shoreline nearby, but to no avail. He was ordered to stop work.

Admittedly there were other holiday cabins in the vicinity, but they were inland of the shoreline and on raised land. But to the west of the harbour facing Portnalug cove, a fisherman's cottage, since remodelled as a holiday home, is located near the shoreline, so there may have been a precedent for Penprase's siting of the single-storey building in 1935.

4.4

5'x3" H by 11 lb per ft.

5"x3"

5"x3"

I. Roof
I. Rest

Feet

Proposed Bungalow for Newton Penprase. To be erected on the plot of ground between the shore and the cart track at the N.W. of Bendo Bay, Ballintoy, Co Antrim.

The alleged illegality of building on the shoreline raises a number of issues. Had anyone misled Penprase into believing that the land had permission for building a house? Did Penprase jump the gun, beginning construction before his solicitor had completed the conveyance? Or did he assume that he had permission from the local council to build when he had not? Pen had prepared a drawing for the shoreline house that he probably sent to Ballycastle Council for bylaw approval – though whether before or after casting the foundations is open to question.

Richard Penpraze, Pen's son, told the author that the sale of the land was a genuine mistake on the part of the vendor. He believed that it was part of the land holding he had bought from the Fullerton estate, whereas, Richard believed, the shoreline site belonged to the Crown, and in this scenario the vendor did not own the land.[6] In fact the title deed of McCurdy's land holding at Ballintoy confounds this view, and does include the shoreline site, which is shown in the land registry plan. So selling the plot was a legal transaction between the two men, but the permission to build on it was another matter.

Relations between Daniel McCurdy and Newton Penprase were at one stage extremely cordial in correspondence, though there are also stories that the two men fell out over the aborted building and shoreline site, which perhaps they did for a period. In any event the outcome was settled within a matter of months, when McCurdy offered Penprase another site, larger and more advantageous in outlook, on a higher situation. It was a honourable settlement.

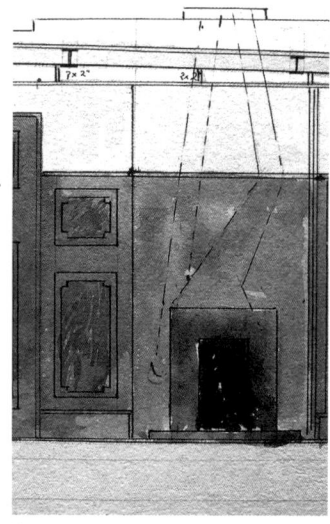

4.5

The cessation of works and the expense involved in the abandoned foundations were seen at the time, by Pen and his family, as a disaster. The foundations had been cast and much of the budget had already been expended – Mildred's interest and commitment to the project cooled considerably after this debacle.

One might assume that a single-storey holiday retreat at Ballintoy in the mid-1930s would be built as a traditional cottage with rendered walls and a pitched roof of thatch or slate tiles; or walls and roof in corrugated iron, as were other holiday shacks built nearby, but Pen's design for the unbuilt shoreline building differs considerably.

The flat-roofed house, unusual for the time and questionable in the exposed marine

4.5
Interior detail,
shoreline design

location, encloses two rooms 12 feet square, the living room and main bedroom or dining room (a matter of speculation as room names are omitted on plan) and two smaller rooms roughly 8 foot square that appear to function as kitchen and second bedroom. A separate water-closet compartment has access from the hallway. Day rooms could double as extra sleeping space for visitors.

The drawing for the 1935 shoreline building is entitled: *Proposed Bungalow for Newton Penprase*, to be erected on the plot of ground between the shore and the cart track at the N.W. of Bendo Bay, Ballintoy, Co.Antrim. The drawing is signed Newton Penprase, A.M.C., F.I.B.D. College of Art Belfast.[7] Undated, it measures 22 x 30 inches, and is executed in pen and colour wash on art paper, at a scale of ½" representing 1 foot.[8] It clearly communicates the character and aesthetic of the building proposed, its materials and mode of construction.

Various details are shown: walls are load-bearing blockwork 12-inch-thick, built off the strip foundations already described; the blockwork supports 5-inch-deep steel beams at approximately 5-feet centres, with timber rafters between, with roof-boarding and weatherproofing on top – the roof tilted a few degrees from horizontal to aid rainwater run-off to one side of the house, the gulley and down pipe not shown. A level ceiling is hung from the roof structure on timber straps, and the timber floor consists of boarding on 4-inch by 3-inch joists, supported on sleeper-walls at 6-foot centres.

The exterior elevations are highly stylised. The rendering to blockwork is shown profiled at the cornice line with two horizontal streamlined bands sitting proud on the render, with a third band below, this time recessed – the recessed bands continuing downwards at 90 degrees to frame each window in elevation. The flat roof contributes to the 1930s aesthetic of the design that is Moderne in style rather than Modern.[9] Windows are distinctively drawn, showing large panes of glass and brass-framing in the top section. This fenestration is virtually identical to the actual windows installed some years later at Bendhu, except that in the later design the top framing and opening lights are in bronze-framing, with stained-glass

AN INTEREST IN THE NORTH ANTRIM COAST 045

incorporated. Other drawn details resemble the later building to a marked degree – most noticeably the steeply inclined window cills on the exterior, shown in sectional view. Additionally the teak-louvered shutters to the windows prefigure those later incorporated in the ground floor windows of Bendhu, the shutters providing security and privacy.

The proposal is explicit as to the materials and character of the interior. Panelling in timber is shown in elevation and section, oak for the living room and mahogany in the bedroom or dining room, and timber grounds built into blockwork to provide fixing for the panelling. Two of the three fireplaces are detailed: a six-foot-wide mantel of polished stone on matching supports in the living room, and a smaller hearth in the main bedroom or dining room, backing on to flues serving the kitchen behind.

This drawing of the shoreline building, therefore, shows Pen's early intentions. It was probably deposited with the Building Surveyor's office at Ballycastle for byelaw approval – the cramped inclusion of a site location plan added to the drawing appears as an afterthought, perhaps indicating that it was produced, or demanded, after the foundations had started. Stylistically the aborted design is remarkable in its chosen aesthetic, a variant of mid-1930s Moderne, flat-roofed with streamlined elevations and unusual window design – all contrasting with a traditional interior of timber panelling. While the design for the abandoned house anticipated Penprase's next building – Bendhu, the larger and more ambitious project that was to arise on the new site – the formal composition became increasingly complex and idiosyncratic.

ENDNOTES

1. In the company of Ben Cowser – who in 1923 had designed the family house for Mildred and Newton in Grasmere Gardens, Belfast.

2. Information from Dr A P W Malcomson.

3. Title No 18667, registered in June 1934. The site for Bendhu, as later transacted, is registered under Title No 22073.

4. The sum of £100 in 1934 is equivalent to between £5000 (using retail price index for calculation) and £19000 (based on average earnings), at 2007 figures. Source (2 Feb 09): http://measuringworth.com

5. Penprase received orders to stop work from Captain Fullerton's agent: *I ceased building after receiving instruction from Mr Hunter [in] Ballycastle, then the agent of the landlord, Capt. Fullerton.*

6. A view made emphatically in conversation with Richard Penpraze, 23 March 1995.

7. AMC is the Art Masters Certificate; FIBD stands for Fellow of the Institute of British Decorators (source: Oxford Dictionary of Abbreviations). Ivor Beaumont, the headmaster of the School of Art in Belfast, also suffixed FIBD to his name and qualifications.

8. Building Regulation or Byelaw applications in the 1930s would more usually be drawn at ⅛" or ¼" representing 1 foot – the larger scale chosen by Penprase, ½" representing 1 foot, commonly reserved for details.

9. Moderne – see Preface.

The first 40 years

A NEW SITE,
A NEW DESIGN

A LIVING
WORK OF ART

RECOGNITION
& FINAL YEARS

5 A new site, a new design

"I have purchased the present piece of ground for £26 from Mr Daniel McCurdy and have built a bungalow thereon. The ground is ... high up on the projecting plateau known locally as Tent Green – [from] the days of big regattas" ... Newton Penprase[1]

After the fiasco of the shoreline building, Daniel McCurdy offered Penprase a choice of sites from his Ballintoy land holding. Pen chose an elevated site with a fine prospect, accessed from the steep winding road that descends to the harbour. The new plot, at three-quarters of an acre,[2] was substantially larger than the site for the shoreline building, and commanded a magnificent outlook with views to Rathlin and Sheep Islands to the north-east, Inishowen and Donegal to the west, and Islay, and the Mull of Kintyre, to the north and north-east. A sharp bend on Harbour Road gave restricted access to the new building plot. Pen later negotiated the purchase of an additional piece of land giving better access and more amenities to his site, though not without a protracted dispute with a neighbour over rights-of-way.

All of concrete is the concise description noted on the 1936 building plan, indicating Pen's chosen material of construction – the plan enclosed with his letter dated 14 April 1936 to Ballycastle District Council. The letter, sent from Belfast, notes Pen's temporary base in Ballintoy at the Coastguard Cottages, which was rented accommodation overlooking the site for Bendhu.

5.1

5.1
Ballintoy in the context of the north coast of Antrim and Scotland – the Mull of Kintyre and the tip of Islay

5.2
The site for Bendhu is on the winding Harbour Road leading to Ballintoy Harbour

OVERLEAF
1936 building plan compared with the 1986 survey

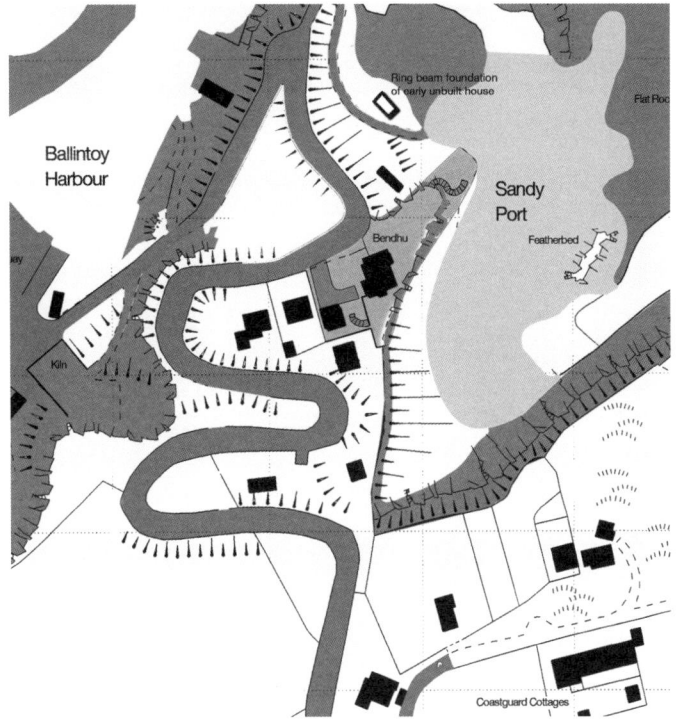

5.2

What is referred to in this account for convenience as the 1936 building plan is more correctly entitled *Proposed plan of Bungalow for Richard Newton Penpraze to be erected on the farm of Daniel McCurdy, Ballintoy, Co Antrim*. The local council received the plan on the 21st April, and the Ballycastle Council's surveyor signed it off three weeks later as 'Approved subject to [the] approval of Co. Surveyor'. This referred to Antrim County Council, based in Belfast, which was the regulating authority for planning. There is no record that Antrim County Council ever gave its approval to the 1936 Building Plan, though critically, neither did it refuse the application. As the sole extant drawing submitted for approval under byelaws, during the

A NEW SITE, A NEW DESIGN   051

1936 BUILDING PLAN

EAST ELEVATION

GROUND FLOOR

FIRST FLOOR

1986 SURVEY

EAST ELEVATION

SECOND FLOOR

GROUND FLOOR

FIRST FLOOR

A NEW SITE, A NEW DESIGN

The 'Battleship' goes up

PENPRAZE'S DREAM—BIT BY BIT FOR 23 YEARS

Express Staff Reporter

FOR 23 years at week-ends and during holidays, Mr Newton Penpraze has been building his dream house on the cliffs at Ballintoy, Co. Antrim.

At 71 the nimble, retired art teacher is still patiently adding to the 14-roomed concrete house, though the country folk say: "He will never finish it because he enjoys the work so much."

Much else to do

To that the tanned, grey-haired builder replied yesterday: "To me it is

5.3

forty years of Pen's construction, the drawing was still being referred to in the 1950s, some twenty years after its first submission, when departure from the submitted plan remained a matter of contention between Pen and the local authority. In effect the plan might be regarded as 'approved by default' in the absence of any formal refusal. As such the drawing could be considered as a commitment by the applicant to conform to the plans shown in relation to layout, elevations, main dimensions, as well as materials and general detail. The building as constructed varied considerably from these parameters.

5.3
Daily Express article, 10 August 1959,

OVERLEAF
Entrance to Pen's Den from first floor terrace, photographed in August 1993

It may be surmised that there was some prevarication by the authorities on the matter of whether to grant approval. The design for the house was highly unusual in shape and form, and in its proposed material of construction – concrete. The design did not relate to any established type-forms, residential or otherwise. The distance between Belfast, where Antrim County Council had offices in the Crumlin Courthouse, and Ballycastle where the Rural District Council was based, was perhaps sufficiently great for the matter to fall into limbo. In subsequent years Penprase maintained that the plan that he had submitted (i.e. the 1936 building plan) had been approved by the Council, and that he had departed from the layout shown in the drawing only on account of "war conditions and material [shortages]".[3]

The title of the 1936 building plan – *Proposed plan of Bungalow for Richard Newton Penpraze to be erected on the farm of Daniel McCurdy, Ballintoy, Co Antrim* – merits further comment on two counts. Firstly, if a bungalow is a single-storey house with a pitched roof, arguably the norm at that time, the design in the 1936 building plan shows a substantial two-storey building, flat-roofed with Classical scrolls – hardly a bungalow in any usual sense. Secondly, the project is dedicated to Pen's son, Richard, who was nineteen at the time. Pen most likely hoped that Richard would get involved in the project – as his only son and heir it was a natural aspiration for a father – but Richard did not enthuse about the Bendhu project in the years to come, often resenting the time his father was away from home, or being commandeered to drive Pen back and forth to Ballintoy.

The ground floor layout shown in the 1936 building plan is substantially what Penprase built at Bendhu, in the layout of dining room, kitchen, three bedrooms, bathroom, WC, and entrance hallway. There are minor variations in the layout of doors and partitions as actually constructed, and the 1936 plan also includes a small internal staircase between the kitchen and first floor that was omitted. Nonetheless the ground floor plan of the 1936 drawing is recognisable as that which exists today. In construction too, the arrangement shown in the 1936 plan is partially what was built. A timber ground floor is supported on sleeper-walls, air-grilles on the east elevation provide

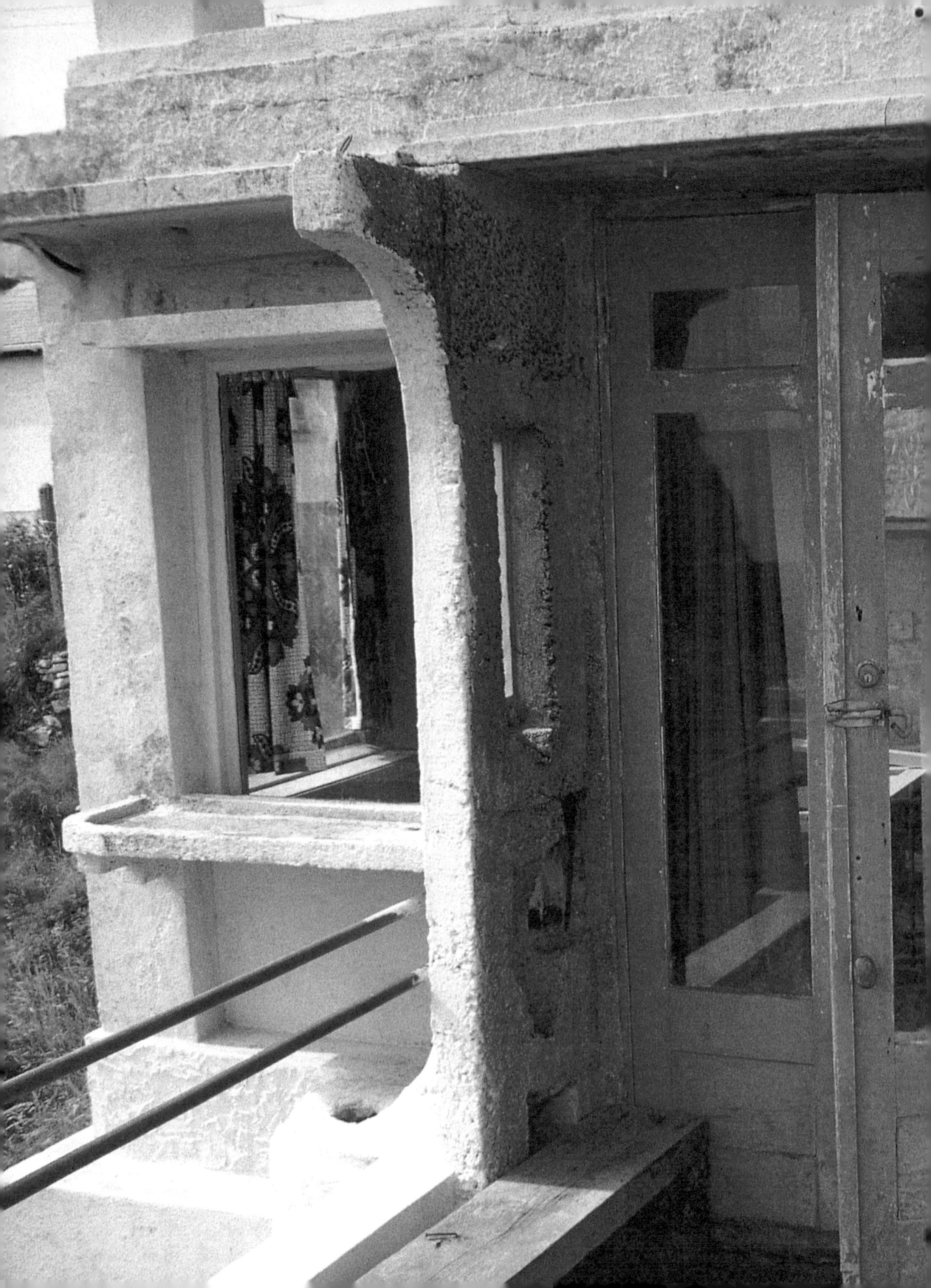

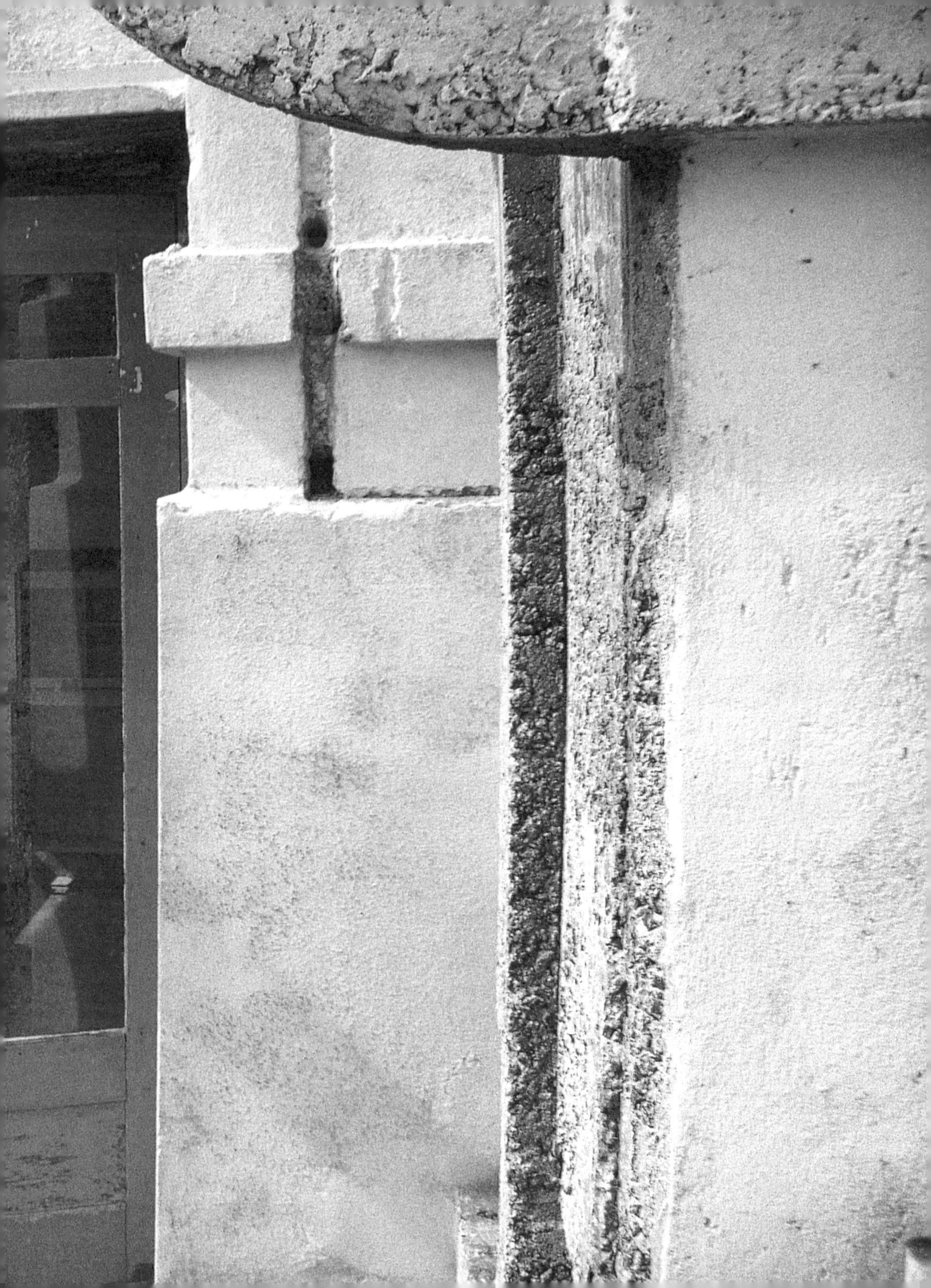

ventilation to the under-croft, the reinforced concrete roof differing in being more complex as built, but still inclined to direct rainwater to a storage tank built into the concrete structure. This latter feature was a practical necessity, as connection to a mains water supply was not possible until the mid-1960s. The nearest source of water prior to that was either sea water obtained from the beach, or fresh water from a well that was located in a cave near the harbour, a good hundred yards downhill from the site in either case. The rainwater storage tank built in to the structure thus saved considerable effort for the builder.

But if the ground floor as constructed was similar to that shown in the 1936 building plan, compare and contrast the first floor layouts shown in the 1936 plan (p 52) and the 1986 record drawing of the building as constructed (p 53). At first floor level there was a radical change in design, namely the incorporation of a large roof terrace.

In the absence of documentation or contemporary accounts one can but speculate on the reasons for the alteration. Having completed the ground floor construction and made it habitable as a self-contained unit that could sleep up to eight people, the 'roof' to the ground floor accommodation formed a platform from which to build the next storey. It must have been important to waterproof this platform temporarily, to safeguard the lived-in accommodation below. The temporary waterproofing probably saw service over one winter at least, before the first floor masonry construction was started in springtime – the waterproofed platform serving as a temporary terrace in the interim. But the spectacular views and orientation enjoyed from this vantage point, more apparent as the building gained

5.4

5.4
Pen's Den exterior, showing the bird-table shelf outside one of the five windows to the Den, May 1995

5.5
Pen's Den, interior photographed in August 1993

5.5

height, coupled with the privacy the building enjoyed on the east side away from the road, arguably promoted the terrace as a compelling change of plan.

Creating the terrace had an inevitable downside – a loss of floor space inside the building – that led to a complete re-plan of the first floor. The drawing room and bedroom disappear, to be replaced by the new roof terrace. The external entrance and stair on the west side of the house survives from the 1936 building plan, as the entrance to the upper floors. The garage and workshop on the first floor are replaced by an artist's studio – in effect a piano nobile – structurally completed during Pen's tenure, but only as a building shell.

Inevitably, perhaps, space was made up by adding a second floor to Bendhu – an additional storey never envisaged in the 1936 building plan that consisted only of ground and first floors. The new second floor was conceived as a self-contained living / sleeping attic, accessed from the terrace by a narrow external stair constructed in concrete. A fine view of the stars at night time was intended through a roof opening glazed with the transparent dome from a wartime plane – reportedly modelled on the air gunner's look-out of a Lancaster or Blenheim bomber from World War Two. Templates for this feature, with astrological symbols decorating the circular opening for the glazed dome, survived until the early 1990s, though the dome was never installed. This new second floor was the result of Pen's increased confidence in building when he reached first floor level. Adding complexity to complexity, the second floor is a key element in the overall shape and form of the building, giving Bendhu its scale and presence. Without the second floor, notwithstanding its limited accommodation, the building would appear much diminished.

Mains electricity did not become available until the mid-60s. Pen hired the services of a local electrician, who provided a temporary supply to the building that consisted of a consumer fuse box and single socket outlet mounted on the plywood meter panel. As soon as the Electricity Board had tested this temporary supply Pen abandoned the electrician's services. His grandson David Penpraze, then 17 or 18 years of age, was commandeered to install the electric circuits in the house. Pen typically addressing David with the injunction "Boy, see the switch is here," Pen pointed to a doorway, "and the light is there", another gesture from Pen pointing to the midpoint of a ceiling, "join the two".

It was then up to David Penpraze to devise a method of accommodating the wiring, and for many weeks he installed the first electrical circuits serving the ground floor.

Bendhu is not an ambitious building in terms of structure. The ground floor living room at 5m x 4m plan dimensions, and first floor studio[4] at 7m x 3m, are the largest volumes built by Penprase, and most other spaces in the house are considerably smaller. However, spaces appear larger, viewed in combination, and especially on the upper floors where many different roof-lights, small and large windows, built-in shelves, and structural recesses combine to make an intricate spatial experience. Pen determined the dimension of roof and floor spans by the size of components that he was able to handle physically; roof and floor joists at 3m to 4m in length were a practical limit to size. The ground floor is a collection of rooms with modest spaces, defined in the main by load-bearing walls. There is no framed

5.6

060   BUILDING BENDHU: FIRST 40 YEARS

5.6
Scallop-shaped hearth, early 1960s

5.7
'Dolmen' fireplace, 1993

5.7

structure, or free plan. Wall construction generally is in concrete cast in formwork, or built in blockwork. The ground floor is built in suspended timber construction as already noted in the drawing. The first floor slab and flat roofs above are made of reinforced concrete, the roofs set out at various levels to incorporate clerestory glazing. External walls incorporate piers made of concrete or blockwork, expressed as pilasters, with similar profiles surrounding window openings on the first and second floors, contributing to the Art Deco styling discussed in Chapter 12.

The changes in design that Pen made during construction (the first-floor terrace and additional second floor) caused some consternation with the local authority. From the mid-1940s onwards, officials acting for the County Council wrote to Pen periodically requesting that up-to-date plans be deposited, on occasion communicating through the Council's solicitor.[5] Matters lingered on for almost a decade, with the correspondence concluding at the end of 1956.

In a memorandum dated 7 December, twenty years after Pen started building, the County Planning Officer for Antrim recorded the decision made at a

A NEW SITE, A NEW DESIGN   061

meeting of the Planning and Highways Development Committee, three days before; the Council file note records:

It was decided that there was little point at the moment in trying to force Mr Penprase to comply with the plan which he originally submitted to Ballycastle R.D.C. The Secretary reported that he had been through the house recently, that no part of it is finished, and he feels that Mr Penprase will never complete it. The Committee decided that in the circumstances they should do nothing in the case.[6]

While this may have been a source of celebration for Pen, effectively ridding him of further surveillance by the local authority, the chances are that the Committee's decision was never communicated to him. The internal memorandum ends by clarifying another long-standing issue, noting that the "excavation at the side of the house is not for the purpose of erecting a garage, but is simply to provide space on which Mr Penprase's car is parked". This allegation over the unauthorised erection of a garage at the side of the house had originated eight years previously, and was finally put to rest. A plan for a garage had in fact been made by Pen, though it remained unbuilt.[7]

5.8
Ventilation holes in ceiling panel, bedroom 2

Pen's building attracted local and even national interest. An article in the *Daily Express*, dated 10 August 1959, by an unnamed staff reporter shows the building in its raw concrete state, structurally almost complete (5.3).

For 23 years at weekends and during holidays, Mr Newton Penpraze has been building his dream house on the cliffs at Ballintoy, Co Antrim. At 71 the nimble, retired art teacher is still patiently adding to the 14-roomed concrete house, though the country folk say "He will never finish it because he enjoys the work so much." ... To that the tanned, grey-haired builder replied yesterday: "To me it is enjoyment, not labour. But I want it finished for I have so much else to do. I want to go back to my painting."

Mr Penpraze is the architect, cement mixer, bricklayer, carpenter, plumber, electrician, decorator, gardener and navvy. One snag with this labour force of one was that when he was designing the house he could only plan for work he was capable of doing himself. All the cement, bricks, and stones he has to carry in a bucket as the monument of 23 years' dedicated toil rises on the cliff overlooking the rugged limestone coast that reminds him of his native Cornwall.

"The Battleship" is what they call it around Ballintoy, because of its three levels with their exterior staircases, and the sun terrace on the first floor ... Ben Dhu [The Black Peak] is the name Mr Penpraze has chosen.

When they go to Ballintoy from their home in Belfast he and his wife live in the "Den", an air-conditioned, self-contained flat full of gadgets and hidden cupboards. Its french windows open on to the sun terrace with a breathtaking view of Sheep Island and the Atlantic.

Mr Penpraze is at present chiselling steps down the cliff face for quicker access to the beach. When will "The Battleship" be finished? No one knows. Said Mr Penpraze: "What they do with it when I am gone, I don't care. The main thing is that I am here enjoying it now".

Pen's Den – referred to in the *Daily Express* article, was one of the most intriguing rooms in Bendhu, and the only part of the first floor that was habitable and lived-in during Pen's lifetime. The Den was a compact multipurpose living and sleeping area, the dining table doubling as an office desk and workbench, on top of which could be found sandwiches, building invoices or iron filings from metalwork in progress. The space, 4m x 3m,

5.9

contained built-in furniture and fitments – a wardrobe, a drying closet for wet clothes, a built-in sofa that also doubled as a bed, an open fireplace, various storage spaces, and a separate toilet. Four windows and a clerestory roof-light provided daylight to the small space so it was marvellously bright in daytime, all within a caravan-like interior. But unlike a caravan it was coloured in Pen's favourite hues of turquoise, lemon and mauve. Beyond repair, Pen's Den has not survived.

Contrary to the report in the Daily Express, there was no "air conditioning" in Pen's building, at least not in the accepted sense of the term that involves heating or chilling air

5.9
Bendhu in mid-construction, c1973

and adjusting its humidity. Nonetheless there was a unique ventilation system in the house that addressed the dual purpose of providing fresh air ventilation, while also assisting in drying out the structure where there was moisture ingress.

Damp in the house was a recurring problem, partly due to the construction of walls built as single skin without cavity, in blockwork or in-situ concrete. While most of the structure was dry, moisture seeped through the building fabric in certain areas. It was often difficult to trace the source of the problem, and Pen's solution was both original and daring. The inner wall surfaces in all the main rooms on the ground floor were panelled in timber or fibreboard, fixed to timber battens, making an air-space between the panelling and wall. Not only did this prevent the direct passage of moisture to the inside linings but on an exposed site where opening windows were kept to a minimum, a room-ventilation system was effected behind wall and ceiling panels. Outside air was introduced to the building by means of small openings, usually located under window cills, on the different elevations to the building. The air thereby introduced was naturally distributed behind the wall and ceiling panels and entered rooms through gaps and slots at the junction of ceilings and walls. The wall and ceiling panelling thus served two functions, to provide a plenum for fresh air ventilation, and additionally to prevent moisture ingress to the inside wall surfaces from a damp structure behind. The ventilation thus assisted in drying out the masonry that had become damp, and provided a relatively draught-free supply of fresh, if cool, air. This form of passive ventilation is one of many innovative features in the house.

Heating the house was spartan by today's standards but typical for the time. A main fireplace in the living room heated the principal living area; portable electric appliances were used to heat other rooms. Pen's Den had its own fireplace and chimney. In the living room the dolmen-style fireplace, a one-off design constructed by Pen from precast concrete elements resembling ancient stones, was a double-sided arrangement that also served the kitchen in the adjoining room. Ventilation was introduced from the base of the hearth, and Pen explained to visitors that a fuel hopper above the fire grate directly stoked the fire.[8]

There were frequent problems with downdraughts from the chimney, which made Penprase take drastic action. A neighbour relates the occasion when walking by the house he encountered Pen at the top of a precariously positioned ladder. With chisel and hammer he was taking down part of a chimneystack he had recently built. His neighbour, who was many years his junior, offered to come over with a sledge hammer and take the offending structure down with a couple of blows, which would leave Pen free to sort out the chunk of masonry more conveniently, wherever it might fall on the ground. Pen rather brusquely rejected this offer, saying that he had "built the offending structure brick by brick, and it would come down brick by brick".[9] The reason for this partial rebuilding was the downdraught on the fireplace serving the living room and kitchen, a problem that remained, despite rebuilding the flue.

An additional feature of the fireplace was the overmantel. This was made as a semi-circular cut-out matching the shape of the fireplace opening, with legs hinged to the underside of the fitment that was attached to the wall. This was lowered to provide a dining table in front of the fire, an original and social arrangement, appreciated at the often chilly but famously convivial gatherings of friends, students, and family.

Many people have visited Bendhu during its construction and been intrigued by the building and its creator. The following are extracts from the journal of architect John Gilbert recording his impressions when visiting in the 1970s:

Well, there he was, standing at the gate, an old, smallish man. We stopped and praised his house. He was quite lively and when we talked, his top row of teeth tended to part with his jaw. Formalities over, we were inside and breathing faster than before. First room had a gorgeous painted ceiling of the signs of the zodiac. The star in the middle had been cut out from a solid piece with a jackknife. When he did that [carving] he had blisters all the way up his palm. The room was panelled from a ship called Bermuda. Muted colours of 1930-1940s style. The other room panelled differently - more Victorian [in] ornament - the ceiling painted with Prometheous stealing fire from the Heavens. All the panelling had a ventilation system directly underneath the cornice line. The wardrobes all had

OVERLEAF
Newton Penprase
in 1965

hot water pipes going through the back of them. Trapdoors in the floor [for fuel storage]. The main room has the best view. He sat us down, one on either side of the window looking over Ballintoy bay and said as he lit up and looked out, "well, what's wrong with that". When asked if he'd ever thought of painting the house he said "I plan to paint from this, not this." The house is designed for most eventualities save coffins and prams.

In a later journal entry:

Went also to see Newton Penprase. He hasn't changed, still chain smoking, sitting, looking out of the window at the pounding sea, his left hand completely arthritic now. His wife had died and he was wondering if he had the stamina left in him. He reckoned she would have outlived him. I offered my help working on the house but he said he didn't expect it. Pen [now in his 80s] talked about how he had started the house when he was about 50, how his wife never liked it, but he seemed content with that. I was hugely impressed by the house and him. [10]

The ingenuity and invention that went into the practical affairs of building, the output of Newton Penprase's fertile and busy mind, found further expression in the varied artworks and decorative features built into the fabric of Bendhu, discussed in the next chapter.

ENDNOTES

1. Letter from Penprase to the Land Registry, undated – probably 1939.

2. 0.3 of a hectare.

3. Letter from Penprase to Mr Anderson, County Solicitor, 4 July 1949.

4. In the 1998-2001 fit-out the studio became a new kitchen and dining area.

5. For transcripts of correspondence see Appendix 3.

6. Planning and Highways Development Committee, *Note for File, re: R N Penprase*, 7 December 1956, signed by the CPO (chief planning officer).

7. Conversation with David Penpraze.

8. Conversation between Joe Fitzgerald and Newton Penprase in the early 1960s.

9. Conversation with William George McGonaghie May 2006.

10. John Gilbert took the staff of his Glasgow office back to see Bendhu in 2004, 30 years later. "It was great to see that the building had been saved and made into a comfortable home. But I miss that afternoon I spent with Newton".

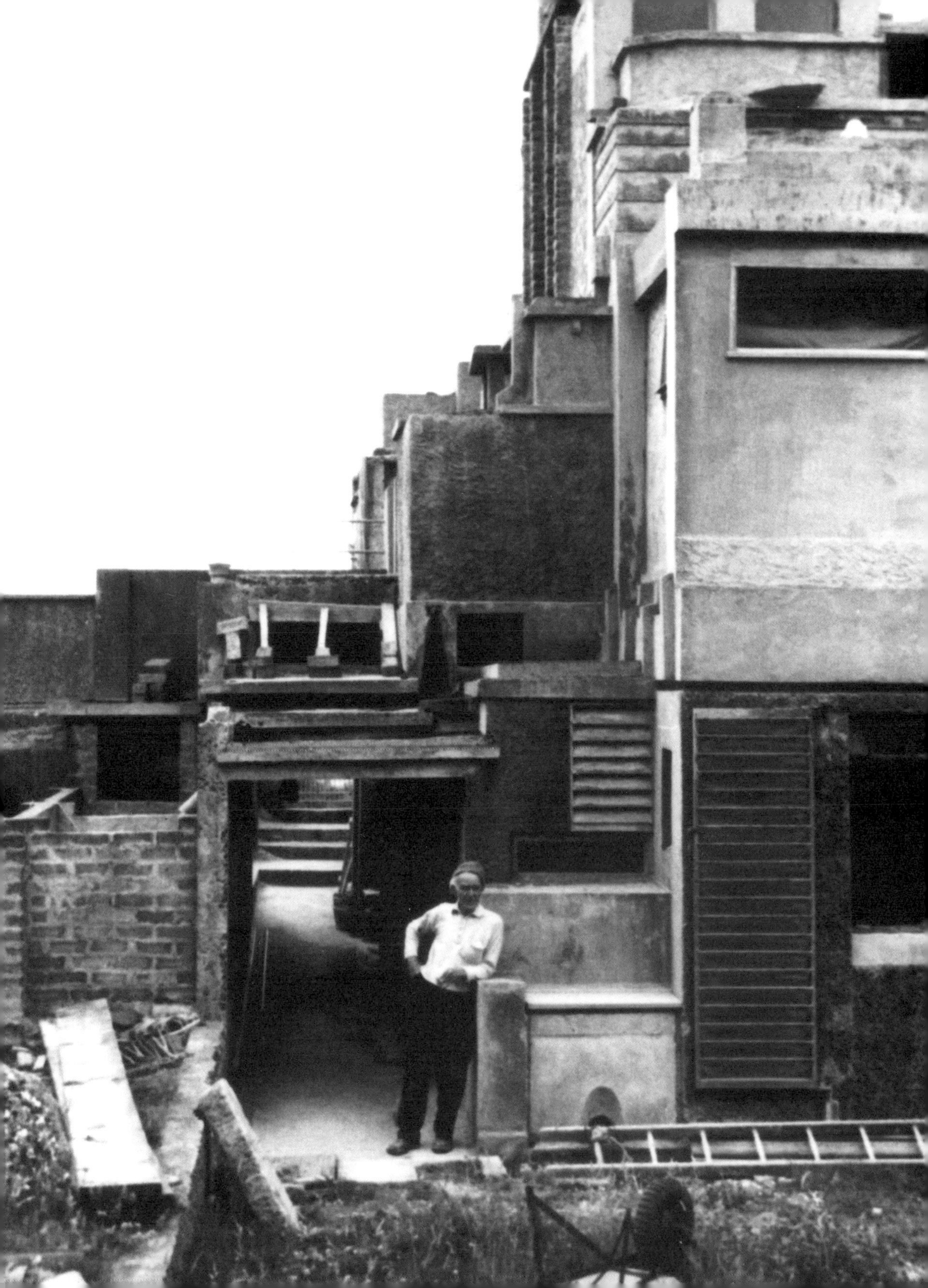

6 A living work of art

Hand-in-hand with building Bendhu incrementally (a room at a time as the seasons allowed), Newton Penprase engaged in painting, sculpture, and applied decorative work for the building. This artistic activity cannot readily be separated from the physical act of building Bendhu. Contemporaries observed that Pen would abandon building work periodically to pursue other activity, often artistic, and then return to construction refreshed. The structure itself sometimes required special components of interesting design, sculptural in nature, such as pre-cast concrete elements for balcony brackets and corner posts. This chapter gives an overview of the artwork and applied decoration incorporated at Bendhu, most of it carried out by Penprase.

The most noticeable artworks built into the fabric of the house are three sets of external sculptures: the Neptune group, Phoenix Rising, and the Maritime relief panel.

The Neptune group surmounts the entrance porch of Bendhu and is visible from the road. The sculpture comprises a group of three creatures representing the elements: a bull symbolising rough seas, a sea-horse symbolising windy conditions, and a dolphin (now missing from the group) calm weather. The figure of Neptune emerging from the sea and dominating the other figures appears in the preparatory maquette for the sculpture, but not in the final work. The sculpture is made of a plaster or cement mixture reinforced with wire, and in recent years has been painted in with the external decorations of the house.

6.1

6.2

6.3

6.4

6.1
Phoenix Rising
sculpture,
mounted above
studio window,
mid-1960s

6.2
Maritime relief
panel, 2007

6.3–6.4
Neptune group
sculpture, above
main entrance,
1960s

Located above the studio window on the first floor terrace was the striking sculpture of a large and intricately modelled bird-like figure, known as Phoenix Rising, reportedly made in celebration of the construction having reached the top floor.

The sculpture's fabrication was a remarkable feat in casting cement mortar (reinforced with light steel wire) in a mould. It has survived the elements to this day and now surmounts the extension on the east side of the building.

On the west elevation of Bendhu is a maritime relief depicting a sailing ship, which also appears as a (rather unfriendly) pirate's head or skull, in a small panel, about 30 cm. square. Made in terracotta or plaster, it is now painted in with the external wall.

Bendhu was listed in 1992 as being a building of Special Architectural or Historic Interest.[1] As well as the main house, individual external elements, namely the bird table, garden pool, and cliff-face stairway, all on the eastern garden side of the house, were included in the Listing notice. The concrete bird table and garden pool again show Pen's skill in concrete pre-casting, and his interest in the natural world.

Additionally, a sunken seating area, made to provide protection from the wind, circular in shape, was excavated in the grassy headland that forms the garden. The headland was also modified by the addition of a low grassy embankment on the southern side, made by Pen to act as a safety barrier and to show the boundary of his site. This grassy embankment was a bone of contention with the local authority over the years.[2]

A concrete construction that is described in this account as the garden altar measures approximately 120 cm wide x 90 cm deep x 60 cm high, and is constructed of cast concrete units made by Pen. The group survives today, albeit hidden under foliage. Pen used to leave food for birds on the 'altar stone' but rats from the caves below were a nuisance, stealing the food and attacking the birds. So within the hollow 'arms' either side of the altar stone Pen placed rat poison, which apparently solved the problem. Whether there was any religious significance or ritual carried out at the garden altar can be neither confirmed nor denied. Sufficient to say its elemental symmetry suggests an altar stone. Neolithic overtones could also, conceivably, relate to the Mount Druid megalith (dolmen) behind Ballintoy manse. The form of the altar stone, on a raised plinth, arranged symmetrically, evokes images of supplication, if not for Christian worship, then maybe for meditation and private prayer, whilst it conveniently doubled as a place for the birds.

The stairway to the beach at Bendhu seems to grow out of the cliff-face with a fortress-like aesthetic. Penprase carved out the narrow steps from the near vertical face of limestone at the eastern end of the site – a remarkable act of physical labour. The steps twist and turn in direction so that a disabled friend could use the stairs "without help or crutch", and to prevent small children losing balance in running down the steps. He built in-situ concrete balustrade panels for safety, the experience of ascending or descending reminiscent of a medieval structure. The stairway so constructed is brought to life by the play of light and shade across its surface, which merges with the limestone cliff. Much to Pen's displeasure, the public started to use

6.5
Garden altar,
mid-1960s

6.6
Garden pool,
2005

6.7
Concrete
bird table

6.8
Steps to beach,
descending
from garden

OVERLEAF
Steps from
beach, ascending

Newton Penprase
wearing his
favourite
tea cosy hat

these steps as a short-cut across his land, so he carved into the risers of the lower steps the injunction KEEP OUT — YES — STRICTLY PRIVATE, the words carved in an elegant Times Roman script, only noticeable when climbing the steps. Inventive metal work by Pen is a feature of the stairway, in handrails and reinforcement to the concrete panels, and has been further developed in the restoration of the stairs by Michael Ferguson.

The story often told about Pen constructing these steps is that while chiselling out the rock-face the hammerhead came off its shaft and struck him on the head, making him lose consciousness. A little while later he came to, dazed, looked round for the hammerhead, secured it to the timber shaft, and continued the work of cutting limestone unabated.

At the front of the house, Pen built masonry gateposts in a distinctly Art Deco idiom (complete with built-in drinking-tray for thirsty dogs). The metalwork for the gates came from galvanised steel conduit, the material cast out during re-wiring at Belfast College of Art. So accurate was Pen's workmanship in manufacture that the gates are reputed to have required no welding, relying instead on the precise tooling of individual metal parts held together by friction, the tightness of joints holding the metalwork together.

The dragon figure sculpted by Penprase, installed on one of the gateposts, had a chequered and all-too-brief existence. The menacing form of the sculpture was intended to discourage trespassers and unwanted visitors. The figure was

6.8

A LIVING WORK OF ART   073

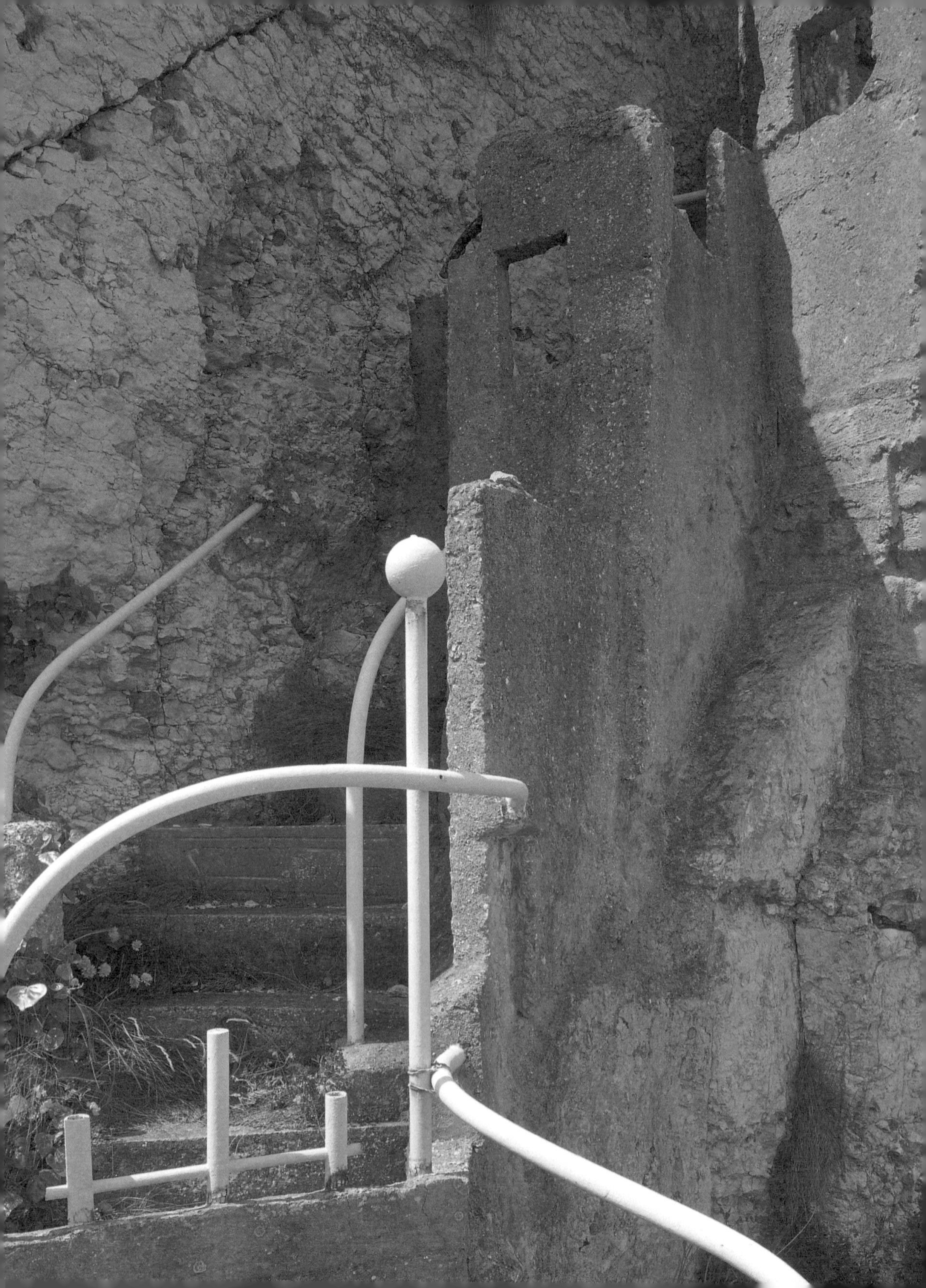

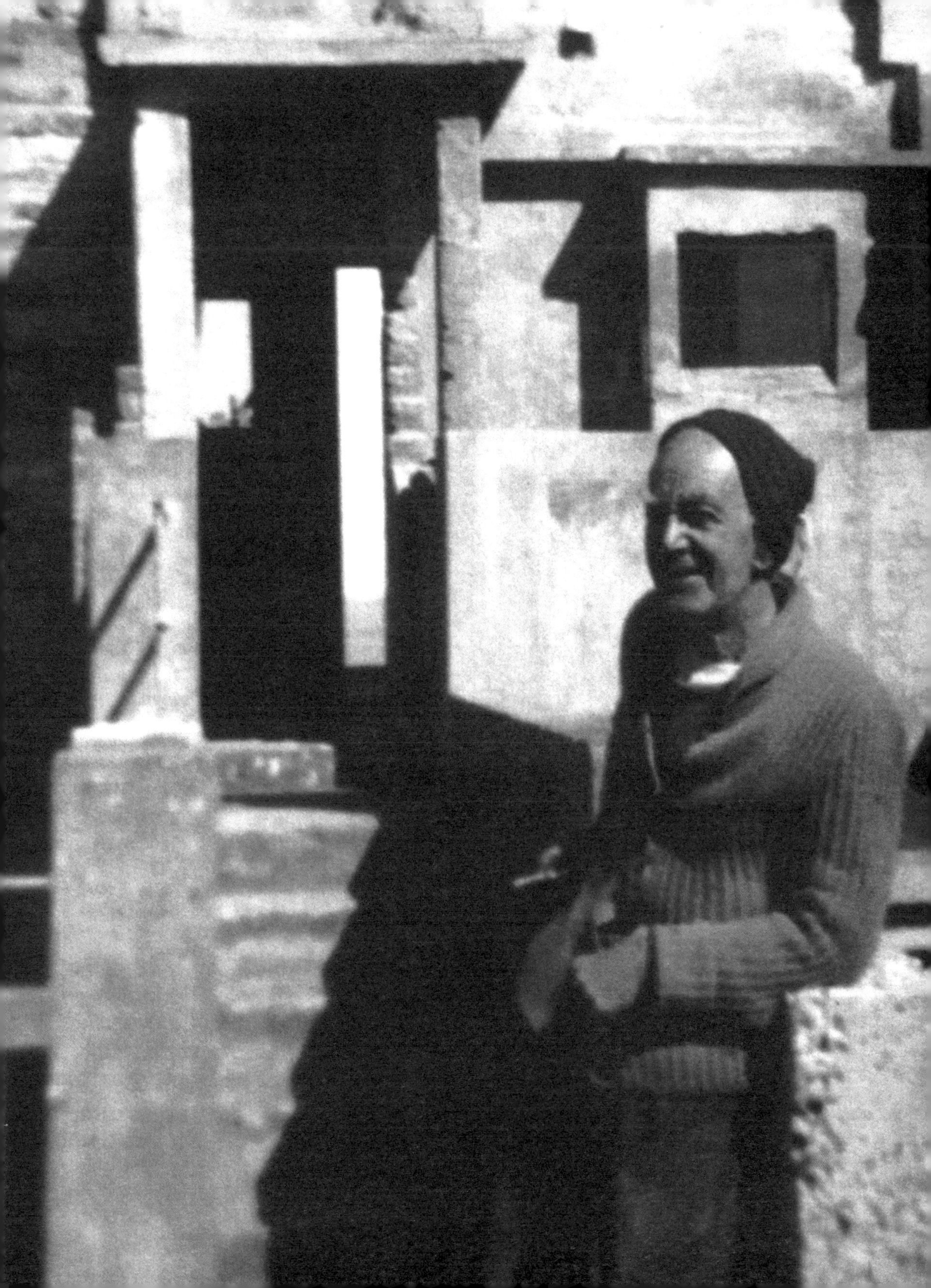

6.9

modelled in clay by Penprase, and then cast in bronze at the Millfield annex of the College of Art in Belfast.³ David Penpraze recollects that it took three people to manhandle the bronze figure for transit, and mount it into position on the gatepost.

It seems the dragon in bronze was too alarming, or too tempting, for someone in the neighbourhood. Ten days after its installation Pen was called to Belfast on business, and on his return to Bendhu discovered that the bronze dragon had disappeared. Having been unlawfully removed, it is hoped that the dragon may one day be re-discovered and returned to Bendhu.

Pen had a wide-ranging interest in the natural world. Having observed birds attempting to

6.10

076 BUILDING BENDHU: FIRST 40 YEARS

6.9–6.10
Gates at Bendhu

6.11
Bronze cast of dragon sculpture, intended for gatepost, early 1950s

OVERLEAF
Twelve cartoon drawings for Stars of the Zodiac lunette panels, by Newton Penprase

build a nest one morning, he redirected his efforts that day to burying in the garden an open-ended tube in which the birds could nest. A student from Belfast College of Art observed in the 1970s that Pen was also interested in flowers, especially orchids, to such an extent that he collected most of the known varieties found in Ulster, cultivating them in the rocks below Bendhu House.[4] The artist Raymond Piper, a past pupil of Pen and famous for his drawings of plants – especially orchids – freely acknowledged his debt to Penprase as teacher. Many of the artworks in the house – paintings, carving and stained-glass – while not having flora or fauna as the primary subject, nevertheless depict the natural world in the design.

6.11

The idea of a building being a Total Work of Art, in which architecture, interiors and furnishings are conceived and executed in complete unity, was held in high regard at the end of the 19th and beginning of the 20th century, ranging from works such as Voysey's quietly mannered vernacular houses in the Home Counties around London, Mackintosh's buildings in Glasgow, Otto Wagner's Secessionist work in Vienna, Horta's Art Nouveau houses in Brussels, to Gaudi's work in Barcelona. The individual spirit and unity of these examples can be traced to the 19th century composer Richard Wagner's concept of *Gesamtkunstwerke*, or Total Work of Art, where there is co-relation and harmony between all the creative elements.

Whether Newton Penprase consciously set out to pursue a comparable sense of unity between building style, decoration and furnishing at Bendhu is open

VIII
Sagittarius Mars Iron
Aquamarine
Oct 24 Nov 23

June 22 July 23.
Leo silver
Emerald

Aug 23.
Virgo Peridot
Gold

XI
Jan 21 Feb 19
Pisces Uranus, Lead Garnet

Capricorn Dec 23. Jan 20.   Aquarius   Saturn

to question, but in effect this is what he embarked on. The impetus for this may have been intuitive and largely unplanned, working on a ceiling painting, or sculpture as the spirit took him. The parts of the house that were completed, mostly on the ground floor, received his creative attention in every aspect, from wall panelling, ceiling painting, use of stained-glass, to the practical items of built-in and loose furniture, not to mention the fireplace, purpose-made ironmongery, and novel heating, plumbing and ventilation systems.

All the main rooms on the ground floor have distinctive artwork or embellishment: some with Classical themes, others apparently influenced by Art Deco, and yet others recalling an Arts and Crafts lineage.

The zodiac bedroom is lined with wall-panelling, constructed from lightweight timber doors of 1930s-1940s Art Deco styling, probably recycled cupboard doors obtained from a re-fit or sale of scrap at Belfast shipyard. The panels were assembled (with additional mouldings by Pen) to make an integrated design, and painted his singular colour combination of turquoise blue, grey, pink and mauve. Gaps in the panelling and holes in the ceiling provide outlets for the ventilation system already described in Chapter 5.

The wall-panelling is background to the main feature of the room – the stars of zodiac ceiling. A two metre diameter circle is divided into twelve zones or zodiacs, with paintings of the astrological symbols depicted in lunette panels, each approx 24 cm high x 37 cm wide (9.5 ins x 14.5 ins). The lunettes are executed in oils, painted on thin ply or hardboard, and depict the twelve astrological symbols: Aries, Taurus, Gemini, Cancer, Leo, Virgo, Libra, Scorpio, Sagittarius, Capricorn, Aquarius, and Pisces. The lunettes were painted studio style, on a table or easel, and may have been executed at the Art College, at home in Belfast, or at Bendhu – but in any case not on the ceiling itself. The lunettes are held in place by small

6.12
6.13

6.12–6.13
Limed oak panelling installed in the second bedroom

6.14
Wall-panelling in the Zodiac bedroom, 1993

6.15
Stars of the Zodiac ceiling

6.14

6.15

timber beads fixed round the edges. Cartoon drawings for the twelve Signs of the Zodiac (6.15) show Pen's mastery in figurative drawing. The restoration of the ceiling is discussed in Chapter 9.

Pen, by all accounts, enjoyed showing the zodiac ceiling to friends and visitors, especially women. He would demonstrate the best position to view the work – lying on one's back on the double bed, directly underneath the ceiling.

Oak panelling is used in the second bedroom to line the walls as it did in the original hallway, the bedroom panelling carved with natural plant forms. The panelling reputedly came from Belfast shipyard, from a vessel being refitted or broken up for scrap.[5]

The oak-lined bedroom also had a remarkable ceiling painting, whose subject was "the second Greek myth: Erebus (darkness) and Nox (night) giving birth to Love and Light".[6] Unfortunately this painting has not survived damage from the leaking structure above.

The living room, with its oak panelling from the same source at the shipyard (but this time unlimed and without carving) incorporated another ceiling painting by Pen, known as *Prometheus stealing Flame from Heaven*.[7] It, too, has suffered irreparable damage from water ingress, and no longer exists.

Small stained-glass panels feature in the top section of the ground floor windows, and ten of these remain intact. The panels (three of which are also shown on pp 149, 156, 164) are of striking design - striking in terms of colour, figurative detail, and condensed imagery. Though worked in a different medium, they are comparable with the graphic style of the cartoons for the zodiac ceiling (pp 78, 79). The upper parts of the windows are framed in bronze, and include small opening lights for ventilation, into which the stained-glass is fixed, the panels measuring approximately 21.5cm x 14cm (8.5 ins x 5.5 ins). They depict Classical themes, and are arranged as follows:

In the zodiac bedroom the subjects are Hope, Prudence, and Power; a fourth panel depicts Terpsicho(re) (the muse of lyric poetry and dancing), and probably replaces one of the damaged or lost panels.

Second bedroom – here the muses are represented by Melpomene (tragedy), and Clio (the muse of history).

In the living room, the four stained-glass panels depict Erato (love poetry), Euterpe (flutes and music), Calliope (epic poetry), and Urania (astronomy).

A larger stained-glass panel Sir Walter Raleigh (originally called *Geography*) by the well-known glass artist Wilhelmina Geddes was installed in Bendhu for a time.[8] Geddes had studied at the Belfast School of Art, and left in the year Penprase arrived in Belfast, in 1911. That same year her Sir Walter Raleigh design had won a Commendation in the National Art Competition. Though designed by Geddes, the

6.16

6.17

6.16–6.18 Details from three of the stained-glass leaded-lights to ground floor windows representing Greek muses. Left to right: Urania, Euterpe and Melpomene

panel was probably made, at least in part, by Francis Hodge who taught briefly at the School of Art.[9] Later, at some undetermined date, the panel was "rescued" from the School by Penprase. The glass was installed at Bendhu, in a window facing Harbour Road. Like much else in the house it suffered vandalism and has not survived.

Penprase made customised ironmongery for Bendhu, including bronze handles for doors and cupboards. These were cast at the Millfield foundry, and are designed in an Art Deco genre. Some of the best examples have been remade in the Ferguson restoration, in cases where the originals have been lost or damaged.

Pen found time for many outside pursuits beyond the building of Bendhu. As Roy Johnson noted in 1977:

In the midst of all this planning, and in spite of the sheer physical effort of building alone, he still had enough energy and time to consider improvements to the general amenities of the [Ballintoy] area. He tried to co-ordinate the efforts of the local fishermen in making representations to the Minister of Commerce for improvements to the harbour, including its dredging, to make it suitable for larger boats. He designed a trophy for the Ballintoy Regatta, and he had plans to provide better facilities for bathing with the provision of a diving-board at the nearby Blue Pool. He also found time to draw and paint, to design for linen damask and stained-glass ... and for [making] a series of rather bizarre sculptures which incorporated various figures encapsulated in the skulls of strange beings.[10]

The latter category of sculptures includes *The Mystic*, depicting a man's head characterised by a third eye, or chakra, in the centre of the forehead (p 219). The sculpture is in the collection of the Ulster Museum.

6.18

Sometime after his retirement in 1953 Penprase had brochures printed advertising the 'Ballintoy Painting School' to run under his direction in July and August. Having described the setting on the north Antrim coast, the brochure advertises: "A pleasure holiday with an interest". On offer was guesthouse accommodation on a weekly basis at Bendhu, and artistic subjects for both the painting beginner and advanced student. "You supply the materials and Ballintoy will supply the subjects", the brochure claims. Weekly rates were nine guineas inclusive of accommodation and tuition. Morning and afternoon working hours were prescribed but excluded Sundays. The brochure states: "The week commences on Saturday at Tea Time and terminates the following Saturday at Dinner Time". Application to join the summer school was to be made to Mrs Stewart, Studio, 22 Grasmere Gardens, Belfast, Pen's home address. Mrs Stewart was a friend of the family.

To what extent the summer school was a going concern is unclear. It probably never was. Family members do not recollect the summer school flourishing, though there may have been individual friends and students who did avail themselves of Bendhu's environment and Pen's tuition, on a less formal basis.

6.19

6.19
Door ironmongery in bronze & copper

6.20
Brochure for the 'Ballintoy Painting School', 1950s

OVERLEAF
Maritime relief panel and facade modeling, 2009

6.20

> From the Studio window
>
> **BALLINTOY**
> PAINTING SCHOOL
>
> July & August
>
> Newton Penprase, A.M.C
> Ex Senior Lecturer
> College of Art
> Belfast
>
> Apply to Mrs. Stewart
> Studio, 22 Grasmere Gdns.
> Belfast

> The world-famed coast road from Larne to Portrush is full of scenic interest throughout, and from its many parts must be selected—as the most varied—Ballintoy, which is situated between and six miles from both Ballycastle east and Bushmills west.
>
> A PLEASURE HOLIDAY WITH AN INTEREST
>
> Studies from
> 9.00—12.30
> 2.30— 5.30
> Evenings vary
> SUNDAYS EXCLUDED
>
> If you have the appreciation and wish to understand the many beauties in Nature, come, and express yourself in any medium and take away with you health, joy and imaginations of beauty and colour.
>
> It matters not whether you are a beginner or advanced, there are plenty of suitable subjects very near "Bendhu", the guest house.
>
> You supply the materials and Ballintoy will supply the subjects

> The week commences on Saturday at Tea Time and terminates the following Saturday at Dinner Time.
>
> Nine guineas inclusive.
>
> Your attention is respectfully drawn to the fact that Two Guineas must accompany your Booking. The rest of the fees will be paid at the commencement of the course.
>
> It is better that you should bring plenty of the various materials, rather than insufficient, and that all your sketching or painting paraphernalia should be so arranged to be easily handled.
>
> Should you give plenty of time, you will be informed how to travel to
> "Bendhu",
> Ballintoy,
> Ballycastle,
> County Antrim,
> Northern Ireland.

In any event, Pen was able to accommodate himself in his Den on the first floor, and to let out the ground floor of the house during summer months, to friends and visitors.

From his retirement in 1953 until 1975, when he effectively stopped work on Bendhu, there was much time to explore creative projects, some of them described in the foregoing account. Perhaps Bendhu as a work-in-progress was more real in Pen's mind than the finished building – which, in the end, eluded him.

ENDNOTES

1. Listing grade B1. Listing reference HB 5/10/13.

2. See correspondence in Appendix 3.

3. The bronze casting was probably done with the assistance of Tommy Watson, who was the technician at the Millfield Foundry.

4. Higgins (c 1977-1980).

5. A possible origin of the timber panelling is the passenger liner Bermuda, built in Belfast by Workman Clark in 1928. She was being reconditioned in Belfast in 1931, following fire damage in Hamilton, Bermuda, when another fire broke out. Thereafter the ship was broken up for scrap. Furniture and panelling from the Bermuda came onto the market from the 1930s onwards, and still appears from time to time.

6. Newton Penprase's description of the ceiling painting, quoted by A.M. Higgins, p 12.

7. Higgins op.cit. p 10.

8. Wilhelmina Geddes (1887-1955) attended Belfast School of Art, leaving in 1911. She lived in Belfast and Dublin until 1922, and there after for three years in Belfast until 1925, when she moved permanently to London. She had a distinguished career as a stained-glass artist, her pupils including Evie Hone.

9. Correspondence with Nicola Gordon Bowe.

10. Johnson (1977).

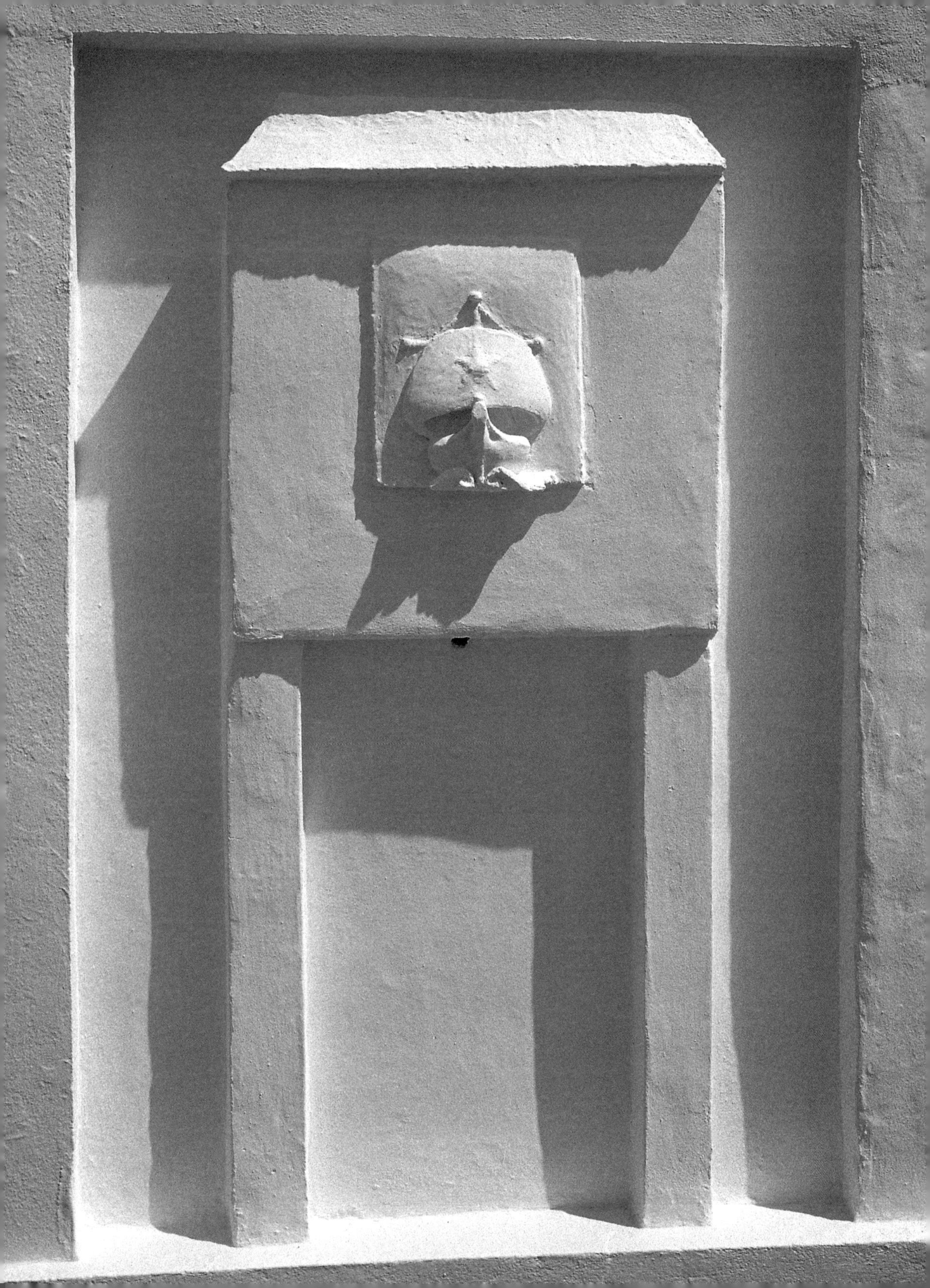

7 Recognition & final years

The 1970s witnessed new interest in Newton Penprase, with the first account of Bendhu to appear in an architectural publication in 1973, and a major exhibition of his life's work held in Belfast in 1977. The retrospective, organised by the Arts Council of Northern Ireland, brought Penprase's work to public view and provided the opportunity for critical attention. Latterly television began to take note of the house, an interest that continues to this day. Pen, an octogenarian, worked at Bendhu until accidents on site and at home in 1975-1976 left him unable to work. His wife Mildred had died in 1974.

Pen's paintings and sculpture had of course been shown to the public and his peers before. As a member of the Ulster Arts Club he took part in the annual and bi-annual exhibitions in Belfast and Bangor from the mid-1940s. The aim of the Ulster Arts Club was to promote

... the social intercourse of Art Workers ... and to further the cause of Art by Papers, Discussions, Exhibitions ... its members consist[ing] of Sculptors, Painters, Architects, Craftsmen, Designers, and those practicising or interested in Music, Literature, and ... Drama.[1]

Penprase took an active part in Club affairs, with periods as Vice President from 1946 to the early 1950s, and as President for the three years 1952-1955.[2] This last honour coincided with his retirement from the Art College in 1953 at the age of 65. Thus at the end of a normal working life he received professional recognition from his peers in the art world.

7.1

7.1
Sir Percival Brown, Lord Mayor of Belfast, at the opening of the Ulster Arts Club spring exhibition in 1953-1954, viewing the work of Mr John Knox, right. Newton Penprase, President of the Ulster Arts Club, on left

7.2
Big A3 Magazine: Issue No 3, May 1973

7.2

Typically, Pen had three artworks hung at the Ulster Arts Club exhibition for 1947: an oil painting *The Cycle of Life*, a watercolour entitled *Moonlight*, and the sculpture *Reverie*, the latter made and worked in local clay, given and fired by the Lagan Vale Terracotta Works. His exhibited paintings and sculpture were seldom offered for sale, except in the later exhibitions of the 1950s.

In 1973, Penprase and Bendhu featured in the Big A3 magazine, published within the Department of Architecture of Queen's University Belfast.[3] The author was Paul Larmour, who visited the building and met Newton, then in his eighty-sixth year. The article was the first published account of the house by an architect or architectural critic. Describing Bendhu's architectural character Larmour observed: "in dull weather its dark bulk sits heavily on the site, but with a burst of sunshine playing over it, it comes to life, its surface animated and light. The sculptural effect is produced by the architecture itself; the multi-faceted appearance determined by the additive building process".[4]

The photograph of the exterior shows a highly textured rough concrete finish, and pre-dates the similar view by Donald Carstairs taken four years later for the Arts Council exhibition, showing the building in a largely un-rendered state. The article records that Penprase "had studied architecture but did not practice, deciding that the tedium of office work was not for him". This is the only recorded instance of Newton Penprase claiming to have had an architectural training,

RECOGNITION & FINAL YEARS   089

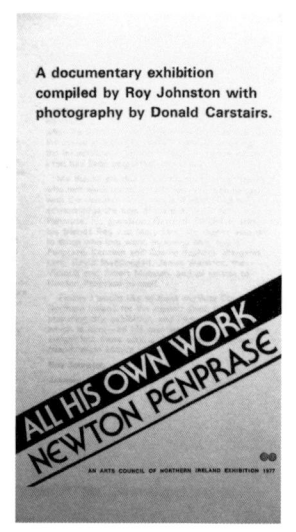

A documentary exhibition compiled by Roy Johnston with photography by Donald Carstairs.

ALL HIS OWN WORK
NEWTON PENPRASE
AN ARTS COUNCIL OF NORTHERN IRELAND EXHIBITION 1977

7.3

and raises a number of questions. Where had he studied and was he a student or an articled clerk? Did he mean he had studied under his father on an informal basis (the term 'architect' at that time having a much looser meaning than today)? Had Pen trained in architecture to some intermediate level in the years between leaving the School of Mines in Redruth and coming to Belfast in 1911? The article goes on to record some of the hostility of neighbours to Penprase and Bendhu, vandalism to stained-glass and the theft of the dragon sculpture in bronze. Pen's crime, it seems, was that he had not built a 'normal house'. The Big A3 magazine article serves as an important first-hand account of the stage building had reached in 1973.

Four years later, '*All His Own Work – Newton Penprase*', was the title of the exhibition mounted by the Arts Council of Northern Ireland, at its Belfast gallery in Bedford Street,

running from Thursday 27 January to Friday 18 February 1977. This was a retrospective of Penprase's creativity in many mediums, covering his life's work as student, artist, teacher, designer and builder of Bendhu. The catalogue sub-titled the event a documentary exhibition, and the curator was Roy Johnson, an artist and teacher at Belfast College of Art. He had met Newton Penprase over a number of years, initially in the company of students from the College staying at Bendhu. On subsequent visits he got to know Penprase well, and admired his work and independent spirit.

The catalogue lists sixty exhibits, of which half are drawings and works on paper, and the other half paintings and sculpture. There were also two trophies exhibited and a work of linen damask. The Victoria & Albert Museum in London lent seven sheets of the nine prize-winning drawings purchased by them in 1905, near 'photographic' in their accurate rendering of three dimensional ecclesiastical wood carving and silverware. Pen's family and friends

7.4

090   BUILDING BENDHU: FIRST 40 YEARS

7.3–7.4
Exhibition
Catalogue, 1977,
front cover and
title page

7.5
Antique dealer
Angus McDonald
of Holywood,
studying Penprase's
sculpture 'Two
Figures' at opening
of Arts Council
exhibition, 1977

OVERLEAF
Architect Robert
McKinstry and
family's visit to
Bendhu in 1965:
Cherith McKinstry
in conversation
with Newton
Penprase, Simon
and Leo exploring
the structure.

7.5

(and Pen himself) lent the majority of exhibits. At the time of the exhibition there were no public holdings of Penprase's work, apart from drawings held at the V&A, a situation that changed with the donation or purchase of drawings, sculpture and paintings by the Ulster Museum in the years following the retrospective. Drawings exhibited included preparatory sketches for sculptures, a design cartoon for stained-glass, studies of religious figures, designs for linen damask, life studies, and drawings of flora and fauna, the latter receiving special praise from the *Irish Times*.

There were relatively few exhibits directly relating to Bendhu, but *Drawings for Ceiling Painting, Bendhu House* (cartoon drawings for the Signs of the Zodiac ceiling),[5] and *Maquette for Sculpture at Bendhu House* were exhibited.[6] The latter was for the Neptune group. Whether there were other exhibits not listed in the catalogue that related to Bendhu, such as drawings (plans /elevations) of the house, or photos taken by Donald Carstairs is, at this remove, unclear. Perhaps by way of compensation, Roy Johnson's catalogue includes a full discussion of Bendhu. A photograph of the house is featured on the front cover, and inside the catalogue are photos of exhibits, and of Pen himself working on site (7.6). Johnson's text is an excellent description of the life and times of Pen, with an account of his building exploits in constructing Bendhu.

RECOGNITION & FINAL YEARS   091

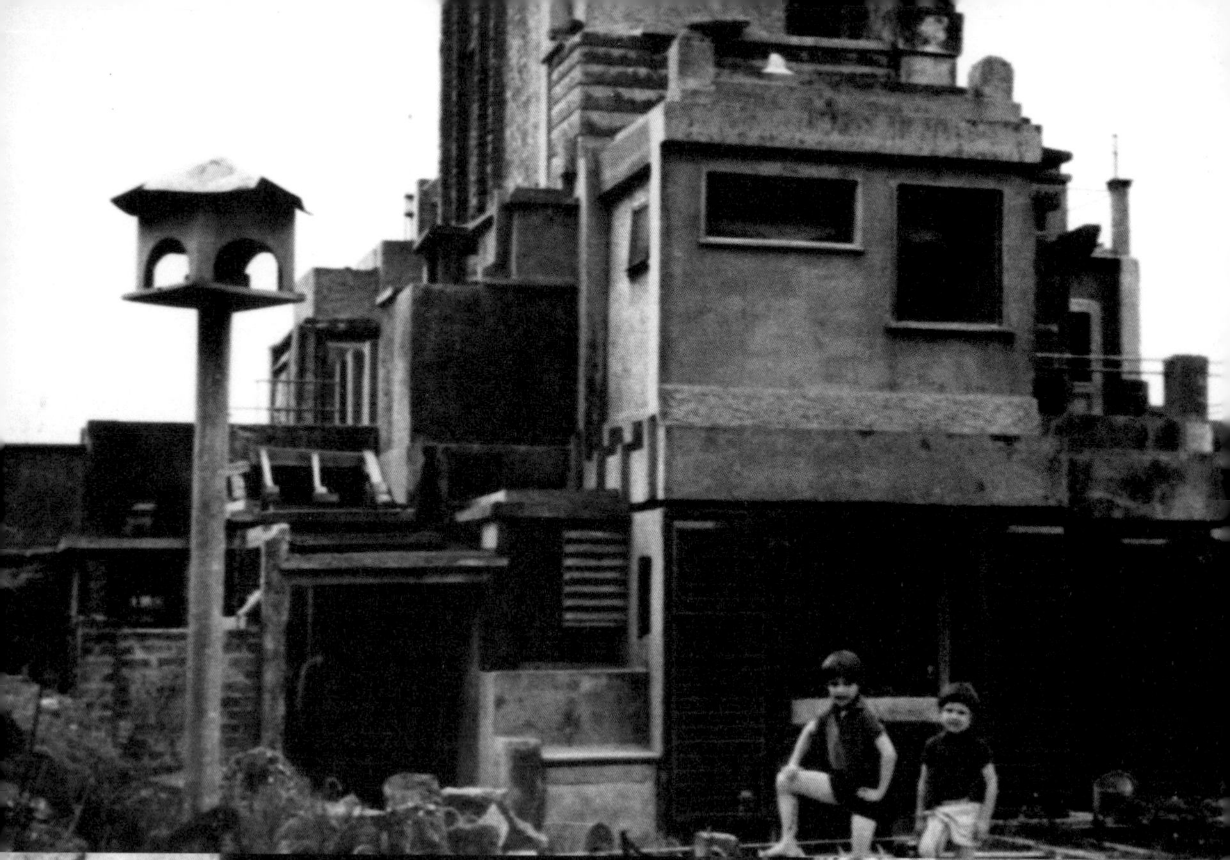

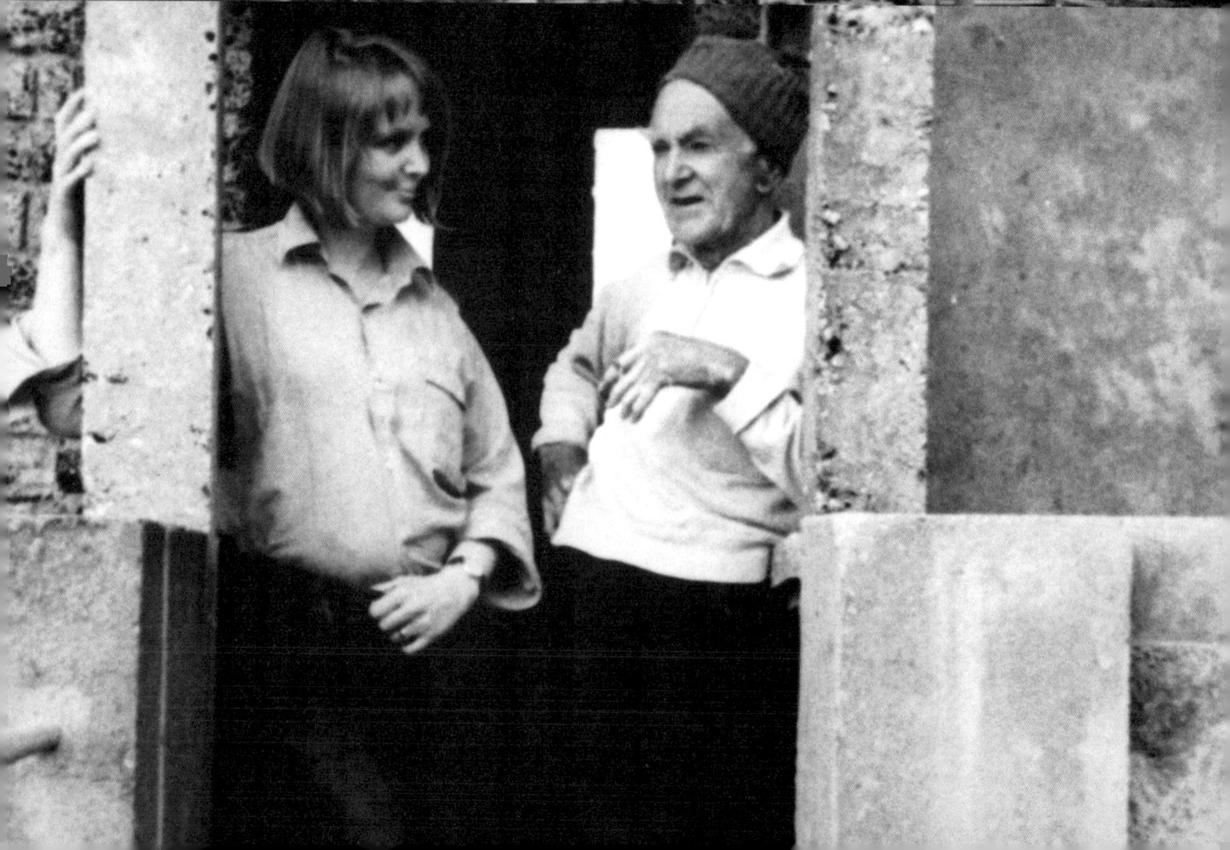

YES

The 1977 Arts Council exhibition was a signal accolade of Pen's work as artist and individualist. Unfortunately he was unable to be there himself. He was confined in his movements and unable to travel from the residential care home in Ballycastle where he had gone to live as the result of a serious domestic accident. This occurred, not on site at Bendhu as is commonly believed, but at home in Grasmere Gardens in Belfast.[7] David Penpraze recounts:

... the accident which stopped [Pen] working was in the late winter/early spring (1975-1976). He got up from his chair placed near the coal fire, and [standing up] blacked out. He fell across the hearth and when he came round his back, which was towards the open fire was badly burnt. This required hospitalisation [at Whiteabbey] where a skin graft was carried out, but ... confinement to bed for an extended period left him almost unable to use his legs.[8]

There were protracted negotiations with his son Richard, about being looked after in a residential care home. Pen resisted the move for as long as possible but finally agreed to move into Rathmoyle Home in Ballycastle in June 1976.[9] He cheered himself up with the proposition that on fine days an electrically-powered wheelchair would enable him to make the journey between Ballycastle and Ballintoy, and perhaps continue some light work at Bendhu around the house and garden. This scheme, equally alarming to friends, family and carers, quietly ignored the distance (6 miles), the precipitous rise of both Knocksaughey Hill and Harbour Road, not to mention transgressing the Highway Code. If his health was fragile his spirit was still strong. Fortunately the electrically-powered wheelchair never materialised.

One can but speculate at this distance what Pen's reaction was to the late interest in his life's work at the Arts Council retrospective – a mixture of pride and astonishment, alternating perhaps with an element of scorn that his work was being exhibited and celebrated in a public place.

In reviewing the exhibition for the *Irish Times*, Ray Rosenfield wrote:

... in all the 65 years he has lived, taught and worked in Northern Ireland, Newton Penprase has never ... had a [solo] exhibition ... In a sense, however, his work has for some 40 years been before the public all the time – a vast eccentric 'work in progress', the still unfinished Bendhu House above Ballintoy in North Antrim ...

7.6
Newton Penprase at work on site, at Bendhu, 1976-1977

OVERLEAF
The Triumph Herald view of Bendhu taken by David Penpraze in 1975

It is the project of a Renaissance man who strayed into the Kelmcott fraternity. Everything of his own making, the house growing, throwing up terraces, balconies, turrets, observation tower as his imagination soared, the ventilation, drainage and sanitation studies as Leonardo might have studied and invented, bricks made by himself and doors, bolts, hinges, screws, furniture designed and made, stained glass for windows and allegorical paintings and plaster work for ceilings and mouldings. Nothing daunted him until advancing years at last took toll and now that he is approaching 89 he has laid aside trowel and knife, brush and chisel ... [10]

7.6

Ray Rosenfield goes on to assess some of the extraordinary paintings and sculpture in the exhibition, observing the mystery, symbolism and complex creativity of the artist, and acknowledging that these works are not always easily understood by the viewer.
She concludes: "the real joy of the exhibition are sheets of drawings and wonderfully delicate watercolour studies of fish, animals, birds and plants. These are perfect, tender and humorous ...".[11]

The 1977 Arts Council exhibition attracted interest from the BBC magazine programme *Gallery* which broadcast a feature on the exhibition, the first television coverage of Pen's work. Unfortunately no copy of the programme seems to have survived.

Newton, confined to Rathmoyle Home, received accounts and photographs of the exhibition from friends and family. His health was waning, and he died in Dalriada Hospital, Ballycastle, on 9 January 1978, a couple of months short of his ninetieth birthday. He is buried at Carnmoney cemetery, Co. Antrim.

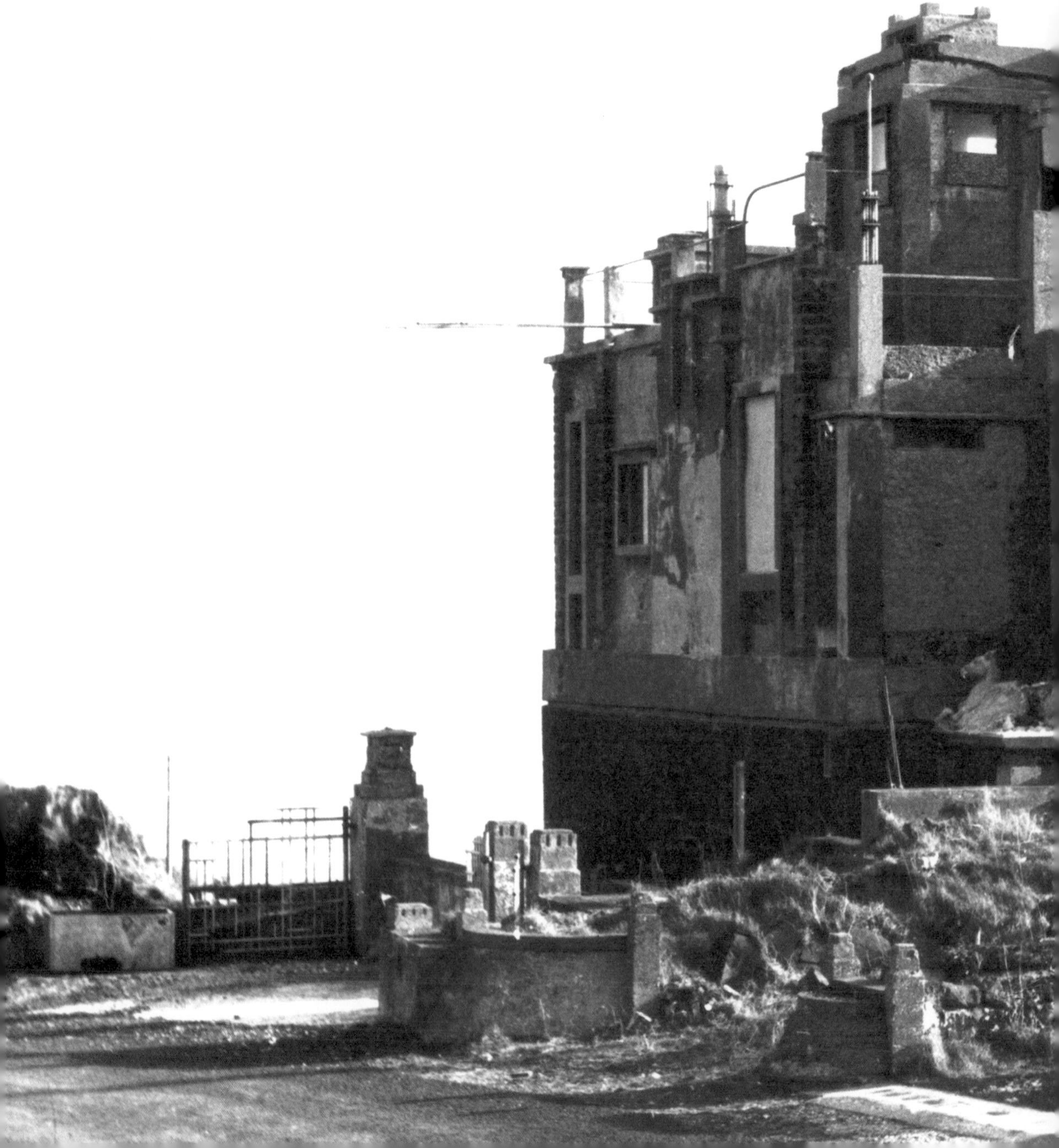

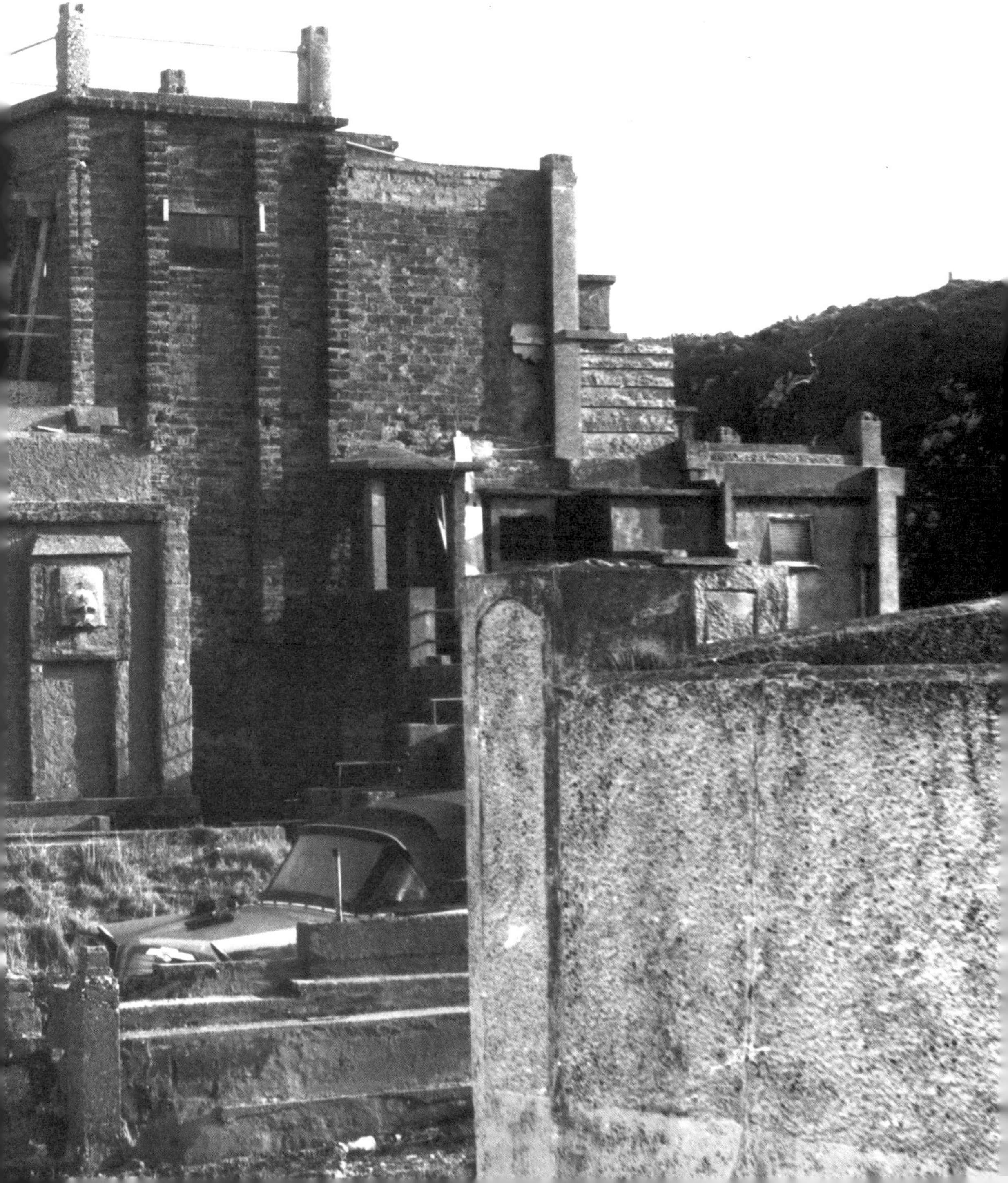

There were many tributes to him. The *Belfast Telegraph* recorded the views of several artists and past pupils, amongst them William Scott. Speaking from his Chelsea home Scott said he held Newton in great esteem: "of all the teachers at the [Belfast] College [of Art] he was the most sympathetic to the pupils. He understood their needs". Colin Middleton added: "He did a great deal to help me. He was an enthusiastic person who infected his students with the same enthusiasm. He was the driving force of art teaching at the College in my time. And he was a man who enjoyed life to the full".[12]

Few would disagree. Yet Pen approached his mortality with some humility and apprehension, putting his thoughts into writing on a number of occasions in his later years. A typical reflection is *'For a Time'* in which he ponders:

The whistle has blown, the game is over, I have played it hard with zest and pleasure. The best of my ability I have given and at times exhausted and, perhaps a few will softly clap their hands and say he has played it justly, and many others will throw their arms about and scream and shout and say it was played [unfairly]. And now, if its [sic] not already done, please fold my arms across my chest; for it is an easy way to rest, for a time. Now, clothe me in my wooden suit and button me up with twelve brass screws, and each will have a Herculean Task to do, for a time.[13]

At the 1978 Annual Exhibition of the Royal Ulster Academy of Arts, Newton Penprase's life was recognised by the display of four of his works in memoriam, the pieces being *The Bubble of Life*, the drawings *Pain* and *Fear*, and the sculpture *The Mystic*.[14]

But the main monument to his creative talents, the project that had occupied him for forty years, would now transfer to new hands. First it passed to Richard Mac Cullagh, and then to Michael Ferguson, who both set themselves the daunting task of completing Pen's vision of Bendhu.

ENDNOTES

1. Ulster Arts Club Exhibition Catalogue 1950 PRONI: D/4300/f/30.

2. Ulster Arts Club papers PRONI: D/4300.

3. Larmour (1973).

4. Idem.

5. See pp 78, 79.

6. The appellation 'House' has generally been lost in recent years.

7. Penprase had an earlier accident on site in the early-mid 1970s, in which he suffered burns from asphalt, while waterproofing the water storage tank built into the upper structure of Bendhu.

8. Correspondence with David Penpraze 26 October 2006.

9. Pen was admitted to Rathmoyle Home on 22 June 1976.

10. *Irish Times* (1977).

11. The watercolour studies are illustrated on pp 52, 53.

12. *Belfast Telegraph* (1978).

13. *For a Time*, private papers Newton Penprase, undated.

14. Anglesea (1981). p 138.

The baton handed on

RICHARD
MAC CULLAGH

MICHAEL
& LORNA
FERGUSON

BENDHU
EXTENDED

8 Richard Mac Cullagh

"It is doubtful if life is worth living without creative work". Richard Mac Cullagh[1]

Richard Mac Cullagh, the second owner of Bendhu, was born in Dublin on 10 February 1913.[2] His father was George Mac Cullagh, a member of the Royal Irish Constabulary, and his mother Evelene (née Dobbyn), who died when Richard was a few years old. Much of his early life was spent in Sligo, where his father, who remarried, was stationed with the RIC. It was in the West of Ireland that Richard's life-long interest in Celtic folklore was nurtured.

After the disbandment of the RIC in 1922 his father moved the family to Buckinghamshire in England, and, after a period, back to Ireland. They settled in Lisburn, Co Antrim, where Richard attended the Technical College. He went on to train as an art teacher at the Belfast College of Art in the years 1932-1938, followed by appointments at the Friends' School in Lisburn, and Rainey Endowed School at Magherafelt, Co Londonderry. A keen sportsman, he delighted in outdoor pursuits: his hobbies including hockey, wrestling and cycling, and, later, sailing, navigation and canoeing.

In 1940 Richard joined the Royal Naval Volunteer Reserve, and, after training, saw service in the North Atlantic patrols. From 1942 to 1945 he was Lieutenant Commander of a flotilla of several gunboats escorting supply ships on active service in the North Sea, and English Channel. Later he was involved in mine-laying operations near the Channel Islands. He was awarded the Order of St. Olav

8.1

8.1
Richard & Claire,
early 1940s

8.2
Richard
Mac Cullagh, 1940s

8.2

by the King of Norway[3] for rescuing a hundred Norwegian seamen from a sinking destroyer. As Richard later recounted to the *Belfast Telegraph*:

> *The gunboat I commanded was guarding a convoy that was passing Falmouth. Suddenly there was an explosion astern and we raced to find the Norwegian destroyer HMS Eskdale torpedoed and on fire. Whilst we were alongside, another torpedo struck. But we managed to snatch more than 100 seamen from the sea and the burning ship, just before it blew up in a terrific blast of flame. Then my overcrowded ship was heavily attacked at so close a range that I could see the incendiary bullets leaving their guns and our gunners could not return fire with the crowd of Norwegian seamen in front of them. Laying a smoke screen and zig-zagging we escaped and landed the survivors at Falmouth ...*[4]

In December 1942 Richard married Claire Hinds the youngest daughter of Edward and Emily Hinds who farmed at Sandymount, the Maze, near Lisburn.[5] They met while Richard was on home leave, and after they married Claire moved to Cornwall, to be near Richard's naval base at Falmouth.

In 1949 Mac Cullagh was appointed to the Art and Light Crafts Department of Stranmillis College (for teacher training) in Belfast. His career at Stranmillis lasted twenty-nine years, until his retirement as senior lecturer in 1978.

8.3

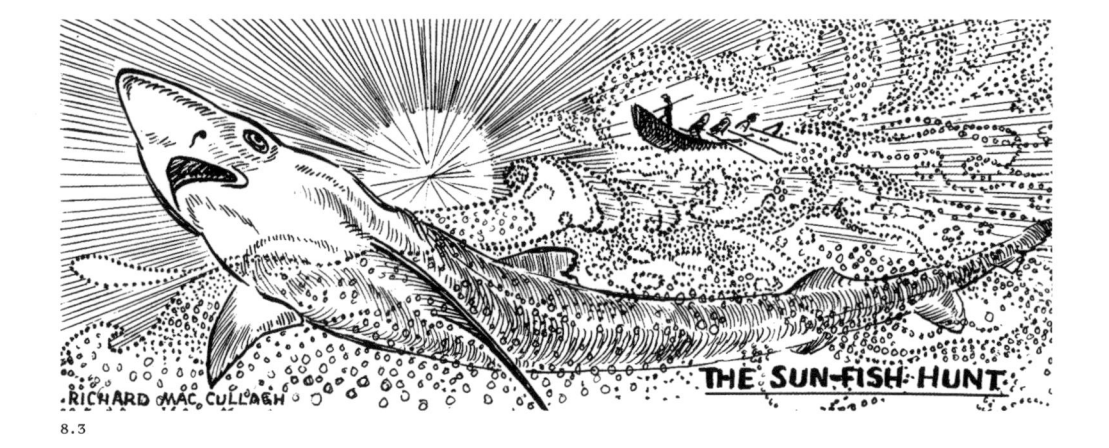

Something of a polymath, Richard had many and various extra curricular activities: fieldtrips to Italy, Greece and Turkey; canoeing and sailing expeditions all around Europe with staff and students. He is remembered as one of the great characters of the College,[6] and many ex-students regarded him as a friend.

A keen sailor, Richard Mac Cullagh's account of his sailing experiences are told in the book *Vikings' Wake*, published in 1958 in both the USA and UK.[7] Illustrated with his inimitable pen and ink maps, freely drawn, the book records Richard's many voyages in the mid- to late-1940s when, having purchased a yacht in Kiel (which he re-named Maid of Mourne), he sailed and navigated in Scandinavian waters. After several summers, he brought the boat back to Ireland via the North Sea and the Forth-

8.3
The Sun-Fish Hunt, illustration by Richard Mac Cullagh from The Irish Currach Folk

8.4
Sea voyage from Derry to Iona

OVERLEAF
Re-enacting St Columba's mission from Derry to Iona in 1963; Richard Mac Cullagh third from left

Clyde Canal. In 1963 he organised a summer school cruise in the Greek ship 'Kolotronis', travelling from Ancona in Italy to Istanbul via the Greek islands.

Mac Cullagh had an abiding interest in Celtic history and customs. He made a particular study of the folklore attached to the currachs – the lightweight boats he first encountered in the West of Ireland, made from animal skin stretched on light timber frames. He was the prime mover behind the Derry-to-Iona currach voyage that re-enacted the fourteen-hundredth anniversary of Saint Columba's missionary journey, the re-enactment taking place in 1963. Richard designed the currach used for the voyage, and was First Mate in a crew of thirteen.[8] On arrival at Iona a reception party that included the Archbishop of Canterbury and other church leaders welcomed Richard and his fellow oarsmen. Pigeons were released bearing messages of peace: the mayor of Derry receiving his two hours later. These experiences, and many others, are recorded in Richard's book, *The Irish Currach Folk*.

Richard Mac Cullagh was a man of modest disposition. He had considerable empathy for the natural world, especially the maritime environment, in which his vivid imagination found expression as both artist and writer. He painted Irish landscapes throughout his life, mostly in oils, at locations all over the country. He also produced allegorical paintings that have some affinity with

8.4

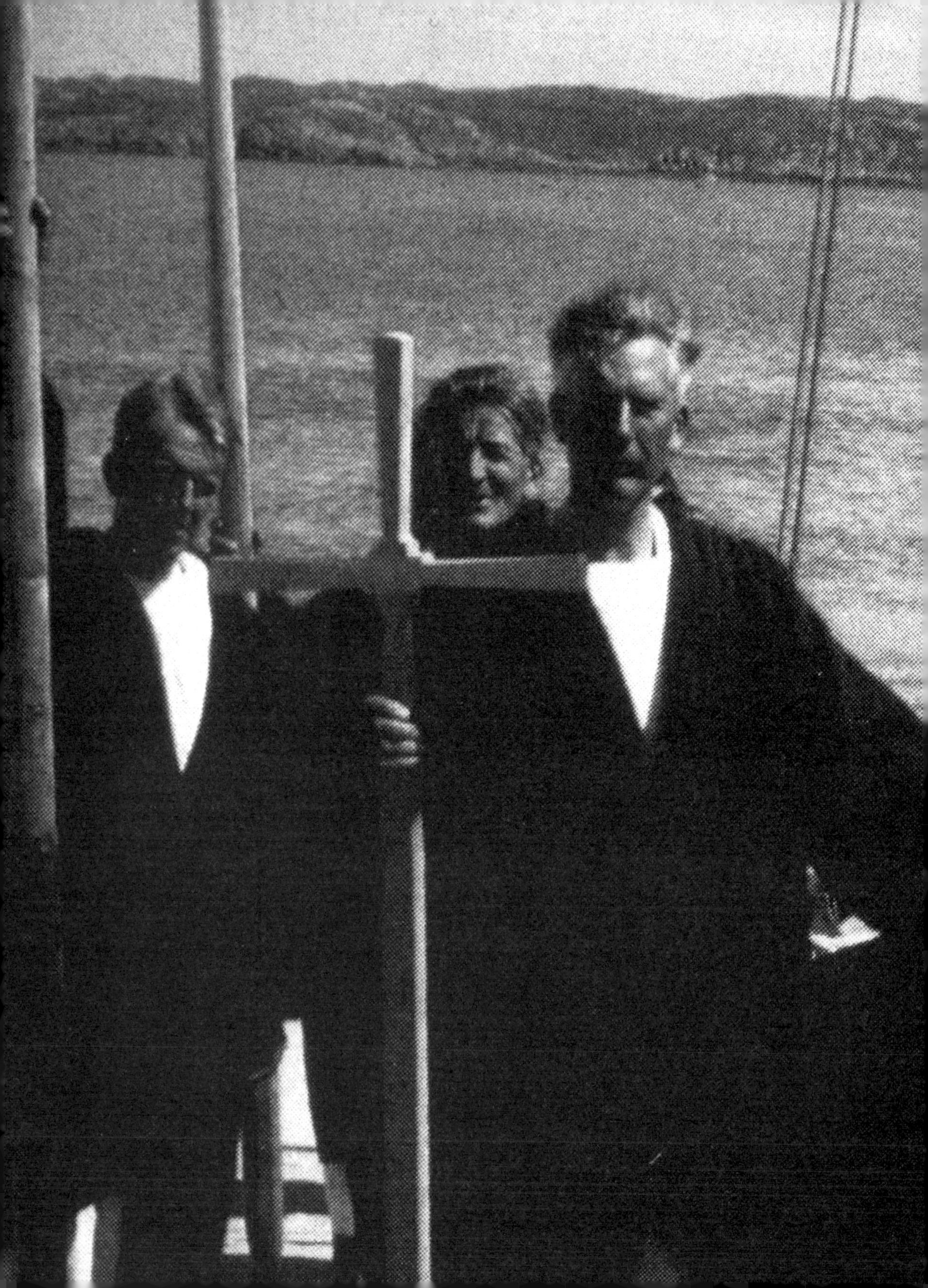

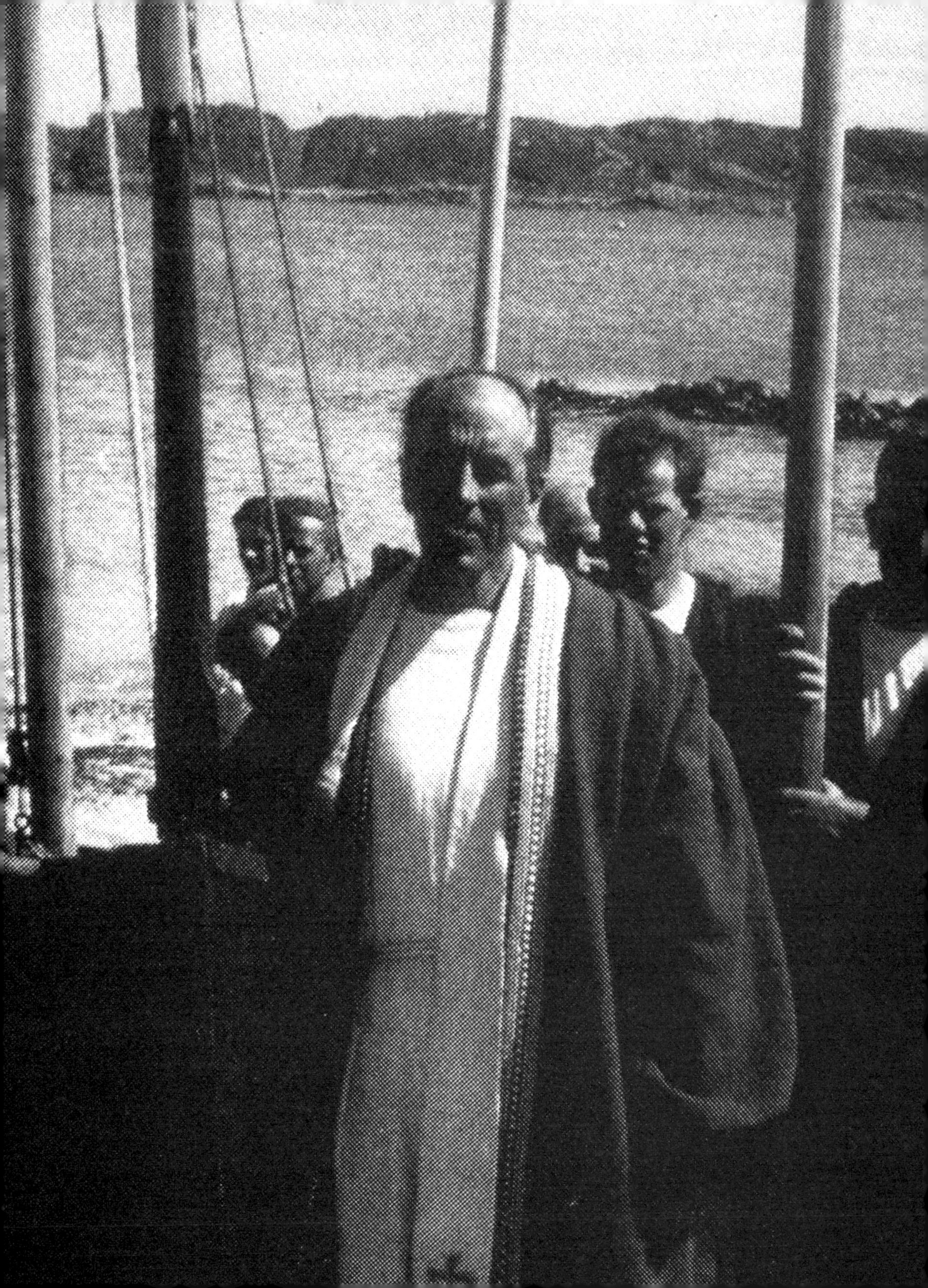

8.5
Richard
Mac Cullagh

8.6
Rendered and cream finish to Bendhu's upper stories, with dark brown below, photographed in 1992-1993

8.5

those of Newton Penprase, his teacher at the College of Art; Richard's paintings in this genre are full of symbolism, and sometimes just as bizarre. Printmaking was another medium he mastered, and correspondents of Richard received wonderful letters, often illustrated, in an unmistakably florid hand, his letters and envelopes still prized by recipients – the subject matter usually celebrating nature's wonders.

Early in his retirement from Stranmillis College, Richard Mac Cullagh considered a new venture: in 1979 Bendhu was on the market, and, knowing Newton Penprase and the Ballintoy house through the Art College, Richard was attracted to the challenge of the unfinished project.

The Penpraze family had looked after Bendhu in the three years since Newton had gone to live in Rathmoyle Care Home in Ballycastle. On Pen's death, in 1978, ownership passed to his grandson David Penpraze, whose father Richard had renounced Newton's will – not wishing to get involved in Bendhu. David Penpraze had always got on well with his grandfather, helping him on site as a teenager with many different building tasks, including the electrical wiring of the house. He considered a number of options involving customising Bendhu for his family's use. However, with many commitments at work and home, and considering the spartan condition of Bendhu with few home comforts to offer

8.6

a young family, he decided to sell the house. In November 1979 ownership of Bendhu passed to Richard and Claire Mac Cullagh, who were to be the custodians of Bendhu for the next 15 years.

Richard was inheriting a building that stood three storeys high, yet was habitable only on the ground floor. This was effectively a self-contained unit, with kitchen, bathroom and habitable rooms (the main zodiac bedroom, a second bedroom oak-panelled, the living room with dolmen fireplace, and two caravan-like bunk-rooms), the ground floor capable of sleeping seven to nine persons. It had been used by Penprase and his family at weekends and holiday times, and sometimes let out to friends, colleagues, and student groups. Two external staircases provided access to the upper floors, the walls of which enclosed empty space, but whose outer form made up the complex geometry of the building. Richard kept to Pen's schema – he did not attempt to extend or alter the design of the building except in one regard, works to the ceiling and roof of the 'studio', discussed later. His son Richard P L MacCullagh remembers the building well:

My father acquired Bendhu when I was 14, so it was obviously a very exciting time to have such an unusual house to stay in and I spent many weekends and longer holidays there during my teenage years ... When we first took over the place, it hadn't been used for some time so my parents set about making it habitable, and before long the ground floor was rewired and replumbed with new bath suite added and we installed a decent cooker in the kitchen. My mother did much of the internal decoration in the Master Bedroom or 'Zodiac Room' respecting the original colour scheme and the other rooms ... My father and I [and sister Nuala] painted the exterior but this was perhaps a few years later on ... this was all done from ladders and from the various ledges and roof levels. This must be where I got my head for heights ... it was exhilarating watching the Atlantic swell roll in with waves crashing on the rocks and cliffs surrounding the house. [9]

There was the perennial problem with the flat roofs, which would leak on occasion and unfortunately never quite, got sorted in our time. I remember various attempts at sealing them and laying a terracotta tile roof on the 1st floor balcony. The 'Captain's Cabin' [or Pen's Den] on the 1st floor was also made habitable but we never got round to fitting out the 1st and 2nd floor studio. My parents spent a lot of their time working on the house ... thankfully we never had a television there, as one would find inspiration in the seascape and Bendhu ... [and] we were never short of visitors, invited and uninvited!

Falling asleep was always a pleasure as you would hear the waves crashing on the shore, and in gales it would be really exciting as the wind would be howling outside but you felt quire secure, [knowing] at least you would not lose any slates! Later ... [I] would have the pleasure of sleeping and waking under the zodiac ceiling, something one never forgets! I believe my parents were good custodians of Bendhu and they appreciated its unique character ... while we never finished the upper floor or completely sorted the flat roof we did manage to preserve its special architectural and historic interest.

The appearance of Bendhu changed noticeably during Richard Mac Cullagh's time with the application of smooth render to the external block walls, and subsequent painting. This radically changed the appearance of the house by covering over the textured finishes of the concrete block construction, and colouring the walls cream and brown.

Most of the other construction work carried out on Bendhu at this time involved repairing or weatherproofing the habitable parts of the building to maintain satisfactory living conditions on the ground floor. This included installing new terracotta paving and a waterproof membrane to the main roof terrace, alterations to the fireplace in the living room made necessary by downdraughts, electrical re-wiring, plumbing in copper pipework replacing lead, renewing sections of flooring, and new tiling to the entrance hall at the front door.

Richard Mac Cullagh's builder carried out the rendering of the upper first and second floor walls in or around 1980, but Pen before him had already rendered the outside walls on the ground

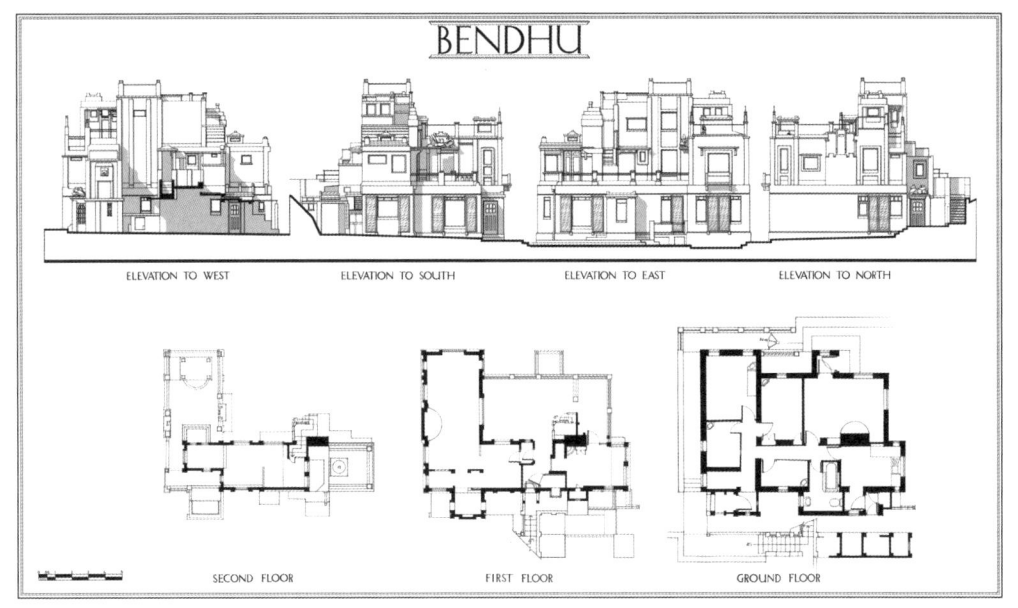

8.7
Bannister Survey
1986

floor.[10] These lower walls were rendered with a cement mixture that included basalt stone chippings as aggregate. The natural colour of this was a dark blue-black, with a sharp textured finish, and in moist conditions of sea spray and rain the render was shiny and glistened. In aesthetic terms this was effectively a base course, or symbolically a rusticated plinth. In practical terms the basalt render assisted in weatherproofing the construction. However, the painting of the basalt render, in dark brown, subdued its appearance considerably.

Pen had constructed the walls to the first and second floors in blockwork (in contrast to the in-situ concrete walls of the ground floor)

8.8

which explains the thinner wall thickness and the frequent use of pilasters to stiffen the construction in the upper storeys of the house. This was a more economic and faster way to build, and one that did away with time-consuming construction of timber formwork. The exposed dense concrete block presented a strikingly textured finish, the utility of which variously shocked or intrigued (and in some cases incensed) passers-by and neighbours alike. Pen had started to render the upper stories, but the west and north elevations, both highly visible from Harbour Road, remained in bare masonry. It was these expanses of blockwork that were smooth-rendered by Richard Mac Cullagh's builder in the early-1980s. The west elevation was probably the largest single area to be rendered.[11] Thereafter the whole superstructure was painted – the smooth

8.8
Richard Mac
Cullagh outsde
Bendhu,
September 1993

render of the upper superstructure in a cream colour, and the ground floor external masonry (rendered with the basalt aggregate mixture) a dark chocolate brown. Except in sunny weather, it was a subdued and somewhat lifeless colour combination, though perhaps appropriate in the context of neighbouring houses; the play of light and sparkle on the basalt aggregate lost in decoration.

Despite all the building work carried out at Bendhu during Richard Mac Cullagh's ownership – repairs, rendering, new installations, decoration – for the fifteen years between 1979 and 1994 the upper floors of the house remained unoccupied, and effectively an empty building shell.

With Richard's encouragement a measured survey of Bendhu was made in 1985-1986 by his son-in-law, Bill Bannister, a graduate of the University of Ulster.[12] The survey comprises a set of three floor plans and four elevations, drawn at 1:50 scale. The survey shows the building as constructed and left by Penprase in the mid-1970s, there having been no major structural changes to the plan layout in the intervening period; so the plans surveyed by Bannister are, despite the time lapse, effectively a record of Bendhu as completed by Penprase during his lifetime. It is an important drawing, one that can be compared to both earlier and later plan layouts, i.e. with Pen's 1936 building plan (p 52) showing his original intentions, and with the 2006 record drawing (p 142) showing Michael Ferguson's renovation and extension.

On 8 May 1992, Bendhu was listed by the Department of the Environment (DOE) as a Building of Special Architectural or Historic Interest.[13] The listing was at Grade B1 and included not only the house but also external elements within its curtilage, namely the concrete bird table, garden pool, and cliff-face stairway. The Listing Notice describes the building:

An eccentric and highly original house designed and built by Newton Penprase, artist and art teacher working entirely on his own over a period of forty years from 1936 to 1975. Laid out on three levels which are connected by exterior stairs only, it was constructed entirely of reinforced concrete. Roofs are flat and serve as balconies which are surrounded by iron railings. Windows are mostly of bronze but there are some of timber.

The house was decorated inside and out by the artist himself. On the exterior are sculptures of a horse and a bull amidst waves above the front porch; a phoenix bird on the first floor balcony, and a relief panel of an ancient sailing ship on the west wall. Ground floor rooms have panelled walls and ceilings.

The decoration of these shows the artist's interest in astrology and Greek mythology. One room has a circular ceiling panel containing a modelled star pattern and painted signs of the zodiac; another has limed oak wall panels carved with naturalistic plant motifs. The stain glass panels incorporated in the ground floor windows depict Virtues and Muses.

The artist also modelled a bird table in the garden and constructed a garden pool and a walled stairway against the face of the cliff at the north point of the garden. Together with these external works Bendhu house stands as a uniquely sculpturesque product of a highly individual and creative artistic personality in addition to containing some accomplished works of decorative art.[14]

The listing of Bendhu in 1992 was official endorsement of its architectural merit and Modernist spirit, and to an extent, of Newton's perseverance and eccentricity. There was a certain irony in this: the Environment Service was listing a building that Penprase had spent much of his life in dispute over with the authorities.

The recognition occurred in the same year as Richard Mac Cullagh's reluctant decision to sell Bendhu. Claire was in poor health, having suffered from Parkinson's disease from the 1980s, and in her last years was wheelchair bound. In addition they both had to deal with the major undertaking of moving house at Jordanstown: because of road widening and the compulsory purchase of their home of twenty-three years at Silverstream House, they were moving to a newly commissioned house, Tideways, a few hundred yards along the shoreline of Belfast Lough. As he turned eighty, Richard Mac Cullagh reluctantly, but probably with some relief, decided the time had come to call it a day at Bendhu.

The Halifax estate agency initially handled the sale. Despite interest, Bendhu proved hard to sell. Notices appeared in the local press advertising Bendhu for sale, detailing the unique qualities of its site and design.

8.9
West elevation, showing large rendered areas of blockwork. (Bannister survey)

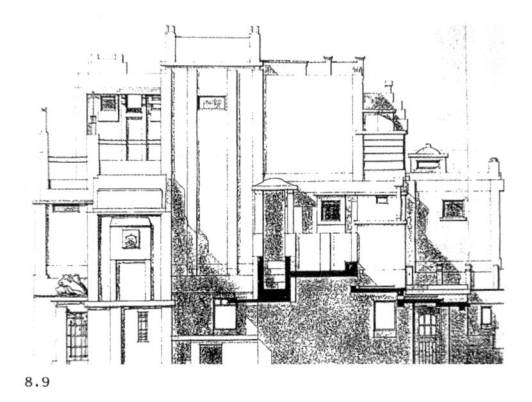

8.9

The *Belfast Telegraph*, under a photograph of Richard Mac Cullagh standing in front of Bendhu on a blustery day, reported:

Seaside curiosity goes on market ... One of Ulster's most eccentric homes ... is up for sale ... The ground floor is a complete dwelling, with oak-panelled rooms and windows containing stained-glass inserts drawn from Greek mythology ... this is one of the finest ... sites in western Europe, commanding [views to] the North Atlantic, the lower Hebrides and a whole array of headlands, islands and skerries.[15]

By September 1993 new estate agents, Agar Murdoch and Deane, were handling the sale.

For a short time the author took part in the Bendhu story. I had joined the staff of Queen's University Belfast as a lecturer in the Department of Architecture and Planning in January 1993. In the previous summer, thirty-two years since my first visit, Richard Mac Cullagh showed me around the house. In discussion, the idea materialised of developing Bendhu as an educational base with public access. Informal discussions took place at Queen's University Belfast and the Historic Buildings Branch of the DOE – exploring the idea of setting up an education foundation at Bendhu for visiting groups and students. Meetings were held with, amongst others, Donald Girvan, David Evans, Colin Hatrick, Laurence Manogue, and correspondence was exchanged with Sir Charles Brett. Brett's view on Bendhu was summed up in his comment ... "I have never been one of the warmest admirers of Bendhu".[16] It was a building that in his view had probably "turned more Ulster people against contemporary architecture than any other building".[17] In a briefing paper the objectives of the proposed Foundation were set out. These were to make the building available as an

8.10

educational resource for student groups, to open the house to the general public at certain times, to disseminate information on the work of Newton Penprase, and to provide facilities for an artist in residence.

Though Sir Charles Brett was not optimistic about the venture, he was helpful in opening various doors for canvassing support, but in the event the proposal for an educational foundation received insufficient backing to be viable. As one door closed another opened. In 1994, a new era began in the story of Bendhu with its purchase by Michael and Lorna Ferguson, whose work at Bendhu is the subject

8.10
Lino-cut print
by Richard
Mac Cullagh,
depicting many
of his interests

OVERLEAF
Phoenix Rising
sculpture by
Newton Penprase

of the next two chapters. The same year, a number of people closely associated with Bendhu were present at the author's illustrated talk on the building's history and design, one of a lecture series organised by ARCSOC, the student architectural society of Queen's University Belfast. Amongst those attending were family members of the three owners of Bendhu – Richard Penpraze, David and Yvonne Penpraze, Richard Mac Cullagh and Richard P L MacCullagh, and Michael and Lorna Ferguson. The Ulster Arts Club provided a social rendezvous afterwards for bringing together the dramatis personae who feature in this book.

In his last years Richard Mac Cullagh was preparing for publication an account of his wartime experiences in *Poems of Love and War*, and collecting together the paintings of a lifetime (over eighty works in oil and watercolour) for exhibition. Another project was the draft of a novel entitled *The Twentieth Century Argonauts*, the title mirroring, arguably, the experience of his own maritime adventures.

If one person can be credited with expressing in prose-poetry the spirit of Bendhu, Richard Mac Cullagh is that person. His love of, and respect for, Bendhu's setting and creator is palpable in his writing:

> *... the rising and setting of the sun, the vast Atlantic horizons, the big seas thundering on the skerries and smashing with terrific force on the cliffs, the galloping white-maned sea horses sweeping in squadrons past, the eerie cry of gulls and their swooping flight – all this activated Penprase's urge to create. Likewise did the quiet beauty of calm seas inspire.*[18]

Richard died on 12th October 2000 at the age of 87. A service of Thanksgiving was held in the Church of the Holy Name, Greenisland on 15 October, followed by burial at the family grave in Ballycarry graveyard, Co Antrim. Bendhu was once again in new hands.

ENDNOTES

1. Correspondence with Richard Mac Cullagh 23 May 1996.

2. Full name: Richard John Mac Cullagh (1913-2000).

3. King Hakon VII of Norway.

4. *Belfast Telegraph*, 14 April 1993.

5. Claire Hindes (1923-1998).

6. *Stranmillis Bulletin* (2000).

7. Mac Cullagh (1958).

8. Mac Cullagh (1992) p 180.

9. Correspondence with Richard Mac Cullagh 30 May 2007.

10. The builder was probably Mr Dan Craig, who lived locally, and did various work on the house for both Newton Penprase and Richard Mac Cullagh.

11. Correspondence with Richard P L MacCullagh, 23 March 1995.

12. William James Bannister enrolled in the HND Architectural Technology and Management course.

13. Historic Buildings List Number 1362.

14. Dr Paul Larmour prepared the report for the DOE that recommended listing.

15. *Belfast Telegraph* 30 September 1993.

16. Correspondence with Charles Brett 21 December 1993.

17. Brett (1996) p 213.

18. From *The Ben Dhu Experience*, compiled by Richard Mac Cullagh, unpublished.

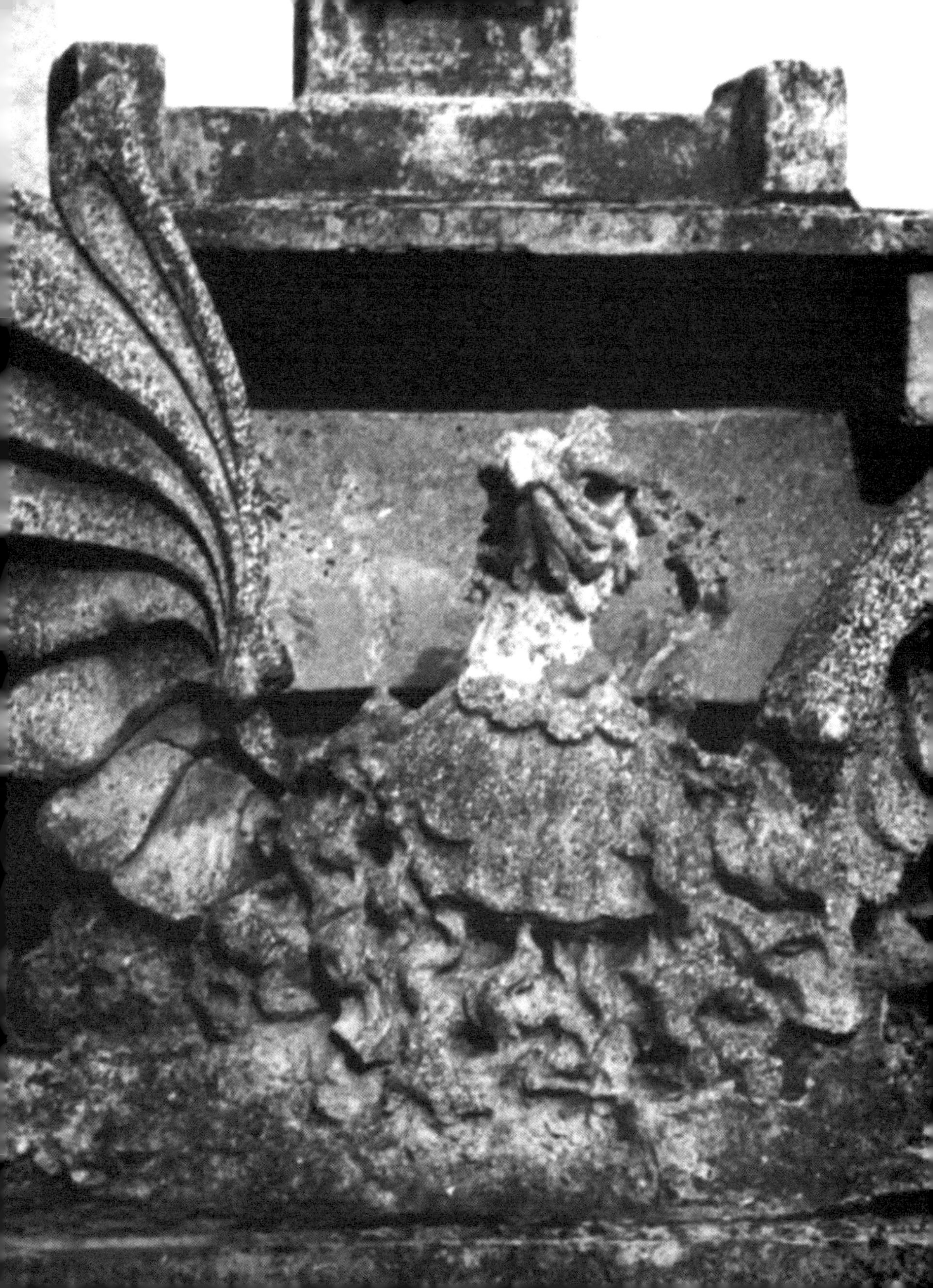

9 Michael & Lorna Ferguson

With the sale of Bendhu in April 1994, Michael and Lorna Ferguson became the new custodians. The building presented a drab and somewhat forbidding presence, the exterior in cream and dark brown and still a shell, largely windowless on the upper floors. To some it looked like a neglected wartime utility. The Fergusons knew they were taking on a daunting task; how would they approach the challenge?

It helped that Michael comes from the third generation of a family of house builders and developers, F T Ferguson & Co, the firm started by his grandfather. He joined the company after attending Ballynahinch Intermediate School, where his hobbies included cars and, what became a life-long interest, photography. Fascinated by the work of the company's in-house architect, he trained alongside him and eventually filled that role himself in all but name. Typically the firm would build 100-200 houses a year, peaking to over 500 in the mid-1960s, together with a number of individual homes each year, depending on land availability and trading conditions. In the 1950s and 1960s many of the dwellings being built were the so-called subsidy houses, for which grants were available under the Northern Ireland Housing Acts. His training with the company thus prepared him for the design and construction of both individual and groups of houses, fostering skills in site layout and landscape design. His enthusiasm for contemporary architecture and modern design was nurtured through books

9.1

9.1
Lorna and Michael
Ferguson at
Bendhu in 2006

9.2
The White House,
Knockagh, designed
by Michael
Ferguson, 1969-1971

9.2

and magazines, and he became aware of Modernist architects such as Le Corbusier and Frank Lloyd Wright. The *Architects' Journal* and a copy of *The Modern House* by FRS Yorke provided further examples of contemporary architecture. Structurally adventurous buildings caught his eye, including two houses by Noel Campbell dating from the late-1950s, the Smyth House at Strand Road, Portstewart, with its unusual butterfly roof, and the Rainey House at Dhu Varren, Portrush, with its pronounced cantilever structure.[1] Other buildings with unusual construction features were noted on his daily travels.

The architect Eric Lyons provided another role model. Lyons' housing designs for Span developments built in the 1950s and 1960s in the London boroughs of Blackheath and Richmond, and at New Ash Green in Kent, set new standards in integrating speculative housing within a landscape setting. These examples encouraged Michael to build housing layouts with a similar approach in Ulster. This ability to work with landscape was recognised in his design for 112 houses at the Ash Green development in Antrim, which won a regional award from the National House Builders' Council in 1979.[2] Michael and his building team have continued to integrate landscape design into housing developments and have received further recognition, including a

9.3

9.3
White House,
Knockagh: living
room interior

9.4
White House,
Knockagh: upper
ground-floor plan

Construction Employers Federation Award in 2006 for the greenfield development of Glencraig Manor in Antrim.

An early demonstration of Ferguson's architectural ability was the design and construction of the White House, built at Knockagh, Co Antrim in 1969-1971, a house that is still his main family home.[3] Taking full advantage of its site with south facing views over Belfast Lough, the building is a confident Modernist work.

The house is arranged as a series of linked pavilions for dining, living and sleeping, built around a courtyard on the north side of the building. A smaller entry court next to the carport provides direct access to the house through the kitchen and utility wing. The living pavilion is an expansive room flooded with daylight, with one long wall of glass, south-facing, with views to Belfast Lough and the Co Down hills beyond. An open fireplace and chimney form part of a 'floating' sculpted block, a Modernist device that acts as space-divider and gives focus to the room. Large pivoted doors, inspired by Francis Pym's extension to the Ulster Museum, connect to the bedroom and dining pavilions on either side of the living space, providing a 30-metre vista through the house when doors are open. From the living room a spiral stair descends to a hallway below and the formal entrance to the house, setting up an arrival sequence culminating in the living room piano nobile.

The steel and glass houses of the American architect Philip Johnson, dating from the late 1940s and 1950s, may have been an influence on the design of the Ferguson home, as may the Californian houses of Richard Neutra of the same period. Many of Neutra's houses have elongated living areas, with glazed walls from floor-to-ceiling along one entire façade, opening up views to the outside landscape and terraces. Additionally, Neutra's open-plan living spaces were often sub-divided into different areas by means of a 'floating fireplace', as here in the Ferguson's home. The house has been described as exhibiting "the joys of elemental expression, light, space and International Style planning characteristic of its period".[4]

The White House received a DOE award in 1988 for 'a house in harmony with its landscape'. In the early 2000s the dining pavilion was updated to make a contemporary studio-kitchen-living area, with new sun deck constructed on the west side of the house.

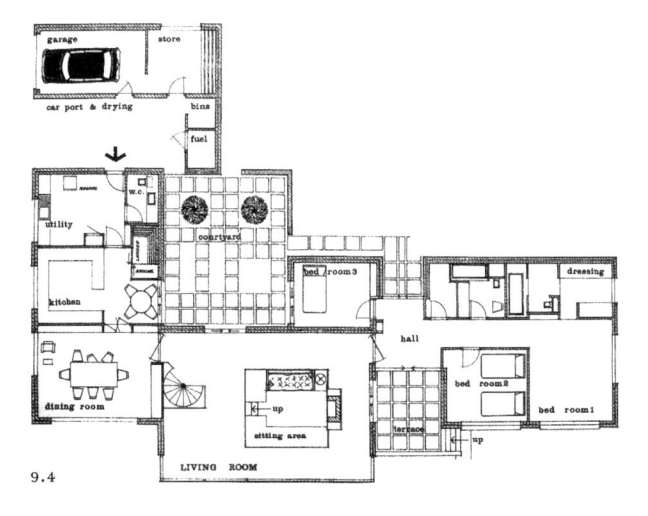

9.4

Thus Michael Ferguson, though untrained formally in architecture, brought to Bendhu the talents of an experienced house designer. His skills in planning, landscaping, construction and management of building sites, together with an unfettered enthusiasm for modern design, were to stand him in good stead in tackling Bendhu.

At the start, Michael's first thoughts were that "the building was bizarre, it will be a challenge, but [Bendhu] had a wonderful location and potential as a site".[5] That the building was different from the norm appealed to him enormously, as did its kinship with battlements and fortified structures. With quiet modesty he says he was not intimidated by the prospect of renovating Bendhu, despite all its technical complexities, and he never had any real doubts about the viability of taking on the project. Perhaps the fact that he had not met Pen during his lifetime, and that he himself had not been conscious of the building in the past, helped put some distance between him and the Newton Penprase legend. Michael relates how he and his wife first came across Bendhu:

Lorna was working in Ballymoney and mentioned that an unusual house at Ballintoy was up for sale. Having a passion for unusual or landmark buildings, I made tracks to view. The building was open to the elements and easily explored. The views were breathtaking, but the building was in a sorry neglected state, being absorbed back into the natural surroundings. Not for Lorna.[6]

But Michael was intrigued with the building, and recalls his early meetings with Richard Mac Cullagh who was then in his eighties:

To gain access to the ground floor, the only part of the building which was occupied, the lock had to be sprayed with WD40, which Richard had in his pocket on each visit for that purpose. I had promised Lorna that I would not buy Bendhu, she wanted a picturesque cottage, not a quirky concrete building, no matter how lovely the outlook. But by then Bendhu had spun its intrigue, and the challenge of recapturing a faded vision together with the views brought Lorna around ... We took possession on April Fool's Day,

9.5

9.5
White House,
Knockagh:
kitchen, living
studio
re-modelled
in 2004

9.6
General view
of Bendhu, on
completion of
first phase of
Michael
Ferguson's
renovations

9.6

and that Easter 1994 was one of the bleakest we have experienced, with horizontal hailstones and chilling winds. At the start we imposed on friends to assist in clearance and stripping out of the building. It took six months to have the lounge in a half-habitable state to stay in, and we don't think many felt [the restoration] was an achievable challenge.[7]

Lorna Ferguson involved herself in the restoration. Her attitude to the house warmed as it was refurbished, room-by-room. By simply living in the ground-floor apartment she was won over. As well as furnishing and interior design, her special contribution was the design and restoration of garden areas, including the boundaries of exposed cliff edges. The planting was chosen to withstand the Atlantic storms and double as a safety-barrier.

Asked about his approach to renovating the property Michael Ferguson says the first objective was to strip the house to the basic structure to reveal its condition, prior to repairs and renewals. This entailed clearing the house of the contents of the two previous owners. Pen had often utilised recycled materials, and subsequently many goods were hoarded for possible reuse in the future. As Ferguson observed "active minds have a tendency to hoard things for future projects".[8] Weeks were spent emptying the building of contents to an adjacent landfill that was later landscaped as part of the garden. This also allowed the bare structure to dry out. Many roofs leaked, being typically flat with minimal incline to deal with the rainwater run-off. The roof forming the external terrace at first floor leaked to such an extent that water cascaded into the hall below during a downpour. The source of water ingress was often obscure, and repairs to the leaks were difficult to achieve because of the exposed site. The complex external form of the building was an added difficulty. In the event roof repairs were effected using a bithuthene membrane, with associated works providing rainwater disposal, including lead soakers and flashings protecting vulnerable edges and forming upstands to prevent water over-spill.[9]

Repairs to the structure were carried out as required – some concrete elements needed to be strengthened and replaced. The original concrete mix for the building in some cases was low in its cement content, and throughout the building the original concrete was reinforced by recycled railway lines, and concrete bulked out with boulders and assorted aggregate.

The uniqueness of Bendhu was paramount in the Fergusons' minds as they went about the task of restoration. At the same time they "wanted the house to be comfortable, special, and enjoyable to live in". They delighted in the hands-on restoration that only a fussy, elaborately detailed building offers the DIY enthusiast.

The next tasks went hand in hand – to decorate the outside of the building and install new windows – both major tasks. The external painting of the building was a group effort carried out by family and friends, that transformed the appearance of the building – in white render, with, initially, light cream banding on string courses and cills. The new colours replaced the former scheme of

9.7–9.8
Michael and Lorna Ferguson at work on Bendhu, 1995

9.9
Phoenix Rising sculpture on the east terrace, before extension, 1995

OVERLEAF
Bendhu restored in 2000-2003; gates and railings added later

9.7

9.8

126   BUILDING BENDHU: THE BATON HANDED ON

cream and brown. Over fifty windows have been installed throughout the building - new double-glazed units for the upper storeys, replacing the plywood boarded-up openings, and single and double glazed units fixed direct to masonry on the lower floor. The new window installation and exterior decoration contributed greatly to the sense of progress in restoring Bendhu, barely a year since work began. Aesthetically the double-glazed PVC frames co-ordinated with the new white pristine appearance of the rendered masonry. On the ground floor, double-glazed units replaced where possible the frameless single glazed windows installed by Pen, with the glass as before fixed directly to the rebated concrete.[10] Repairs were carried out to the bronze opening lights, and the stained-glass cleaned.

9.9

These were major undertakings carried out by Michael and his team, and he acknowledges that the building refurbishment was very much a cooperative effort:

Raymond Gilmore, a local builder, helped out during the first months of exploration, and we imposed on other friends and relatives to assist. Because of this support the project never seemed that daunting — we had a vision of Bendhu being renewed, and the hope that one day it would be a comfortable house. Ballintoy has lots of men involved in the building industry, and there were those who knew the house and the history well, thinking fondly of the quirky building and its original builder. Fortunately Lorna and I made many friends in the area willing to help with the restoration. Pen had been well liked, and was fondly remembered by the community, and several local builders were willing to put their skills into the various building challenges. Lyle Taggart and his men did the first phase, in replacing

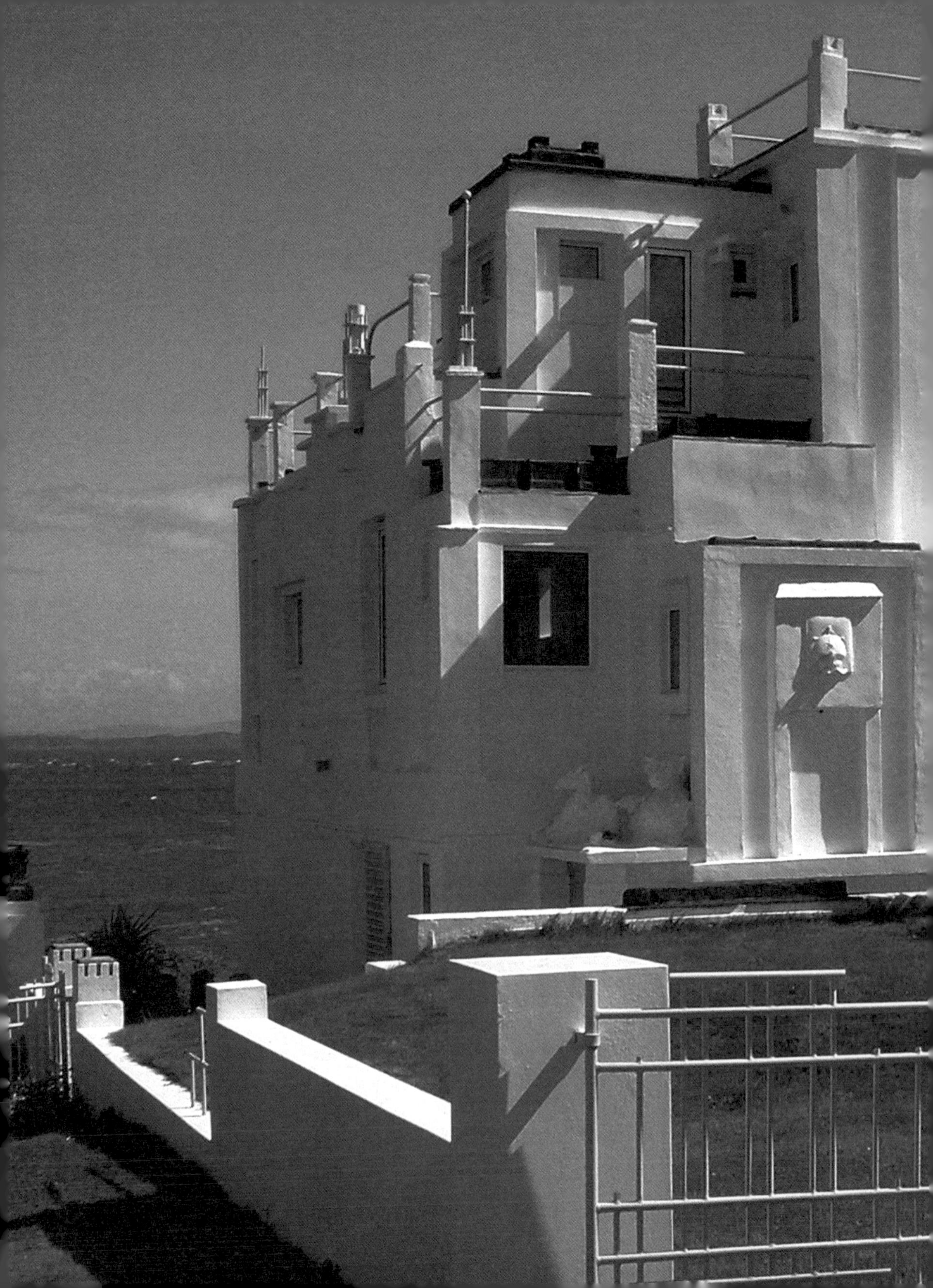

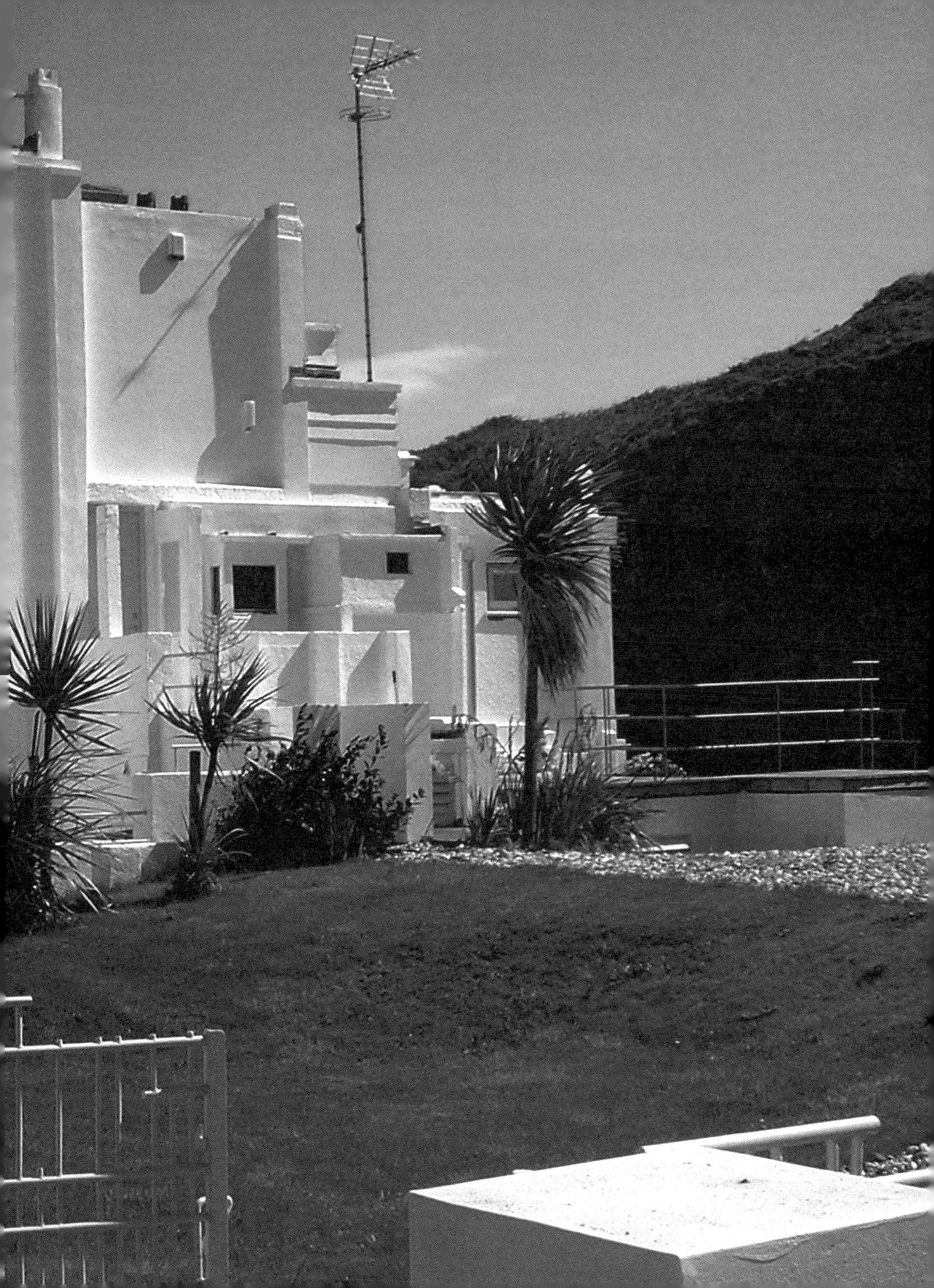

the living room ceiling, building the shower enclosure to the ground floor and replacing the outside doors. Raymond McCaw, who also worked for Lyle and later started his own building company, built both the sun lounge and garage in the second phase, and installed the internal concrete stairs to the first and second floors. These were all skilled and enthusiastic tradesmen. Jeffrey Cupples from the village, a plasterer, became good friends and for many years has helped with the project. Some of Penprase's ironmongery was missing from the ground floor, notably bespoke handles in handcrafted metal from the bedrooms, and I was fortunate that Ken Gilmore was able to make identical handles. He also made over twenty brass and copper matching ones for the replacement ground floor kitchen.[11]

The process of building, with the designer on site involved with every decision, has its own dynamic, as Michael observed:

You learn from what was built before, and all the refurbishment and restoration projects looked back to what Pen would have done had he been here today. Bendhu was never a house to remain in the past. Pen's creation of light and shadow in the structure gives the building vibrancy, playing a large part in arriving at solutions for many of the rebuilding features. Having got the building almost watertight, the jobs became more enjoyable, each finishing a piece of the puzzle and bringing the building back to life, not in an eccentric way, but in a youthful and playful manner — as a place to enjoy, admire and live in.[12]

While Michael was building, Lorna was exploring and finding hidden garden features concealed behind rough grasses. Penprase's orchids still managed to grow through the ivy now covering the limestone, and more decorative plants – red-hot pokers and wild daisies – all did well. Pen had created a garden that offered shelter to wind coming from all directions, the garden framing the many unique views that the site enjoys.

With the exterior of the building sealed from the weather, and outside decorations complete, attention could shift to the interior. Here the plan was to complete one room at a time. Thermal insulation was installed to the interior face of all external walls and roof slabs, with 50mm polyurethane board mechanically or foam fixed to the structure, following the shape of the existing built form. Bendhu's eccentric geometry, with multiple roof-lights, window recesses, and ad hoc openings made this a demanding and time consuming task, but has kept

9.10
Bathroom
mosaic design
in shower tray

the geometry intact and has retained the original spatial quality of the house, in all its complexity and delight.

Early in the renovations an important decision was made about the air ventilation to the ground floor accommodation. Pen had designed a hidden ventilation system, introducing fresh air to the building from small circular openings in the outside wall, usually concealed under window cill projections. With air-pressure differentials between the windward and leeward sides of the building, air entered these openings and passed through the inter-space between interior wall panelling and external masonry, or in the ceiling space between hardboard panelling and the structure above. These spaces provided an air-plenum, that distributed fresh air to individual rooms, terminating in gaps between the ceiling and wall panelling which acted as grilles. This invisible passive ventilation system dispensed with the necessity of opening windows. The plenum also served in assisting drying out the structure in areas of damp. This ingenious system, however, suffered a number of drawbacks. In winter the air thus introduced was unacceptably cold, the quantity of air could not be controlled, and the air movement encouraged the open fire in the living room to smoke.

9.10

In the renovation, this method of ventilation was abandoned, and the inter-space behind wall panelling filled with thermal insulation. Fresh air ventilation to ground floor rooms is now provided by the small opening-lights framed in bronze at the head of the existing windows.

Where rooms were lined in timber panelling in the ground floor apartment, this was removed temporarily, the walls insulated, and the panelling replaced on new battens. There were various types of panelling, painted hardboard (much of it rotten) in bunk rooms, oak panelling obtained from a Belfast shipyard in the living-room, second bedroom and hallway, and a third type of panelling in the zodiac bedroom, made from 1930s-style cupboard doors. All panelling was removed, repaired, re-battened 50mm from the wall, insulated in the inter-space, and re-fixed.

Once the living room and second bedroom were renovated, it was possible to stay in the house at the weekend, and for work to proceed on the other rooms, including the zodiac bedroom with its remarkable ceiling. Sandra and Des Neill renovated this in 1996-1997. The wall and ceiling panelling were repaired, and decorated in a new colour scheme of light cream and gold leaf. Bit by bit the house was made habitable, and the unique environment of Bendhu opened up for a new generation of family and friends.

New kitchen fittings were installed on the ground floor, with a direct opening made between the living room and the kitchen. The dolmen-fireplace was still problematic with the recurring problem of down-draughts, and, with regret, the Fergusons replaced it with an enclosed wood-burning stove. Hinged openings in the floor revealed, as at Grasmere Gardens, built-in fuel storage-compartments for the fire. The still-intact fold-away dining table, also by Pen, acts as an over-mantel to the fireplace, which was reinstated and continues to be used. Newly bought, mostly second-hand furniture was chosen for the living room, to

9.11

9.11-9.12
Living room
on ground
floor, restored

9.12

be sympathetic to the Arts and Crafts feel of its interior, whereas in the zodiac bedroom Art Deco inspired furniture and accessories were selected. The 1920's oil painting *Portrait of a Lady* by Newton Penprase was brought from Greenisland, and has pride of place in the living room. The Art Deco theme is continued in furnishings including glassware and objects d'art, and in a pair of remarkable Art Deco chairs with side arms that accommodate bottles and glasses.

Commenting on the interior style and character of the ground floor interiors, Michael observes that Bendhu defies easy classification:

The building, we feel, is Art Deco but with a Penprase twist. Art Deco was the style of the period and the art that we felt reflected the brightness and imagination of the artist Penprase.[13]

Another change to the ground floor accommodation was the removal of one of the bunkrooms. The space created made a generous hallway, and, with the original timber panelling removed, was finished in plastered walls with recesses for contemporary ornaments and bookshelves. A few years later this hallway was further reworked to incorporate the new internal staircase joining the ground and first floors.

The bathroom refurbishment revealed Penprase's original concrete bath, which had been covered over with an inelegant fibreglass substitute that required less water and was arguably more comfortable. The concrete bath had been partially cut out of the rock base, and the stones used for aggregate, but it required huge amounts of water to fill, and typically provided a cold, spartan and sharp-cornered experience. In the renovation the concrete bath becomes a generously sized shower tray, its surface newly tiled in mosaic with an aquatic design, which is based on the graphic of the Pisces lunette panel in the zodiac ceiling.

The original stained-glass panels in the bronze window frames by Penprase have mostly survived intact, and the opening-lights have been repaired as necessary.[14] Additionally, new stained-glass has been installed in the interior of the later phase, its design picking up the Classical themes of Pen's originals. The new stained-glass work was made by David Esler.

By the end of 2000, the first phase of Michael Ferguson's refurbishment was complete. The superstructure of the building was now waterproofed and insulated, new windows had been installed, and the exterior finished in brilliant white. Inside, the ground floor accommodation, effectively a self-contained apartment, had undergone a complete refurbishment with plumbing and electrical installations, a new kitchen and bathroom installed, wall-panelling insulated and re-fixed, the zodiac ceiling conserved. Both the Arts and Crafts and Art Deco characteristics of the interior had been renovated.

To public view the building presented a new image – pristine white. Still unique and eclectic in form, Bendhu was now more contemporary and above all friendlier in appearance. A passer-by might assume the building was now fully renovated on all three floors, but in fact it was still an empty shell on the first and second levels, the interior awaiting fit-out.

During the first phase renovation Michael and Lorna Ferguson had had plenty of time to contemplate the future of these upper floors, and having renewed Penprase's interior in the lower floor apartment as faithfully as possible, they could now allow their imagination free rein for the next stage of building.

ENDNOTES

1. Larmour (1997), pp 18-30.

2. The NHBC prize was the Sir Stanley Morton Award for the best housing estate of the 1970s, the winner for Northern Ireland, Category 1, December 1979. Chairman of judges: Sir Hugh Casson.

3. Brooks (1996) pp 42-44.

4. Idem.

5. Interviews with Michael Ferguson, July / August 2004.

6. Michael Ferguson notes prepared for *Coast* programme on BBC1, autumn 2006.

7. Idem.

8. Correspondence with Michael Ferguson, 14 Sept 2004.

9. Interviews with Michael Ferguson, July / August 2004.

10. Two frameless windows on the ground floor were replaced with framed units – in the double bunk bedroom and in the kitchen.

11. Précis of Michael Ferguson notes, December 2008.

12. Idem.

13. Interviews with Michael Ferguson, July / August 2004.

14. The stained-glass panels are described in Chapter 6 and Appendix 2.

10 Bendhu extended

'After five years getting the ground floor habitable and stemming the leaks, we thought it was time to create a space for ourselves on the open balcony ... How to build, and what material would be appropriate, were discussed and discussed'. Michael Ferguson

Extending a Listed Building is a challenging task, the more so when the original structure is as idiosyncratic as Bendhu. An extension might attempt to replicate the architectural language of the original building, or alternatively, be carried out in design and materials of the present time. The result of the first approach is likely to be an unconvincing imitation, one that risks compromising the integrity of the original. The contemporary approach of extending in a modern idiom allows the old and new structures to speak for themselves, but a satisfactory union between the two is by no means certain.[1]

In planning the fit-out and design for the upper floors of Bendhu, Michael and Lorna Ferguson had dual objectives – to work with the form of the house in a way that respected Penprase's building, and to provide a contemporary living space for themselves. They had long been at home with Modernism, as seen in Michael's design of their house at Knockagh.[2] Thus a modern, present-day design was their approach of choice in adding to Bendhu.

The structural shell of the upper floors, with its complicated geometry and multiple windows

10.1

136 BUILDING BENDHU: THE BATON HANDED ON

10.1
The all-glass proposal for the terrace extension included a lean-to roof, one of many designs considered: south elevation. Drawing by Michael Ferguson

10.2
East elevation incorporating the extension

10.2

and roof-lights, provided the basic container and starting-off point for planning the extension. Other considerations were the utilisation of the unoccupied studio space, what to do with Pen's Den which was now in a dilapidated condition, and the existence of two external stairs that gave sole access to the first and second floors.

The space within the structural shell was modest, the largest area being the Studio having dimensions 3m wide by 7m long, while the second floor attic measured only 2.5m by 5m. These spaces were envisaged by the Fergusons as part of a self-contained living unit that could be linked at a future stage to the ground floor accommodation, already in use, with the insertion of a new internal staircase. The idea of building an extension on the first floor terrace had emerged early on, the new space initially conceived as a large kitchen / dining area, and subsequently as a central living space and sun lounge.

Michael Ferguson drew up a number of designs for the extension. These varied from partially glazed additions to an all-glass enclosure. This latter design was to be built in planar or framed glazing for walls and a sloping roof, allowing the form and features of the existing building to be visible. The design was abandoned, partly due to difficulties in the supply and delivery of the large glass units required for construction,[3] but mainly due to concern regarding comfortable thermal conditions. These were likely to be too hot or too cold, without special provision for controlling or utilising solar gains, or additional means incorporated to prevent heat loss.

10.3

10.4

The scheme that prevailed is a hybrid structure, built in materials and form sympathetic with Penprase's work, the roof cast in reinforced concrete supported on a lightweight steel frame. Glazed walls are held in timber-framed mullions. Projecting from the new roof is a glazed box enclosing the replacement staircase to the top storey, previously an external stair but now incorporated within the extension. As built, the addition is a brightly lit living space that takes full advantage of the views through a 180-degree panorama, and forms the centrepiece to a series of living spaces on the upper floors. The transparency of the extension reveals the existing form of Bendhu. Asked whether he was concerned about losing the original terrace Michael comments:

10.3
New stair from first to second floor

10.4
New stair linking ground and first floors

10.5
South-east corner of extension: concrete roof overhang with stepped edge profile, on light steel frame, and timber window joinery

OVERLEAF
Construction photos of the extension

138 BUILDING BENDHU: THE BATON HANDED ON

The balcony faced east, and while we enjoyed relaxing and appreciating the setting, we kept that for evening and the wonderful sunsets over the Atlantic ocean [on the other side of the house]. Part of the original balcony was retained as open terrace, a perfect spot for al fresco breakfasts and, architecturally, adding depth and detail to the new addition.[4]

A welcome practical consequence of building the addition was finally to weatherproof the terrace that had always leaked, despite the efforts of all three owners.

The remodelling of the first and second floors was conceived as the major unifying factor in renovating Bendhu. With the new internal staircase to the ground floor inserted towards the end of building operations, the glazed addition effectively connects all three levels of the house into a unified spatial sequence. Now the house can be used as one residence, or as two units independently. The ground floor apartment (fitted out by Pen and refurbished by Michael) is cellular and traditional in character, the first floor (the piano nobile) is a light-filled contemporary living space with dramatic sea views, spatially linked to the new kitchen / dining area formed in the studio. An ingenious stair, with treads and winders of minimal thickness constructed in concrete, rises from the new living space to the second floor bedroom eyrie, or Crow's Nest. Moving through these areas is the culmination of a progressively more engaging spatial experience as one ascends the house. A new bathroom is incorporated where Pen's Den was previously sited, the new facility enjoying unique views to the beach cove, Bendoo cliff, Sheep Island and Rathlin beyond.

10.5

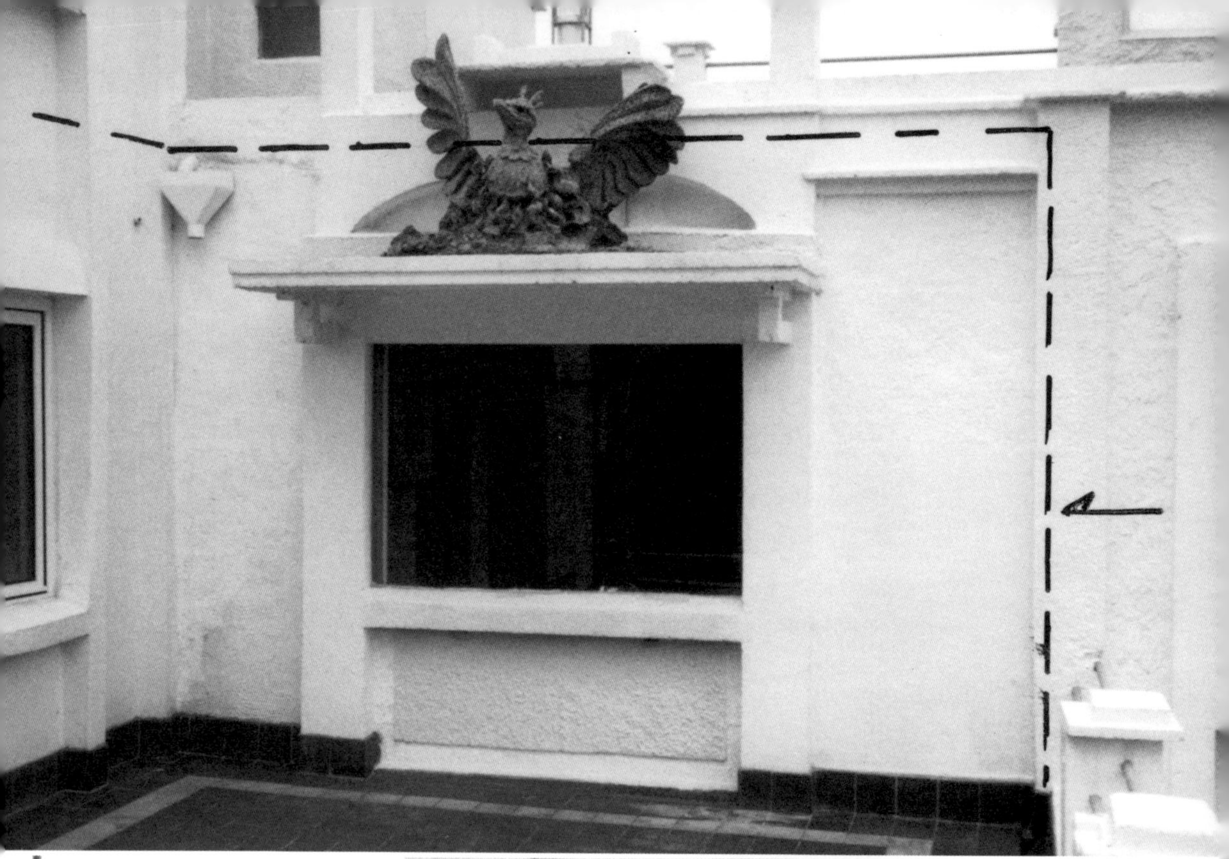

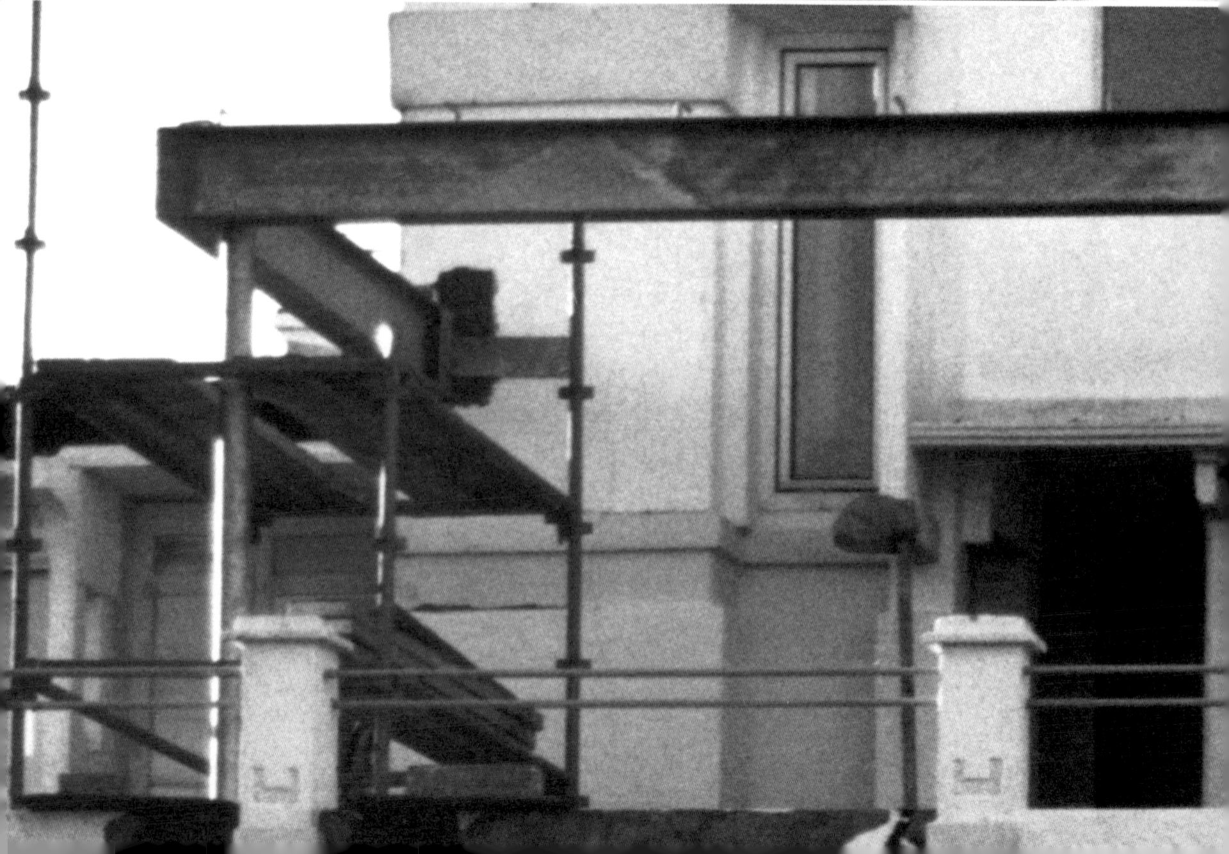

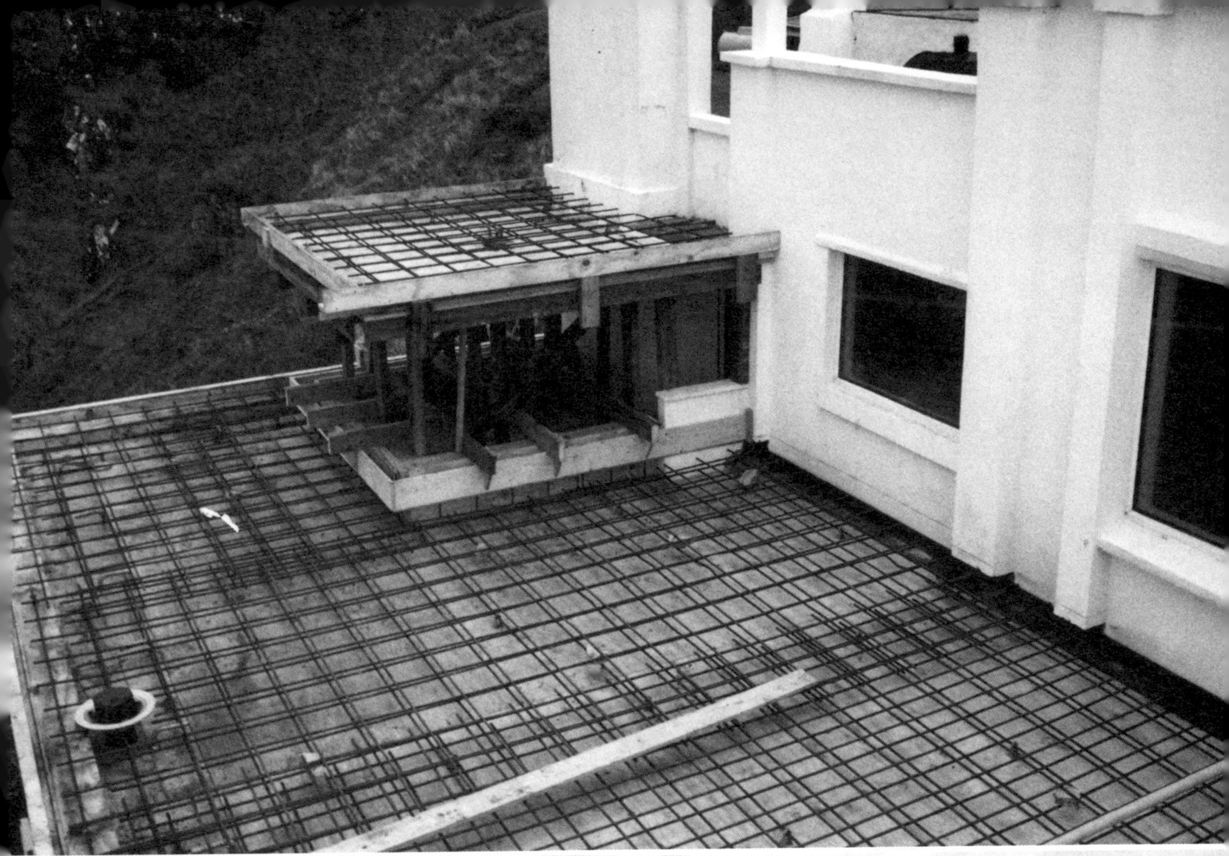

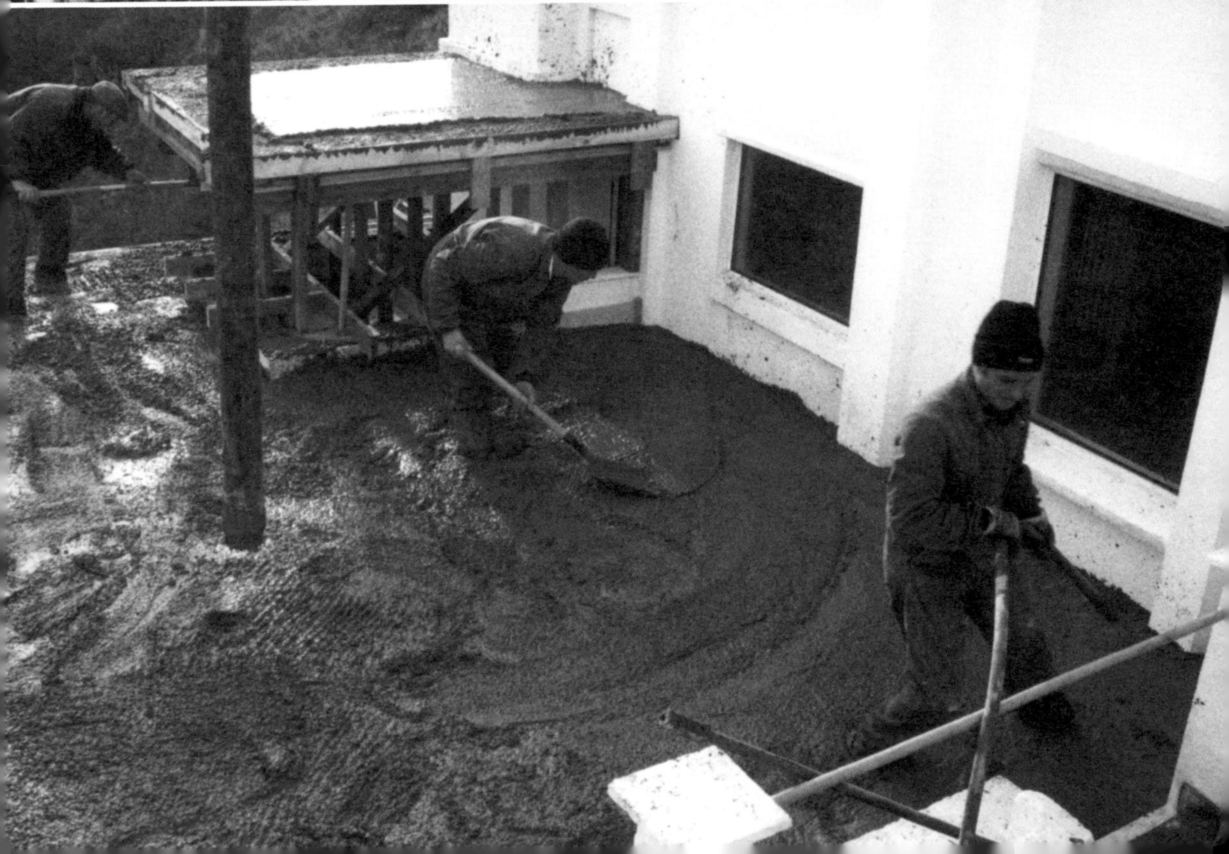

2006 RECORD DRAWING

EAST ELEVATION

SECOND FLOOR

GROUND FLOOR

FIRST FLOOR

142   BUILDING BENDHU: THE BATON HANDED ON

10.6
2006 Record drawing, showing plans of Bendhu after renovation and extension. Drawing: Nicholas Allen

The design and construction of both the extension and the existing shell areas, newly fitted out, have been handled with skill and sensitivity. Michael describes the design ethos of the new work as "crafted modern of the late twentieth century, using Penprase's palette of materials". While the general feel is minimalist, the extension acknowledges Pen's original design. The dialogue between old and new is seen in the window layout for the family room, where large glazed areas alternate with narrower bays incorporating opening lights, positioned to reflect the rhythm of the existing masonry piers on the edge of the balcony. The Fergusons have also succeeded in retaining the mystery and idiosyncrasy of Pen's design - the recesses and projections, internal and external shelves, pilasters and features, and the delight in all the unexpected and multiple sources of daylight entering the building.

The extension and upper floor renovations were carried out in the years 1998-2001; the ground floor hallway and building the new internal stair to the first floor in 2003-04, probably the last major work to be carried out in the house. Opening up the first floor for the staircase involved cutting into a massive concrete structure that also buttressed the tall exterior masonry of the west elevation. The central spine of the staircase, cast in reinforced concrete, supports cantilevered limestone treads, and ties together the structural opening for the staircase. Glass

10.7
Interior view from second floor

10.8
West façade and new terrace platforms

10.7

balustrade panels with steel handrails give a high-tech feel to the stair, a transition zone between the traditional character of the ground floor and the Modernist interiors upstairs.

A boat store, equivalent in size to a double garage, has been constructed on the site to the west of Bendhu. The only stipulation planners made in considering the application for the house extension was to "tone down the garage" – to break up the massing so as not to compete with the form of Bendhu. Thus a fairly large structure is articulated with a central pillar, earth-coloured and incorporating glazed blocks, breaking up the building mass. The profiled overhang to the concrete roof, and a roof lantern reminiscent of Bendhu, provide links to the main house. The dialogue with Bendhu continues with new boundary walls in white render finish that extend from Penprase's Art Deco-styled gateposts to the newly constructed double entrance gates in tubular metal, again contextual with Bendhu, hung from new square entrance piers. On the west elevation, a metalwork balustrade around new deck areas takes its cue from Penprase's designs in tubular metal construction. These external works (the boat store, new gates and boundary wall, the outside seating decks) have the effect of further integrating Bendhu into its site and setting.

Bendhu has attracted many visitors and groups over the years. In 1996 a group from the Belfast Naturalists' Field Club visited the house, making a return visit in 2005 to see the completed extension.[5] In May 2006 thirty-five members of the Ulster Architectural Heritage Society visited Bendhu, a visit that promoted much interest and discussion. Summer programme students from the University of Ulster visited in August 2008.

Bendhu continues to attract attention in the media. The article in the *Daily Express* on 10 August 1959 was typical of the coverage during Penprase's time.[6] During the Fergusons' ownership the house has attracted more interest from both local and national television. In 2006, a feature on Bendhu appeared in the BBC-tv nation-wide programme *Coast* in the second series presented by Neil Oliver.[7] The programme explored the coastline from Dublin to Derry, and was broadcast on 23 November. Suggesting that many mavericks have been attracted to the north Antrim coast, Cornishman Newton Penprase is singled out for special mention; the reporter Alice Roberts takes the viewer on a tour starting at the steps to the beach, ascending to the garden of Bendhu to

10.8

meet Michael and Lorna, proceeding to the first floor extension, then downstairs to Penprase's ground floor apartment to see the zodiac ceiling. The piece concludes with long distant views of the house in its wild coastal setting, the narrator asserting that true individualists like Newton Penprase have had the last laugh, with public recognition made manifest by the statutory listing of Bendhu.[8]

Asked if there is anything else that he would like to do to the property, Michael says Bendhu will require ongoing maintenance in the years ahead, and that is an agreeable prospect.[9] He reflects that Richard Mac Cullagh left him a list of unfinished projects for Bendhu, and he hopes to do the same, observing

> ... it is not a building that will ever be maintenance-free, and there are still lots of unfinished projects that spring to mind if feeling creative, or in need of a project. We still have mice that visit each year and it remains a mystery as to how they get in. It would be great to have castings made for the hardwood shutters and catches that would enable them to be readily opened and closed. The metalwork and exterior rendering needs re-painted every other year and we do change the colour scheme each time, although mostly white.[10]

Taking stock he feels the renovations show Pen's work in a good light, making the analogy to a famous painting, that requires a proper setting, good framing and lighting, so that the work can exist and be seen, enjoyed and experienced. He recalls that when he first took over the property, passers-by on seeing the building for the first time often had a concerned look, and avoided eye-contact. Now they stop to view, and often to photograph, with smiling faces. That indeed has been Michael Ferguson's singular achievement in remodelling, completing and extending Bendhu.[11]

ENDNOTES

1. This approach is typified by Foster Associates' Sackler Galleries at the Royal Academy of Arts in London completed in 1991, where high-tech steel and glass lift and stairs provide access to modern galleries at roof level, contrasting with the restored 18th and 19th century courtyard spaces. More locally, the Ardhowen Arts Centre in Enniskillen, designed by Tom Mullarkey in 1987-1988, is uncompromising in its use of curtain wall steel and glass, different in material yet geometrically in harmony with the adjoining 19th century house from which the Centre grew.

2. The White House at Knockagh, see Chapter 9.

3. Michael later built an all-glass planar domestic structure for a house in Co Donegal.

4. Notes prepared by Michael Ferguson for BBC-tv programme *Coast*.

5. The Belfast Naturalists' Field Club was established in 1863. The Club's visits to Bendhu followed a well travelled path to north Antrim, in the steps of previous members such as R L Praeger, Robert Welch, A R Hogg et al, exploring the flora and fauna, geology, archaeology and history of the coast.

6. See Chapter 5.

7. BBC-tv programme *Coast*, first broadcast 23 November 2006, with subsequent repeat viewings.

8. Listing by DOE: see Chapter 8.

9. Interview with Michael Ferguson 20 August 2004.

10. Précis of Michael Ferguson notes, December 2008.

11. Cowser (2004). This chapter is updated from the article by the author published in *Ulster Architect*.

Bendhu in colour

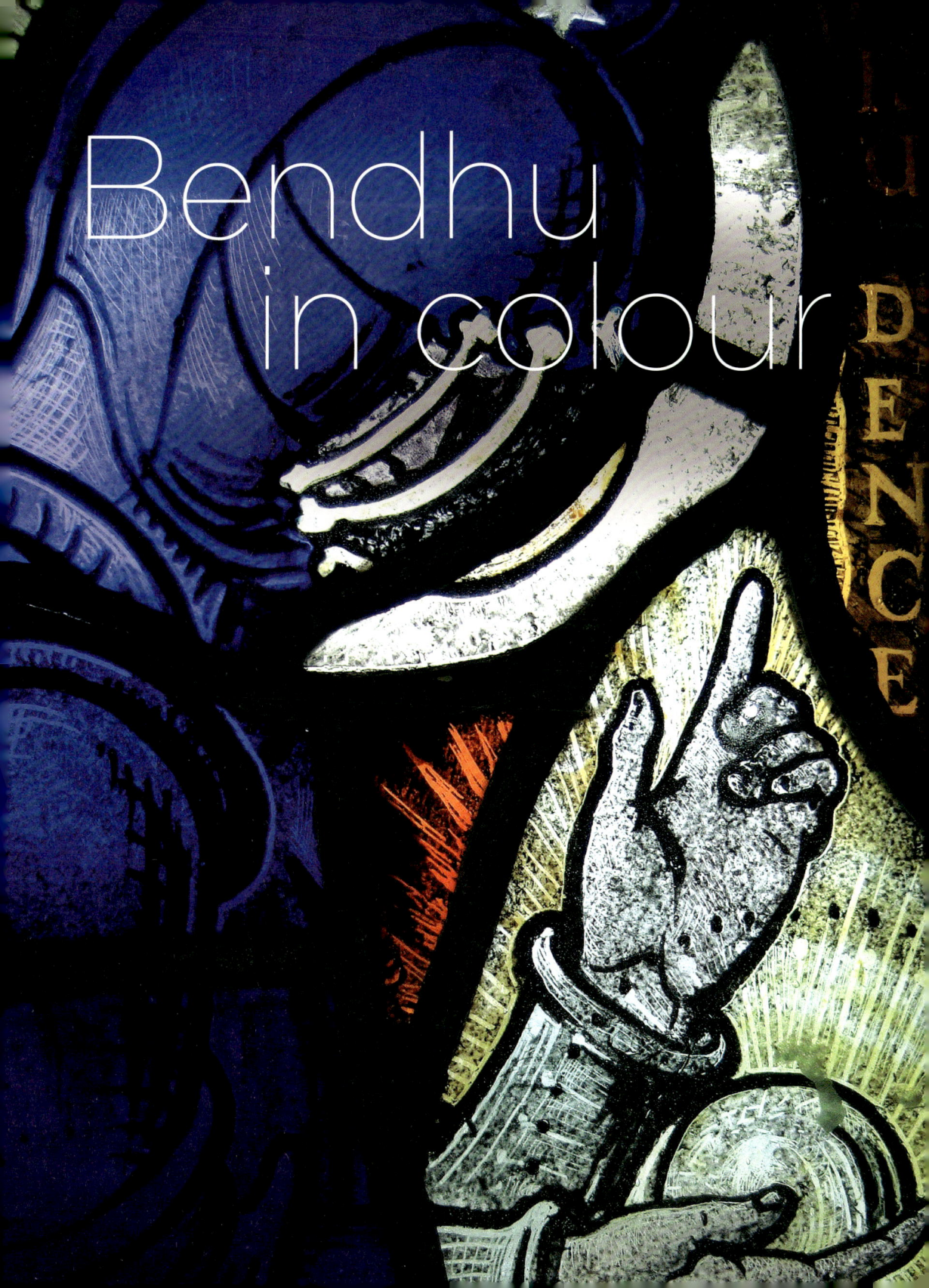

C.1–C.2
Drawings of church silverware by Newton Penprase that won a Gold Medal in 1905

C.3–C.4
Antiquities of Cornwall - prize winning drawings by Newton Penprase depicting wood carving from Cornish churches, 1905

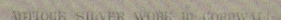

C.1

C.2

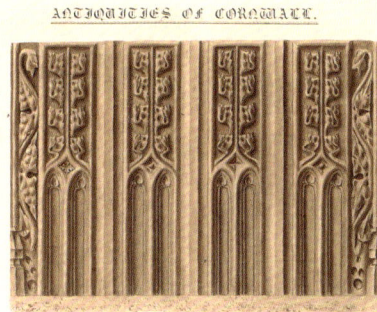

ANTIQUITIES OF CORNWALL

ANTIQUITIES OF CORNWALL

PARTLY OPENED
BACK VIEW
ABSTRACT
BUTTERFLIES
FROM LIFE
FROM PRESERVED SPECIMENS
ABSTRACT
ABSTRACT
DRAGON-FLY
ABSTRACT
BAT
FROM LIFE
ABSTRACT
ABSTRACT
SNAIL SHELL
KINGFISHER
ABSTRACT
FROM A PRESERVED SPECIMEN
ACOCK FEATHER
PHEASANT
FROM A PRESERVED SPECIMEN
ABSTRACT
SPIDER
ABSTRACT
EGG OF GUILLEMOT
ABSTRACT
LIZARD
TAIL LOST
FROM LIFE
EGG OF RAZORBILL
ABSTRACT
ALL NATURAL
STUDIES
NATURAL SIZE
GURNET
ABSTRACT
ABSTRACT
CRAB
FROM LIFE
FROM LIFE
FROG
FROM LIFE
STUDY OF BACK LEG

C.5

C.5
Bird, fish, animal studies, Watercolour, 75x55cm, by Newton Penprase

C.6
Plant studies, Watercolour, 76x55cm, by Newton Penprase

C.6

C.7
'Progress – the dawn of a new day', oil on canvas, 143x192.5cm, by Newton Penprase, undated, Ulster Museum collection

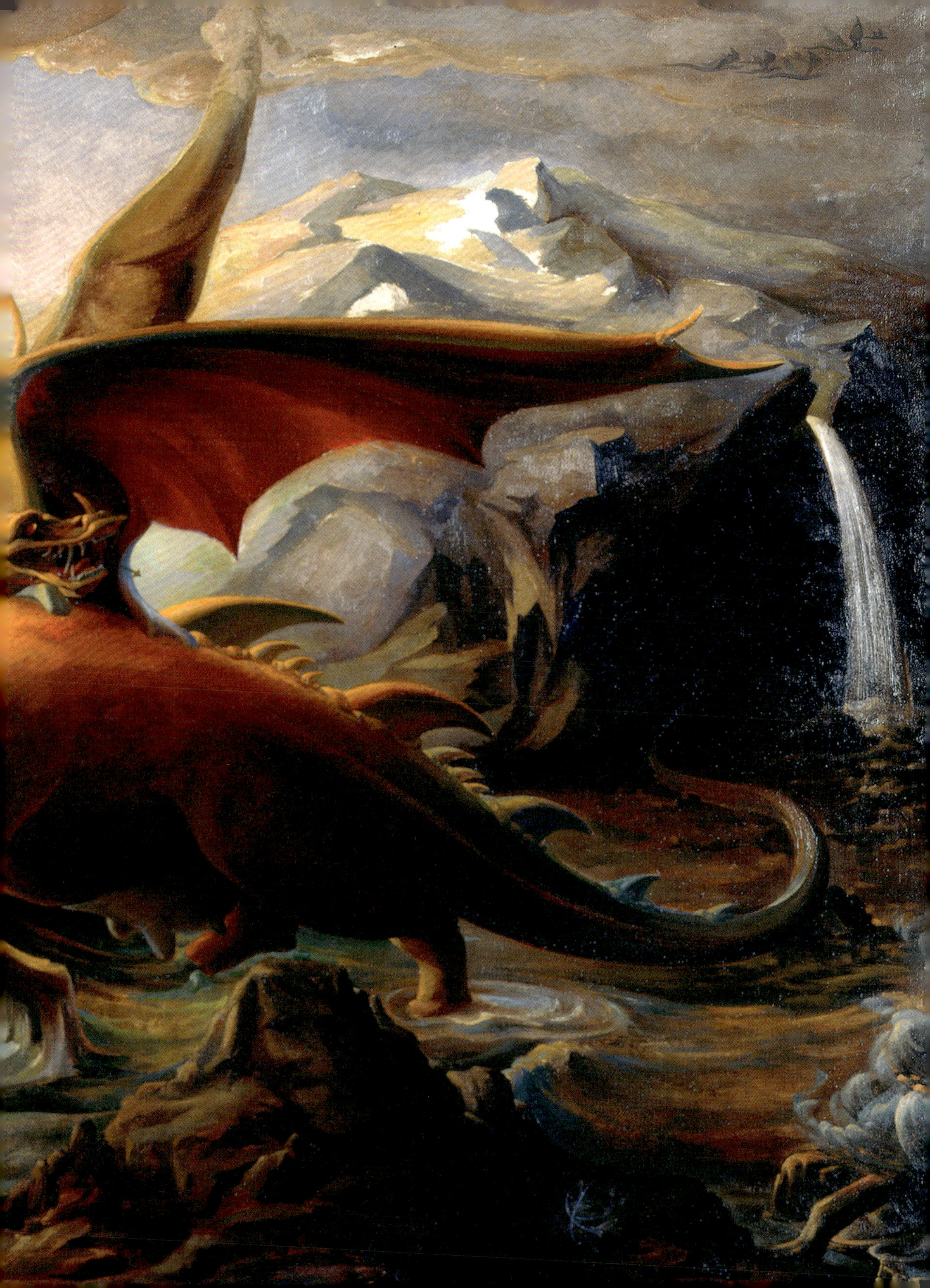

C.8
Detail of stained-glass leaded-light, 21.5 x 14cm, depicting Classical muse Euterpe.

C.9
The Pilgrims' Chorus - Tannhauser, painting by Newton Penprase 99.5x84.5cm

C.9

C.10–C.11
Panelling and
ceiling in the
zodiac bedroom,
Penprase's colours

C.12–C.13
Zodiac bedroom
with restored
decorative scheme

C.10

C.11

C.12

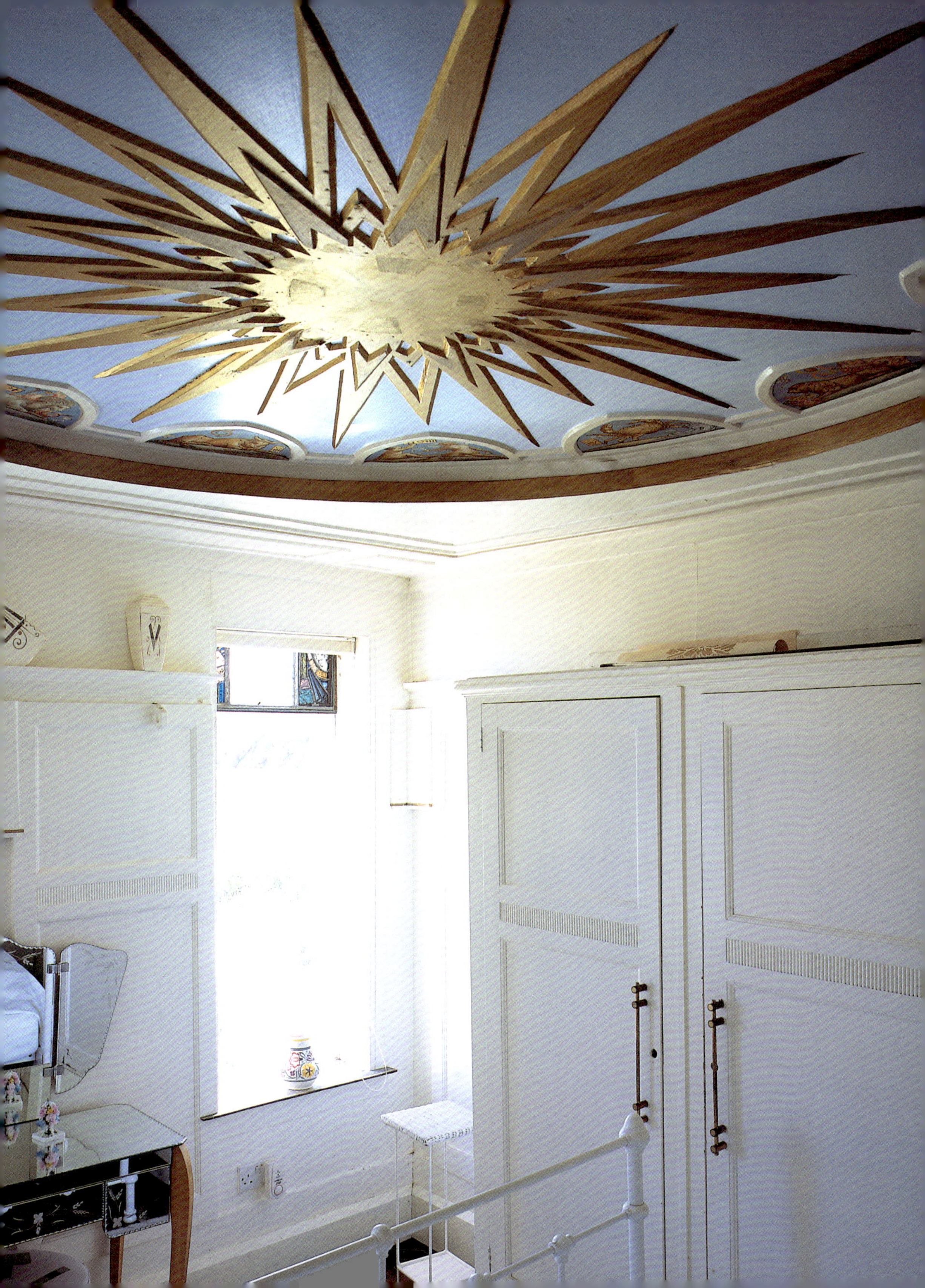

C.14

C.14
Rendered cream
coloured finish to
upper storeys,
with basalt
pebbledash below
painted dark
brown, 1992-1993

C.15
Blockwork
construction, 1957

C.15

C.16
West entrance to
first floor - in situ
concrete and
exposed blockwork
juxtaposed, early-
1960s

C.17
East elevation of Bendhu, 2009

C.18
Interior of the extension, 2009 by Michael Ferguson

C.19
West elevation of
Bendhu from boat
store, 2009

C.20
Bendhu from boat
store, 2009

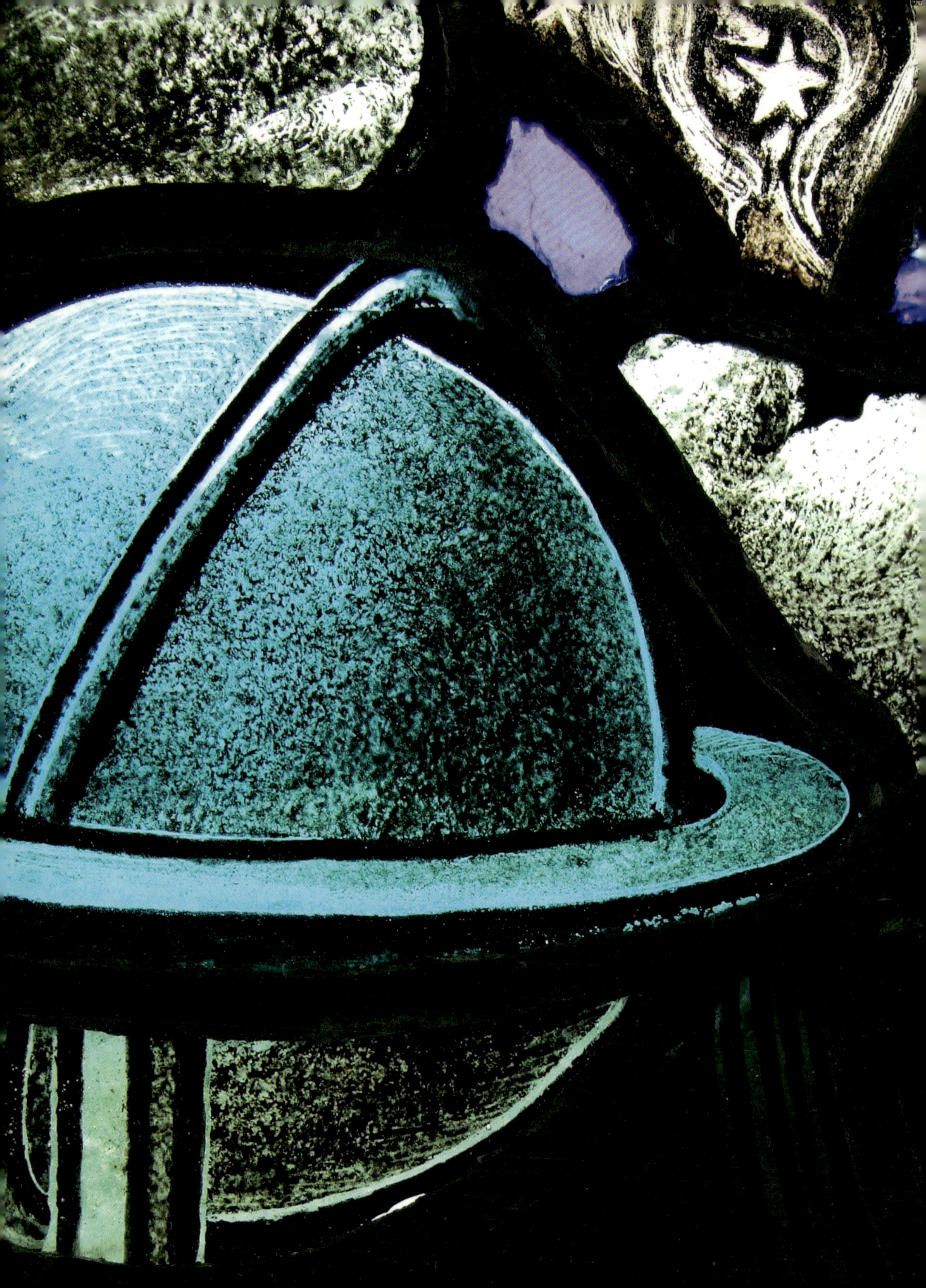

Appraisal

BENDHU IN
ITS TIME

DESIGN
ELEMENTS
CONSIDERED

END PIECE

11 Bendhu in its time

As noted in the Introduction, John Hewitt likened Bendhu to "a Turkish fort assaulted by a cubist task-force", a description that highlights Bendhu's enigmatic character. Notwithstanding the difficulty of classifying Bendhu stylistically from an architectural viewpoint, this chapter investigates possible precedents and influences at home and abroad, particularly in relation to contemporary buildings of the mid-1930s that might provide links with Bendhu.

In attempting an architectural assessment of Penprase's building there are pitfalls. If its designer and builder did not conceive of Bendhu as a work of architecture in the first place, it is perhaps hardly fair to appraise it as such. In that case Pen's endeavour can be viewed as a personal odyssey to build a concrete house, without reference to architecture or stylistic allegiance, the task and programme a personal quest that evolved with time. However, as already discussed, Penprase did claim on one occasion to have had an architectural training although where or when and to what level remains a mystery.[1] In either event it is worth reviewing other residential designs, contemporary with Penprase's proposals of 1935 and 1936, and Bendhu as built, in order to see what connections, if any, there may be.

The extent of Pen's awareness of contemporary architecture in Ireland and Britain, or the wider Modern Movement abroad in the 1930s, is unknown. When he started building the foundations in 1935, and then again, a year later started Bendhu, we can but speculate what

11.1

11.1–11.2
Bendhu viewed
from south-east,
in 1949
and in 2004

11.2

was in his mind by way of precedent or example. Yet there is considerable confidence in the cubist forms that emerged in the building of Bendhu, and some specific stylistic attributes that suggest precedents. That he was aware of architectural developments in Europe, where the architectural experiments of the 1920s had been disseminated more widely by the mid-1930s, is perhaps unlikely. According to his family Pen did not travel beyond the shores of Ireland after his arrival in 1911. Pen may well have had access to contemporary architectural thinking through the library at the Art College,[2] though there is no record of this. More probably he was untutored in the development of the Modern Movement in architecture, and approached the building of Bendhu from a quite different viewpoint, that of an artist and sculptor, the merit of this approach being that it gave unfettered rein to his creativity.

If Penprase's approach was intuitive, Bendhu can be regarded as a work of naïveté, using that term in a non-pejorative way: naïve in the sense of being untrained in building or architectural design and yet in effect engaging in both those activities while enjoying the freedom of expression and action that the untrained background gives; naïve in the sense of being admirably straightforward and uncomplicated and to a degree innocent and unaffected, not using the conventional styles and techniques of the trained builder. In all these ways Penprase could

11.3

11.4

be described, affirmatively, as an artist of naïveté, bringing his own unique forms and aesthetic to a project with seemingly elastic boundaries.[3]

To put Pen's work in the context of architectural developments in Europe and Britain, it is worth looking briefly at other one-off houses of the period. Pen's building started in 1935, an interesting time in relation to European modern architecture. 1929-1931 had seen the completion of two landmark buildings – Le Corbusier's Villa Savoye near Paris, and the German Pavilion by Mies van der Rohe in Barcelona. Both buildings were seminal in demonstrating new principles of spatial and formal relationships in architecture, and both were iconographic in demonstrating alternative Modernist approaches.

11.3
German Pavilion
Barcelona, by
Mies van der
Rohe, 1929

11.4
Villa Savoye,
Poissy, by Le
Corbusier, 1931

But Bendhu bears no resemblance to either exemplar, being a construction with loadbearing walls enclosing domestic sized rooms. In contrast, both the Villa Savoye and the Barcelona Pavilion are reliant on framed structures. The first demonstrates Corbusier's five points of a new architecture, and is built in concrete frame and blockwork infill, all rendered as a white 'purist' form, juxtaposing the cubic volume with free-form elements at base and roof.[4] The second exemplar, designed by Mies, is constructed in steel, glass and stone, and frees the boundaries between interior and exterior by overlapping spatial layers.

From an Irish perspective, another contemporary building is worth noting. This is the house 'E1027', built at Roquebrune near Menton in the south of France, completed in 1929 – a tour de force by Irish designer Eileen Gray. This house, looking "like a ship anchored on the shore",[5] sited at the cliff face on a narrow site overlooking the Mediterranean, is an imaginative distillation of Le Corbusier's five points, uniquely interpreted by Gray in a virtuoso composition of architectural elements and spatial arrangement. Interiors are both luxurious and practical. A comparison between E1027 and Bendhu highlights the Modernist experimentation with spatial concept, form, layout and furnishing, all of which were well developed in Eileen Gray's building, contrasting with the more modest cellular spaces and traditional finishes of Bendhu, the Cubist exterior of which arguably suggests a more radical interior.

A building in Paris by the Austro-Hungarian architect and polemicist, Adolf Loos, has some resonance with the design of Bendhu. In Loos' house for the writer Tristan Tzara, a complex internal plan of changing floor levels and spatial volumes has a much simpler expression on the exterior, with masonry rubble walls picking up the still-rural surrounds of Avenue Jeunot in Montmartre. From the stonework emerges a white cubic form. This is given fuller expression in the smooth-rendered rear façade, where south-facing terraces overlook one another, and the composition of flat roofs, railings and masonry corner-posts arguably bear some resemblance to the external form of Bendhu. The rear of the house (11.7) is now almost impossible to see, hidden from view by subsequent additions and neighbouring structures.

11.5–11.7
House for
Tristan Tzara,
Paris, architect
Adolf Loos, 1926

11.8
Aerial view of
Bendhu, 1995
showing additive
cubic-built forms

11.9
Maison
particulière,
axonometric study,
by Theo van
Doesburg and Cor
van Eestern, 1923

However, if a later work by Loos is considered, for example the Müller house in Prague from 1930, the similarities with Penprase's work recede. Loos' house is almost a perfect cube in external form, with a projecting bay and recess for the balcony on the second floor. Inside, the villa is organised as a dramatic sequence of spatial volumes, culminating in a double height living space, all part of a Raumplan or 'plan of volumes', a complex interlocking of rooms on different levels that forms a continuous living space, contained within the simple cubic form of the building's exterior.[6]

European debate on modern architectural form provides a surprising connection with the design of Bendhu. One study stands out, made graphic by the de Stijl architects Theo van Doesburg and Cor van Eesteren in 1923. In a series of axonometric drawings and models, they explored the form of an asymmetrically planned house, with a staircase volume placed centrally, around which the various rooms connect. The house is planned as a group of inter-locking volumes, with a series of flat roofs, terraces, projecting cills (and light shelves at windows) shown in orthogonal composition (11.9). The aerial views, while differing in detail, bear a strong resemblance to the external form of Bendhu. In the de Stijl sketch, no effort is made to line through the levels of the roofs, or tidy up the composition into a simpler geometry. Quite the reverse. Individual volumes are deliberately varied according to function – all making a sculptural architectural form that has its parallel in Bendhu, where, for example, the first floor studio and Pen's Den have entirely different functions, and therefore individual volumetric expression.

A second point of comparison between the De Stijl study and Bendhu is the ground floor plan, as form generator of the building. Seen in van Doesburg's projection of the house viewed from below, the asymmetry of the plan form is clearly indicated – to the left a corner is cut into, at the bottom of the plan a projection juts out and at the top a corner is removed. All this has its parallel in the ground floor planning of Bendhu, where a basically rectangular plan is cut into and extended in a similar way.

A third point of comparison between the design of Bendhu and the axonometric study is the design of windows and their 'pairing' off side-by-side, as one medium size window adjacent to a small linear one, with the window heads lining through. This occurs in the windows lighting the top of the staircase cube (11.9). At Bendhu this unusual arrangement appears in Pen's Den on the south elevation (11.8), and is further recorded on the east and north elevations of the Bannister survey (8.7).

Another drawing in the same series by van Doesburg and van Eesteren depicts the same house, but this time re-interpreting the form as a series of elemental planes (walls, roof, floors), each component having its own identity, and seemingly floating in space. This elemental approach would be realised in built form a year later, in the celebrated Schröder House in Utrecht, by architect Gerrit Rietveld.

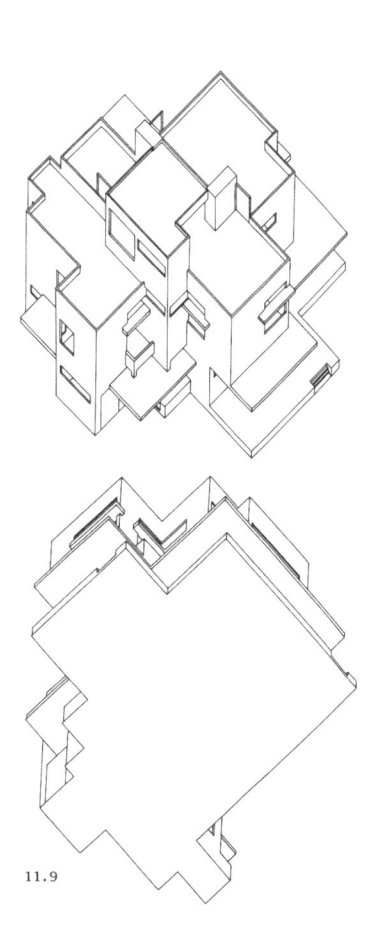

11.8

11.9

An exhibition of the Dutch de Stijl group's work was held at the end of 1923, in a private gallery in Paris.[7] Visitors included Le Corbusier and the artist Fernand Léger, and there was keen interest and journalistic coverage. Did Newton Penprase know of this work, or had he seen images from the exhibition, in a book or journal in the Art College library? There was a twelve year interval before Pen started work at Ballintoy. We can only surmise.

In England the Modern Movement in architecture had gained some acceptance for public buildings by the mid-1930s, though less so for private houses, which were often the subject of fierce planning battles. A younger generation of architects was eager to build in the Modern style and with high social ideals (designing public housing, schools, health and community buildings), many of them influenced by ideas and contemporary forms gleaned from the continent. Some of the architects who designed these buildings were themselves émigrés from Europe, relocated or in transit in England – architects such as Serge Chermayeff, Walter Gropius, Berthold Lubetkin, and Erich Mendelsohn.

One-off houses by Modernist architects in England, in the years before Pen started Bendhu, often interpreted the 'white cubist' idiom. Typical of the bravura spirit of the times are Connell and Ward's design for houses at Saltdean completed in 1935.[8] The three holiday homes, built near the beach, were cubic and white rendered in form, with stairs to roof terraces cantilevered from the façade, expressed externally.[9]

A one-off variant to the cube is seen in Christopher Nicholson's artist's studio for Augustus John of 1934, the cubic design juxtaposed with rounded volumes, raised on columns, with special provision for picture storage and the moving of large canvases. Curved geometries are also at play in Raymond McGrath's design for St Ann's Hill in Chertsey, 1935, a building that

11.10

11.10
The Sun House,
Hampstead,
architect
Maxwell Fry, 1935

11.11
House at Saltdean,
architects Connell
& Ward, 1935

OVERLEAF
House at 20
Lismoyne Park
Belfast, architects
Young &
Mackenzie, 1932

11.11

celebrates its raised site, a significant luxury house set on a verdant hillside, well restored in recent years. Maxwell Fry's Sun House in Hampstead, also of 1935, contemporary with Pen's start at Ballintoy, was an influential south-facing family house with terraces and strip windows, the subject of much controversy with the authorities and neighbours as a result of its Modern design – a cause célèbre of its time.

Each of these one-off and mostly expensive houses was a veritable tour de force demonstrating particular tenets of the new architecture, to the applause of Modernists, but meeting heated opposition from traditionalists and planners, some houses being famously publicised because of their unwitting controversy. However, neither these examples nor other contemporary houses in England of the 1930s serve as obvious precedents, or as a possible aesthetic source of Bendhu.

Nearer to his adopted home, early Modernist architecture in Belfast might have been an influence on the design of Bendhu. In Belfast, Newton and Mildred had built their home at Grasmere Gardens in the Fortwilliam area in 1923, and continued living there until the 1970s. Only a few streets away, in the early and mid-1930s some of the first Modernist houses in Belfast were appearing. These tended to be flat-roofed, white rendered, some of them with elements of Art Deco styling. The nearest of these houses to the Penprase home was built at 20 Lismoyne Park, to the designs of Young and Mackenzie, in 1932. It was a substantial three-bay house, finished in white painted render with Art Deco styling to parapets and chimney-stack, Crittall-style metal windows

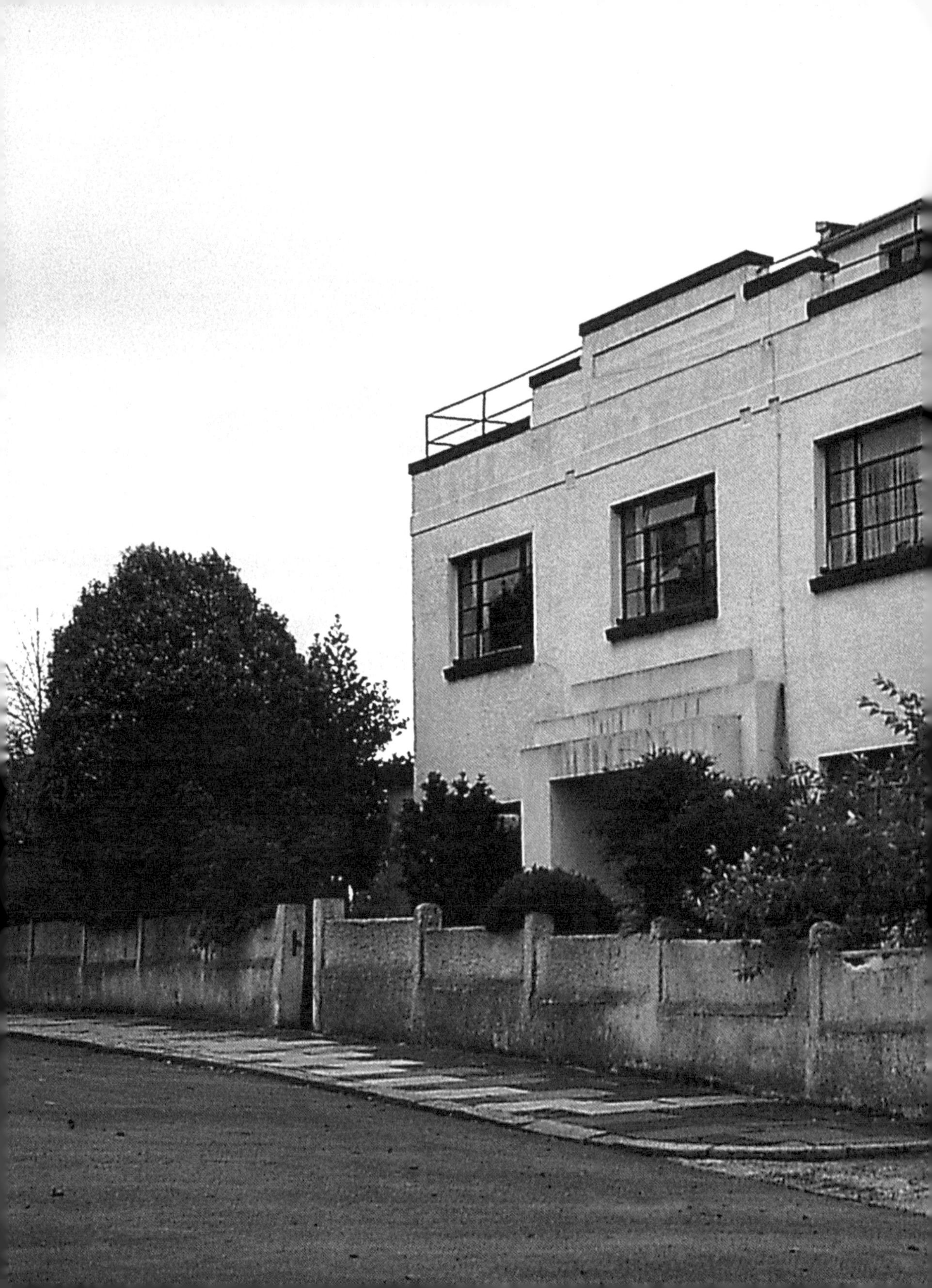

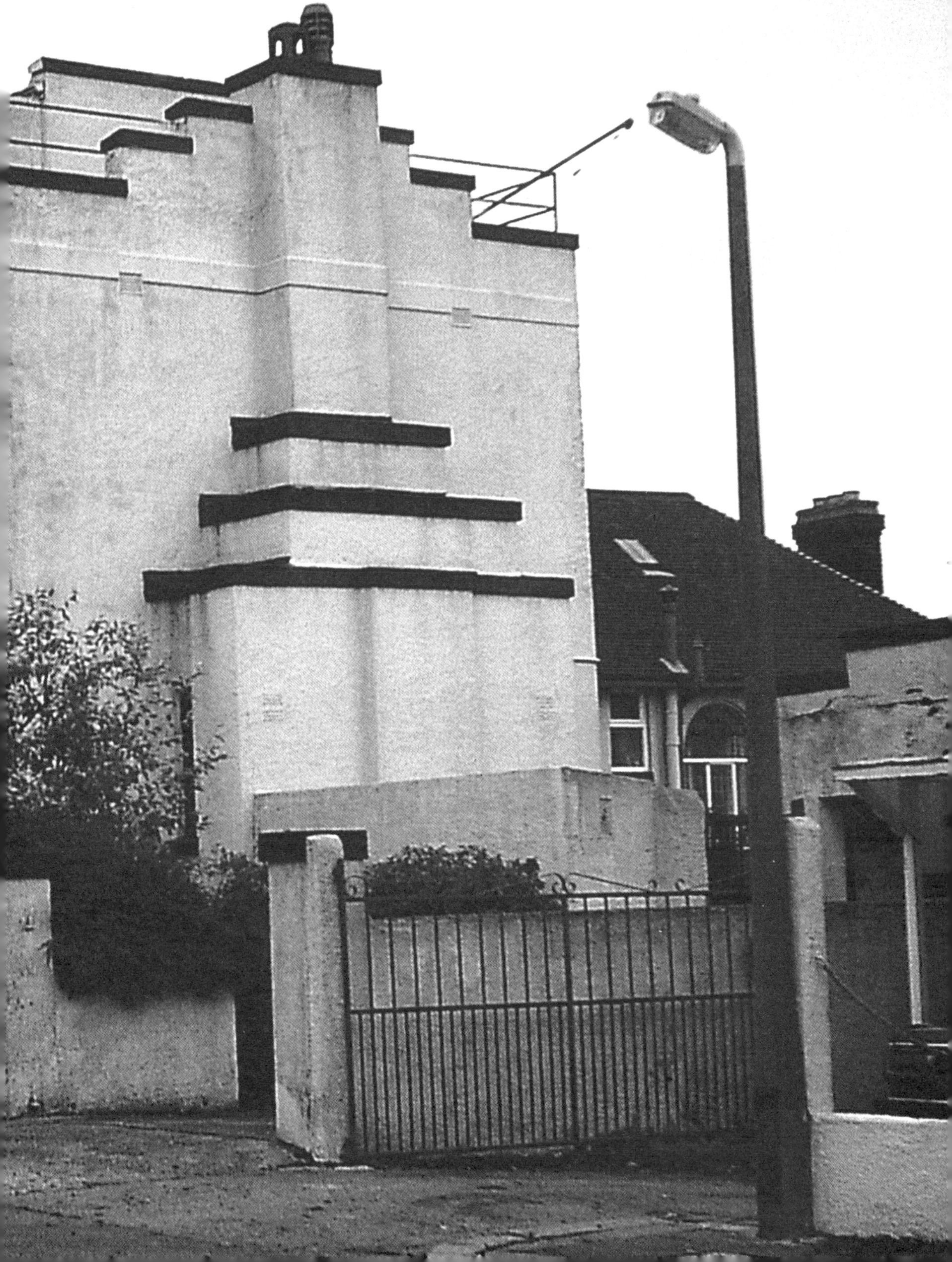

and a sun lounge terrace on the flat roof. It was a strikingly contemporary house of its time, but now much altered. Built a few streets away from where Penprase lived, the house must surely have caught his attention.[10]

In 1934 Hugh Gault was the architect for a house at 736 Antrim Road, which is still reasonably intact. This shows its Moderne credentials in white stucco walls, flat roof terrace, sun lounge and distinctive curved bay windows commanding fine views of the city, with predominantly horizontal styling – all with a nautical feel of look-outs and decking for promenade.[11]

In south Belfast, Hugh Gault was responsible for 4 Cleaver Gardens. A white cubic composition, the house still has its original corner windows and staircase with stained-glass. The modelling of architectural form on its south side resonates to an extent with Bendhu, but dating from 1937 could only have influenced Penprase in the later stages of building.

However, some of these houses in Belfast dating from the mid-1930s can hardly have escaped Pen's notice. Their cubic form, flat roofs, steel windows, roof-top sun lounges and terraces were potentially influential, though their distinctive Crittall-type windows with horizontal emphasis are entirely absent from Bendhu. Despite that, Art Deco modelling appears on façade panels, gateposts, and interior detailing at Bendhu, and conceivably bears kinship with these Belfast houses.

In the same part of the city, a public building of Modernist design was appearing at the top of the Antrim Road in 1936, the year Bendhu started. This was the Floral Hall designed by architect David Boyd, intended for public entertainments – its renowned dances still remembered. Circular in plan, with white painted render and a shallow copper dome,

11.12

11.13

176 APPRAISAL

11.12–11.13
House at 736 Antrim Road Belfast, architect Hugh Gault, 1934. Windows are recent replacements

11.14
House at 4 Cleaver Gardens Belfast, architect Hugh Gault, 1937

the Hall's Modernist credentials were proclaimed. Its location, adjacent to Belfast Zoo, was in keeping with other cities in Britain, where the new Modern style in architecture was readily adopted for zoological gardens.[12]

In the south of Ireland the situation was not so dissimilar from the north. Private dwellings in the modern style started to appear in the early 1930s, but they were not numerous. The best known is probably the architect Michael Scott's home 'Geragh', built at Sandycove, Co Dublin, completed in 1938 two years after Bendhu started.[13] There is little obvious influence between this Modernist house and the design of Bendhu.

If avant garde designers and their clients in Ireland and Britain in the 1930s were coming to terms with the white purist villas of Le Corbusier and other European Modernists, Penprase was in effect doing his own thing at Ballintoy – building a concrete house for which there were few obvious precedents. Concrete, arguably, is the linking factor between the houses considered in this chapter, many Euclidian in their white cubic and cylindrical forms, sometimes streamlined with Art Deco and other 1930s motifs. Though bearing little visual resemblance to Bendhu, the use of reinforced concrete in construction is a common factor that enabled the provision of flat roofs and terraces, but in the case of Bendhu there is little sign of cantilevered or framed structure, forms in which reinforced concrete excels. In Bendhu, the structure is almost entirely of concrete load-bearing walls.

11.14

11.15

This short survey of buildings of the 1930s reveals some possible linkages between Bendhu and contemporary examples. Three influences may be re-stated: the well-established use of reinforced concrete in Modernist houses of the period; the Art Deco styling of houses in the early-mid-1930s, some of them built near the Penprases' home in Belfast; the tradition of a building conceived as *Gesamtkunstwerke*, or as a Total Work of Art. In the latter case architecture, painting, sculpture, stained-glass, metalwork, wall and ceiling painting are conceived as a unity, fully integrated in style and execution. To this list may be added the possible influence of studies in architectural form by members of the Dutch de Stijl group.

11.15
'Geragh', Sandycove, Co Dublin, architect Michael Scott, 1938

ENDNOTES

1. Larmour (1973).

2. Such as Le Corbusier's *Towards a New Architecture,* published in English in 1931, or F.R.S. Yorke's *The Modern House* published 1934.

3. The comparison of Bendhu with work of naive artists is explored in: Thompson (1987). Thompson compares the work of Newton Penprase with that of Ferdinand Cheval (1836-1924), Simon Rodia (1879-1965), and Clarence Schmidt (1897-).

4. The five points for a new architecture:

    raising the building on pilotis (or columns), effectively reclaiming the footprint of the building and returning it to the landscape.

    the free plan: the use of a framed structure to rid internal spaces of loadbearing walls.

    horizontal windows, or *les fenêtres en longeur,* promoting even daylighting to rooms (a spurious claim), but also flexibility in placing partitions.

    the free façade, made possible with a framed structure and cantilevered edge slabs, enabling whole or partial glazing, solid or open facade.

    roof terraces for amenity, taking the view, exercise and reclaiming the landscape.

5. Adam (1987). p 190-237.

6. For a further discussion of Loos' concept of *Raumplan* see Weston, (1996). p 51.

7. L'Effort Moderne Gallery, Paris.

8. Saltdean is between Rottingdean and Newhaven, on the English south coast.

9. Yorke (1937). p 174.

10. This house is now much altered, having lost the original windows, roof terrace and sun-lounge, and gained a pitched roof – all to the detriment of the 1930s design.

11. Larmour in Evans (2006). p 6.

12. For example London, Dudley, and Whipsnade Zoos all commissioned Modernist buildings, some with inventive concrete structures, such as the London Penguin Pool, designed by Berthold Lubetkin and Ove Arup, and the entrance canopy at Dudley Zoo near Birmingham.

13. A gazetteer of modern houses from the 1930s, including Northern Ireland and the Republic of Ireland, is included in *'The Modern House Revisited'* Journal of the Twentieth Century Society, No 2: 1996.

12 Design elements considered

For many years Bendhu appeared as a weather-beaten concrete shell, but in recent times has taken on the aura of a Modernist house, gleaming white and well tended. The appearance of the building today is very much the result of recent renovation and extension. This chapter looks at Bendhu in relation to its evolving plan layouts and changing appearance, stylistic elements that characterize the building, and how the Mac Cullagh and Ferguson eras have further developed the design ethos of the building.

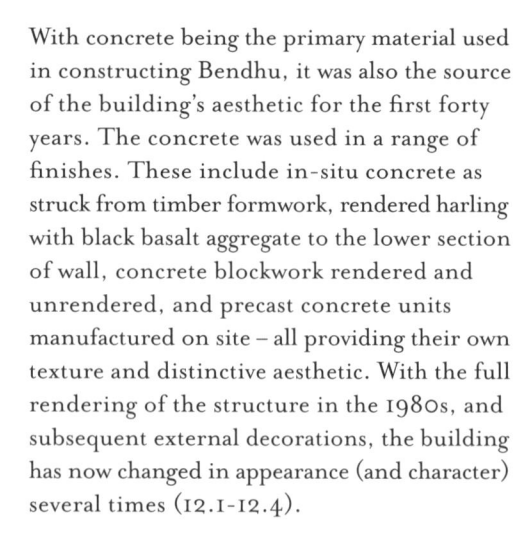

With concrete being the primary material used in constructing Bendhu, it was also the source of the building's aesthetic for the first forty years. The concrete was used in a range of finishes. These include in-situ concrete as struck from timber formwork, rendered harling with black basalt aggregate to the lower section of wall, concrete blockwork rendered and unrendered, and precast concrete units manufactured on site – all providing their own texture and distinctive aesthetic. With the full rendering of the structure in the 1980s, and subsequent external decorations, the building has now changed in appearance (and character) several times (12.1-12.4).

As Bendhu developed over time, the house design became ever more complex, and the drawing of comparative plans (pp 184, 185) shows the evolution of Bendhu from a small single-storey holiday cottage to a three-storey structure on the present site. The larger house started as a two-storey flat-roofed design shown in the 1936 building plan, then, with

12.1

12.1
West elevation - fair
faced concrete
finishes to Bendhu,
mid-1960s

12.2
North elevation -
rendered finishes to
Bendhu, mid-1960s

12.2

the incorporation of a first floor terrace, into the three-storey structure recorded in the Bannister survey of 1986. A further layer was added in 2006 with the fit-out of the upper stories and building of an extension on the first floor.

Bendhu is a house without a 'front' or 'back', and in that respect it is quite different from most other houses. There is no principal elevation, each façade is individually modelled, and from the outside it is unclear which the principal rooms are, or indeed what is the function of any room. The piano nobile, or principal storey, is on the first floor, but only the new glazed extension indicates its position. In Penprase's day the piano nobile was in effect the open-air east-facing roof terrace, which affords the dramatic views of the changing seascape, now enjoyed from inside the glazed extension.

The ground floor accommodation has a constant floor to ceiling height that provided a level platform from which to build the upper floors. But while the plan of the ground floor is orthogonal in layout, as shown in the 1936 drawing, it is not a simple square or rectangle in its outer geometry. Instead, the building has a complex outline of projections and recesses, even on the ground floor. From the first floor upwards the building was designed around the east-facing roof terrace, where, in an additive process, rooms were given whatever

DESIGN ELEMENTS CONSIDERED 181

12.3
Bendhu from the north-west, rendered and painted façades, 1995

12.4
North elevation, with Art Deco relief highlighted, 2007

OVERLEAF
Comparative plans showing 4 stages in the evolution of Bendhu

12.3

dimension and detail they required for their function - additional porches, bays and projections were added to the plan as necessary. This resulted in the sculptural form of the building's exterior as seen today.

Various stylistic elements characterise the elevations of Bendhu, and some of these first appeared in Penprase's drawing of the abandoned shoreline building of 1935 (p 42) and are repeated in the 1936 building plan (p 52), especially in the type of window design that is common to both designs. The window design can be regarded as an *idée fixe*, discussed previously in Chapters 4 and 5. The steeply sloping window cills are also a recurring feature of the design.

The cill serves the purpose of dealing with heavy and driving rain, allowing water run-off from the window glass, and avoiding water collecting on the cill. The source of the detail may be other buildings located in a maritime environment, or, alternatively, ecclesiastical buildings. This latter category may be the lineage of the window cills at Bendhu, as it might be for the Whitla Hall at Queen's University Belfast, a building started after Bendhu, incorporating steeply sloping but more refined projecting cills, that throw rainwater clear of the masonry.

Windows on the ground floor are installed with external shutters. Made in slatted timber, teak shutters are shown in the unbuilt 1935 shoreline design, and again repeated in the 1936 building plan. Penprase clearly intended their use from the start. Though unusual in domestic buildings in Ulster, they provided a degree of security and privacy.

Penprase's earliest proposal shows stylistic elements in a Moderne idiom, particularly the streamline styling shown in the 1935 shoreline design. The rendered masonry is styled with horizontal bands that are projecting and recessed – with the latter turned at 90 degrees vertically to 'frame' the main windows – all drawn in a most singular way as discussed in Chapter 4. This streamlining treatment to the elevations is continued a year later in the 1936 building plan. In this design for a two-storey building new elements are introduced in the elevation – Classical scrolls and acroteria, the latter being corner pedestals sculpted to resemble an acanthus leaf, bearing testimony to Penprase's interest in the Classical. Surmounting both the corner scrolls and acroteria are metal flagpoles, which prevail in the final building, though, as built, simpler piers in square-shaped masonry replace the Classical elements.

The different wall construction used in the upper floors produced further changes in the aesthetic of the building. The 300mm wide concrete walls used in the lower part of the building were superseded by construction in 200mm and 150mm wide blockwork for the superstructure, and led to a new elevational treatment to masonry areas. Built-in piers, mostly located on the exterior façade, strengthened the thinner masonry walls to the upper part of the house, now built in concrete block instead of in situ concrete. The piers stiffened the wall and saved on material content (and cost) and by turn imparted a distinctive verticality to the elevations that previously had horizontal

12.4

1935 SHORELINE DESIGN   1936 BUILDING PLAN

1935
Design for a single storey bungalow. Abandoned *after* the construction of foundations Design and drawing: *after* Newton Penprase

1936
Design for a two storey bungalow. Penprase worked on the construction for almost 40 years, making radical alterations to the upper floors. Design and drawing: *after* Newton Penprase

1986
Part of a measured survey carried out in 1985-1986, showing the stage reached in building when Penprase stopped work in 1975. Survey drawing: *after* Bill Bannister

2006
Showing the alterations and extension of Bendhu carried out by Michael Ferguson 1994-2003. Drawing: *after* Michael Ferguson's design

All plans and elevations re-drafted by Nicholas Allen

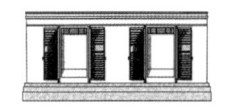

EAST ELEVATION

SECOND FLOOR

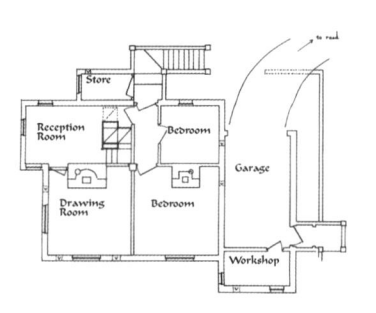

FIRST FLOOR

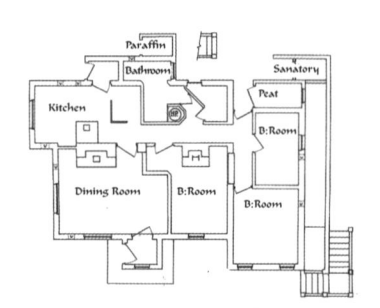

GROUND FLOOR

1986 SURVEY

2006 RECORD DRAWING

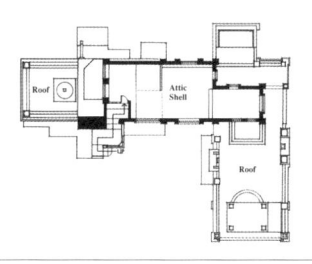

DESIGN ELEMENTS CONSIDERED 185

emphasis. When later rendered, the piers become uniform pilasters, sometimes combined with a wider profile around window openings on the upper floors, making external shutters unsuitable in these areas.

A further characteristic of Bendhu are the corner turrets of metalwork set in masonry blocks, built at the corners of flat roofs and balconies at different levels of the house. Constructed in cast concrete, the corner turrets support horizontal railings at parapets and cills. Metalwork standards emerge vertically at the corners to form a sculptural element that is essentially decorative, from which, as conceived by Pen, flags and pennants could be flown on special days.

Bendhu was always an artist's house, and it is unsurprising that artwork is incorporated throughout the building both inside the house and externally. The individual elements are discussed in Chapter 6. Inside, most of the painting, carving and castings are integrated into the building fabric, including the stars of the zodiac ceiling, wood panelling in several rooms and stained-glass. Of the external sculptures, the dragon gatepost sculpture was made off-site at the Millfield foundry in Belfast, the others possibly in the makeshift workshop on site, or back in Belfast. The Phoenix Rising sculpture on the east-facing terrace (now sited on the roof of the extension) and the Neptune group above the front door were essentially 'placed' on the building. Only the small maritime relief is built into the outside wall.

Other works by Penprase are conceived as part of the landscape: the birdbath and pond, the sunken grass seating area, the garden 'altar' group, and the steep external steps down to the beach, cut from the rock and protected by a 'fortified' concrete casement. These are site-specific elements, some of them listed, most of them with a degree of functionality appropriate to the setting.

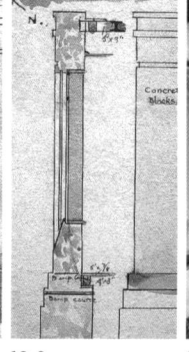

12.5

12.6

12.7

12.8

12.5
Part elevation
detail, 1935
shoreline
design drawing:
Newton Penprase

12.6
1935 shoreline
design detail:
section
through window

12.7
Bendhu, ground
floor window,
mid-1960s

12.8
Sloping window
cills, Whitla Hall
Belfast, John
McGeagh architect.
Built 1939-1949

12.9
Classical
composition of
first floor studio
façade, east gable

12.9

Penprase's external steps cut into the limestone rock at Bendhu, have a resonance with the countless stairways – typically steep and narrow – built into harbours, lighthouses, and rocks in coastal locations. An example of sculpting the landscape is the building of the Minack theatre, at Porthcumo in Cornwall, started in 1932 by Rowena Cade.[1] The construction of this open-air, privately owned theatre (which, like Penprase's building, takes its name from the adjoining rocks) pre-dates Bendhu by a few years, and, as with Bendhu, was built incrementally – in this case over a twenty-five to thirty year period. Since it is sited remotely four miles from Land's End, a considerable journey from Redruth on narrow roads, it is unlikely Penprase had any direct knowledge of the cliff-side theatre, as he remained in Ireland after arrival in 1911. The theatre appears to grow out of the cliff-face, and commands its landscape setting in a manner reminiscent of Bendhu at Ballintoy.

Returning to Bendhu and considering Penprase's interiors, there are perhaps some surprises. The first is the narrow hallway, an intimate space with timber panelling without any sign of the concrete construction or finishes of the outside. The second surprise is the Arts and Crafts character of the ground floor that is further revealed in the principal rooms, particularly the living room. A third and unexpected highlight is the Art Deco style of the zodiac bedroom, in which the focus is the stars of the zodiac ceiling, featuring twelve lunette panels depicting

DESIGN ELEMENTS CONSIDERED   187

12.10

12.11

each of the astrological signs,[2] from which graphic rays burst across the ceiling. In contrast the living room is lined in oak panelling, the oiled oak now matured to a silver-grey, with a much more traditional feel.

With the built-in artwork, panelling, stained-glass, ingenious furnishings – such as the moveable overmantel attached to the fireplace that folds out as a dining table before the hearth – how might Penprase's ground floor interiors be characterised? Arguably they share some of the design ethos of the Omega Workshops set up by Roger Fry and friends in the Bloomsbury Group, during the years 1913-1920. The Omega Workshops produced furniture, pottery, textiles, and other household goods that married traditional methods with a Modern approach. The work was produced anonymously under the trademark of the Greek Omega sign Ω, so as not to take account of the individual reputations of artists in the group. The work produced by the Omega Workshops combined contemporary and vernacular styling, sometimes referring to the Classical world in subject matter or symbolism. This produced interiors that could be comfortably cluttered, traditional and yet of their time, typically with lots of books, upholstered chairs, handcraft and tapestry.[3] In this there are echoes of the timber-panelled interiors, and installed artwork, by Penprase at Bendhu.

Bendhu changed in appearance in the 1980s when Richard Mac Cullagh carried out repairs and rendering to the blockwork façades. He was faced with huge practical problems of leaking roofs, keeping the building warm, and trying to make the upper floors habitable – tasks he was ultimately unable to achieve because of lack of resources, both practical and financial. Stylistically he sought to continue the building in the spirit of Penprase, his former teacher at the Art College. Some of the work carried out under his direction involved radical changes in the appearance of the building. Foremost was the rendering of the superstructure on the first and second floors, in a smooth finished cement render, covering over the textured blockwork and fair-faced concrete wall surfaces, a task that Penprase had started but not completed. The external decoration of the new rendering in a cream coloured paint, a sort of 'mushroom' hue, was a further alteration in appearance, as was the painting of the basalt harling to the ground floor walls in a 'chocolate brown' colour. The external walls now presented a rather drab and lifeless colour combination that only came alive in sunny weather, but was possibly in keeping with neighbouring houses.

Other works carried out by Richard indicated his individual approach and aesthetic, as seen in the work he carried out in the first floor studio, described in correspondence:

… in the long room upstairs I have placed 5 wood encased concrete beams each with 5 no. ¾" (steel) rods as roof strengthener, not because of any crack in the roof but to give a black beam appearance with Venetian red panels between, and I thought that I might as well make these load-bearing as a very nice airy salon might … be made … [4]

Had this approach been applied to the other rooms on the upper floors, the interior of Bendhu would be very different in appearance today. Richard Mac Cullagh's main contribution, however, was his role as custodian of the building

12.10 & 12.12
The Minack Theatre
Porthcurna Cornwall

12.11
Rowena Cade, at the
Minack theatre

12.12

DESIGN ELEMENTS CONSIDERED 189

for fifteen years, repairing the building fabric as resources allowed, and in effect saving the building from possible demolition, had Bendhu fallen into unsympathetic hands.

The work carried out by Michael Ferguson since taking over the building in 1994, includes the repair of the building fabric, the restoration of the Penprase interiors on the ground floor, and, after five years of repairs and refurbishment, the building of an extension on the first floor. He has continued the design intentions of Newton Penprase wherever possible. On the ground floor the timber panelling, ceiling painting, stained-glass, fireplace overmantel and other features have been carefully restored in the Arts and Crafts and Art Deco spirit of the original work. The first phase of Michael's refurbishment of Bendhu also took care of a range of practical matters: insulating roofs and walls throughout the building, upgrading or replacing services, and installing over thirty windows on the first and second floors.[5] The new windows, together with the external decoration of the building, significantly changed the exterior appearance of the house to a Modernist white aesthetic.

Painting the building a brilliant white in 1995 coincided with the installation of white framed double glazed PVC windows to the superstructure on the first and second floors, and transformed Bendhu in visual terms, giving the building a much brighter, friendlier and contemporary appearance both from a distance and at close quarters. Some architectural elements were picked out in colour variants, e.g. horizontal banding in light cream, and plinths in earth red, though in some of these decorative schemes Michael was experimenting, and later reverted to an all-white appearance.

The gleaming white appearance of Bendhu today suggests a closer kinship to Modernism, arguably linking Bendhu to Modern Movement buildings of the 1930s. But this is misleading. Pen, as far as we know, did not intend the house to be finished in render or paint, or as a 'purist' white volume. From comments made to his family he envisaged the concrete and blockwork fair-faced, cement grey in colour, and seen as a textured concrete structure.[6] On the other hand Pen rendered parts of the structure himself, in particular the ground floor 'rusticated

12.13
The zodiac bedroom and furnishings, 1995

12.13

base-course' of harling, shiny black with basalt aggregate. He also smooth rendered a good part of the north elevation. The practical purpose of this work was to assist in waterproofing the building, and perhaps to hide unsightly workmanship. Whether Penprase had plans ultimately to render the whole building is unclear. The cover illustration of the catalogue for the 1977 Arts Council exhibition shows the house in rough concrete block, and in situ concrete. This was the main appearance left by Pen when he stopped work in 1975. Indeed 'all in concrete' was the guiding mantra during Pen's long involvement with Bendhu, and concrete in its raw finish his original intention.

The aesthetics of the extension posed much debate in Michael's circle. Given that the first and second floors had never been occupied or made habitable (except for Pen's Den) the Fergusons chose a Modern approach to the design of the upper areas of the house. The shell interiors have been transformed into a series of bright spaces, making full use of the multiple sources of daylight from windows and roof lanterns, the seascape views framed by windows, and the intricate geometry of Penprase's existing structure retained and continued in the newly built areas.

The glazed extension is at the heart of the new arrangement of spaces for living, dining, cooking, sleeping and bathing – linked by new internal staircases to both the second floor eyrie (the Crow's Nest) and the older ground floor apartment. The extension, sited on the east-facing terrace to form a sun lounge and family room, together with new kitchen and dining spaces within the original building shell, has,

DESIGN ELEMENTS CONSIDERED 191

as already discussed, become the piano nobile of the house.[7] The design evolved through all the different stages of planning and construction by working within the building's limits and possibilities, on a pragmatic step-by-step approach, the one bold late-twentieth century intervention being the new glazed extension, resulting in a practical interior of considerable finesse.

In making a design assessment of Bendhu the inevitable conclusion is reached that it is a one-off work that defies precise classification in terms of architectural style. The building is of its time and includes elements of design characteristic of the 1920s and 1930s: Cubist modelling, Modernist and Art Deco forms, a geometry of flat roofs, lantern lights and terraces, and specific and unusual window styles. The painting of the exterior a brilliant white in the 1990s and the changing plan form over the years, combine with the Arts and Crafts, Art Deco and late-twentieth century modern interiors to contribute to the present-day Bendhu that remains, recognizably, the unique creation of Newton Penprase.

Two other controversial buildings, both very different from Bendhu, are described here by way of final comparison. Each building – the Housden House in Hampstead, London, and the Apollo Pavilion in Peterlee, Co Durham – was, like Bendhu, the creation of a committed individualist, working within a concrete aesthetic that challenged public norms, and both buildings were the subject of strong opposition from neighbours.

12.14

12.14
Bathroom, first floor, 2003

12.15
Studio, kitchen & dining, 2003

OVERLEAF
Bendhu elevations, from top left clockwise: north, east, south, west, 2009

12.15

Built much later than Bendhu, neither example could have influenced Penprase, and the reverse influence beggars belief. However, the bold expression of concrete structure in these two examples contrasts with the relative subtlety, and indeed the complexity, of the exterior form of Bendhu, and makes a comparison with these buildings worthwhile.

The Housden House is in South Hill Park, Hampstead, and was built in the years 1958-1968 by Brian Housden. An uncompromisingly Modern house constructed in concrete, and the architect's home, it is inspired by two icons of the Modern Movement: Rietveld's Schröeder House of 1924 in Utrecht, and Pierre Chareau's Maison de Verre in Paris of 1932. Housden sought out each building, and conversed with Mrs Schröeder about their joint admiration for Rietveld's work. As at Bendhu, Housden's house was built incrementally, much of it by himself, to fierce opposition from the local community, on a limited budget (money was always in short supply), and the building period was protracted over many years.[8]

The building differs in a number of ways from Bendhu: in its uncompromising interior of exposed in situ concrete, sculpted concrete stair and dramatic open plan living spaces. In Penprase's completed interiors there are no exposed concrete finishes, all wall and ceiling surfaces were either panelled, plastered, or decorated with ceiling paintings, with classically inspired themes. Other

DESIGN ELEMENTS CONSIDERED

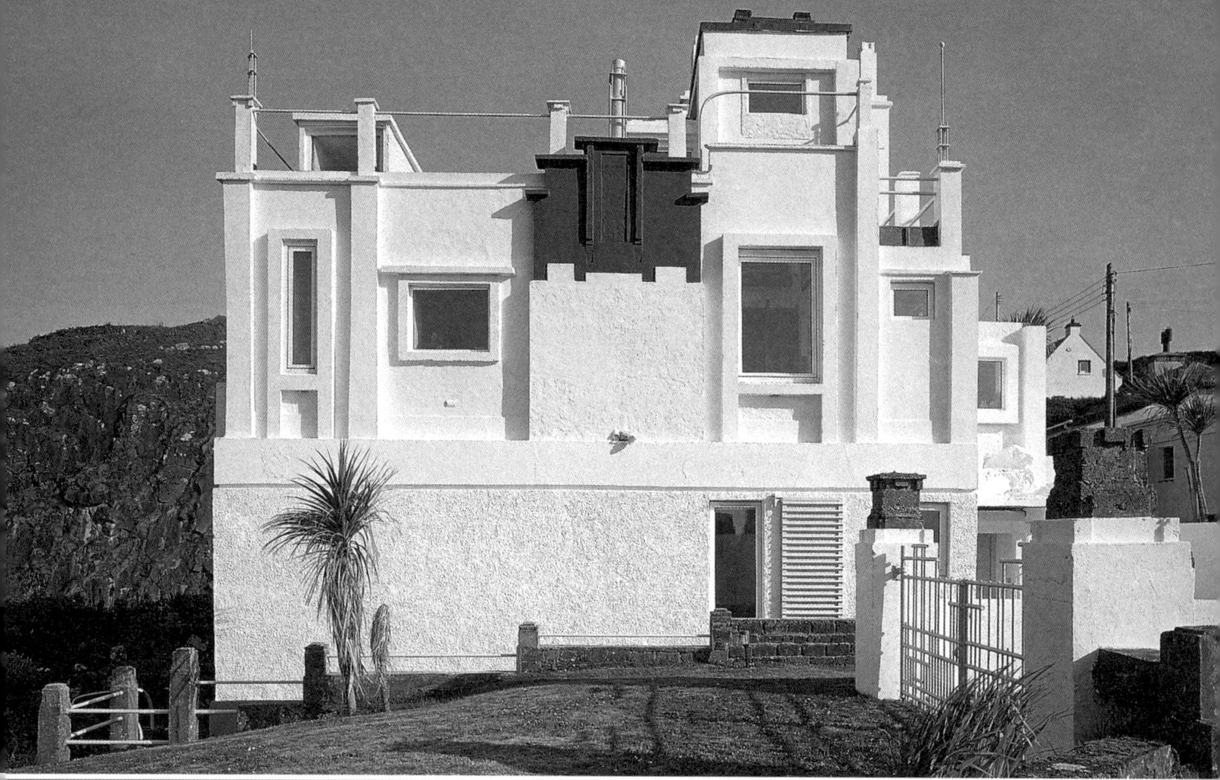

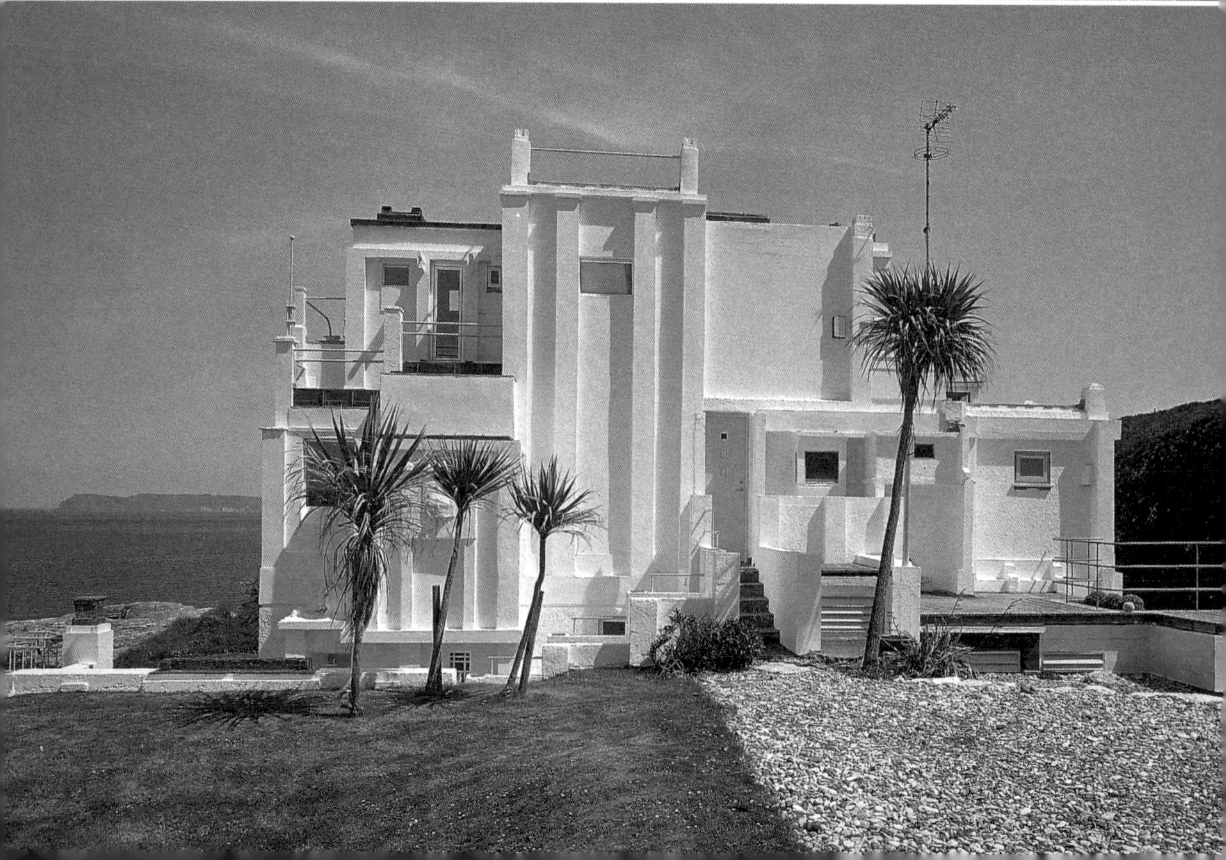

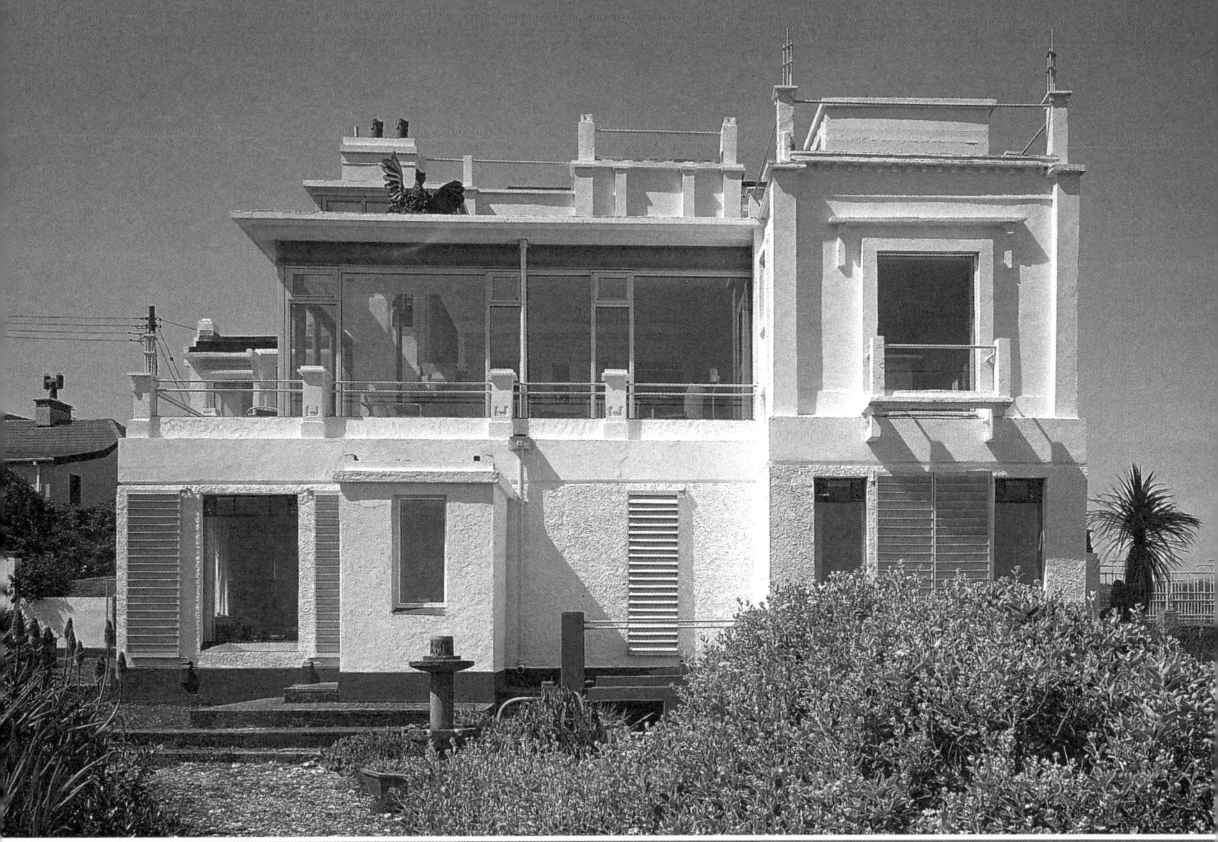

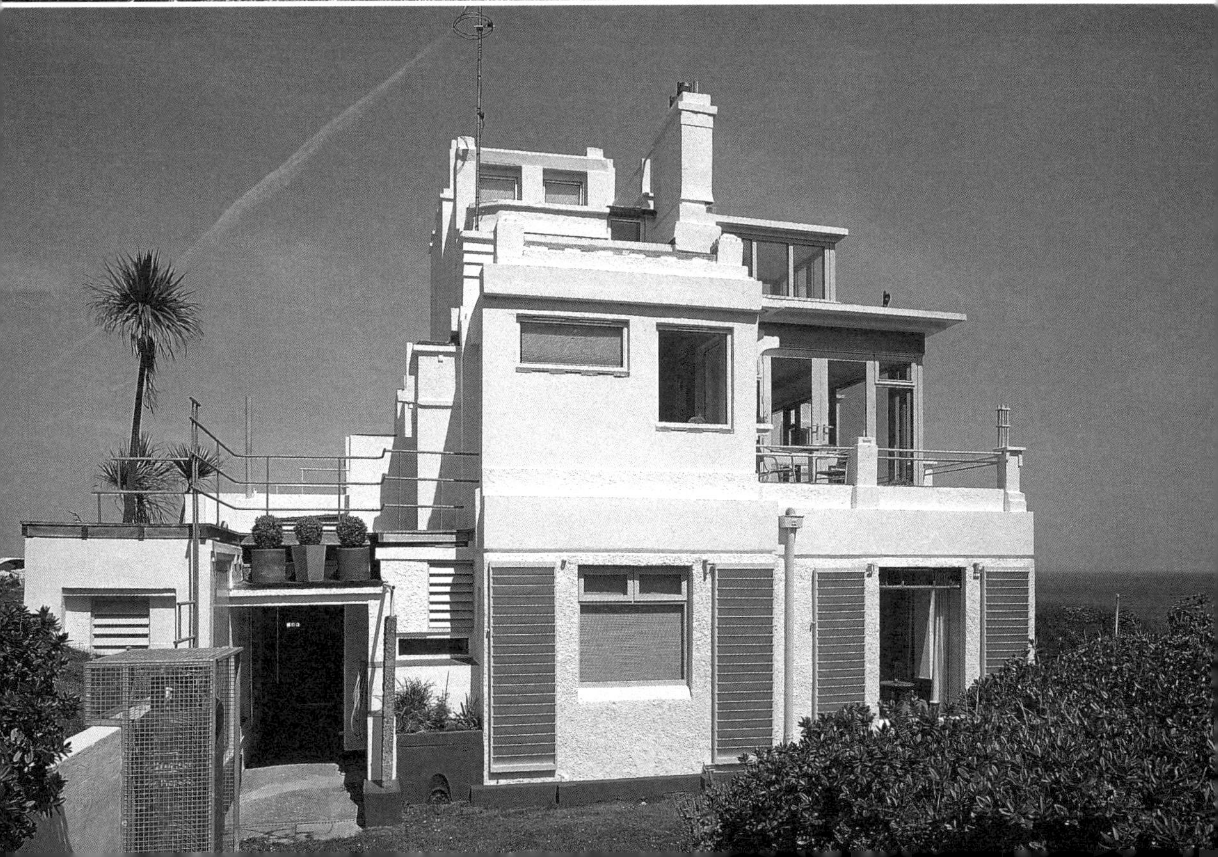

12.16

differences include the use of glass blocks (or Lenscrete) for translucent walls, and clear glazed windows set into the glass blocks, directly influenced by the example of the Maison de Verre; the use of metal mesh and industrial framing for railings, gates and fencing, a Modernist conceit borrowed from the continent. But the way in which Bendhu and the Housden house differ is partly due to the fact that Housden was a trained architect, enthralled with Modernism, and seeking European precedents, whereas Penprase worked primarily as a sculptor and artist with his own preoccupations, that included an interest in the legends and symbolism of the Classical world. But the lone journey of Penprase and Housden over many years in creating a building from their inner vision, often in a hostile environment, was an experience in common.

12.16
Apollo Pavilion,
Peterlee

12.17
Housden House,
Hampstead

OVERLEAF
External steps to
first floor entrance

The Apollo Pavilion at Peterlee in Co Durham was built in the years 1968-1970, to the design of Victor Pasmore.[9] The new town of Peterlee started in 1948, on land previously owned by the National Coal Board. Uniquely, the painter and sculptor Victor Pasmore was put in charge of the team looking after landscape design, and one of the results of this was the building of the Apollo Pavilion, (named after the Apollo Space Programme) to his design, completed in 1970.[10] The concrete sculpture is sited between two of the new town's housing estates, separated by an artificial lake, the pavilion serving as a pedestrian bridge. The bridge sculpture was designed to promote neighbourliness: providing stopping-off spaces, seating and balconies that would encourage the sociability of residents in their daily travels.

Unfortunately a different form of interaction occurred, with vandalism, graffiti, and drug use, resulting in the removal of steps in 1982 to prevent access. Pasmore had described the Apollo Pavilion as "... an architecture and sculpture of purely abstract form through which to walk ... to linger and on which to play, a free and anonymous monument which, because of its independence, can lift the activity and psychology of an urban housing community onto a universal plane".[11] Though derided by local people for much of its time-span, the pavilion has survived. In recent years public opinion has changed, so much so that enthusiastic support secured a sizeable lottery grant in 2008 for the pavilion's refurbishment and renewal.

The Apollo Pavilion and the Housden House are both works of optimism of their time, uncompromising in their powerful architectural forms. In the same spirit the building of Bendhu has been an act of faith and optimism, producing an individually crafted, complex, evolving and unique form.

12.17

ENDNOTES

1. Rowena Cade (1893-1983) was the moving force in building the theatre, working with one or two helpers, usually her long-term gardener, well into her eighties. She shared with Penprase an indomitable spirit, leading the building work for the forthcoming year every autumn, through the winter up to spring-time (summers were for theatrical productions).

2. Discussed in Chapter 6.

3. At Sissinghurst Castle in Kent, the home of Vita Sackville-West and Harold Nicolson, the interiors of the Elizabethan Tower typify the Omega influence.

4. Correspondence with Richard Mac Cullagh.

5. Including the ground floor there are over 50 windows in the house.

6. Conversation with David Penpraze 14 Dec 2005.

7. For a fuller discussion of the extension, see Chapter 10.

8. Overy (2000).

9. Victor Pasmore (1908-1998).

10. For information on Peterlee see: http://en.wikipedia.org/wiki/Peterlee

11. Quoted from:www.nothingtosee here.net/2006/11/the_apollo_ pavillion_peterlee.html (accessed 26 February 2009).

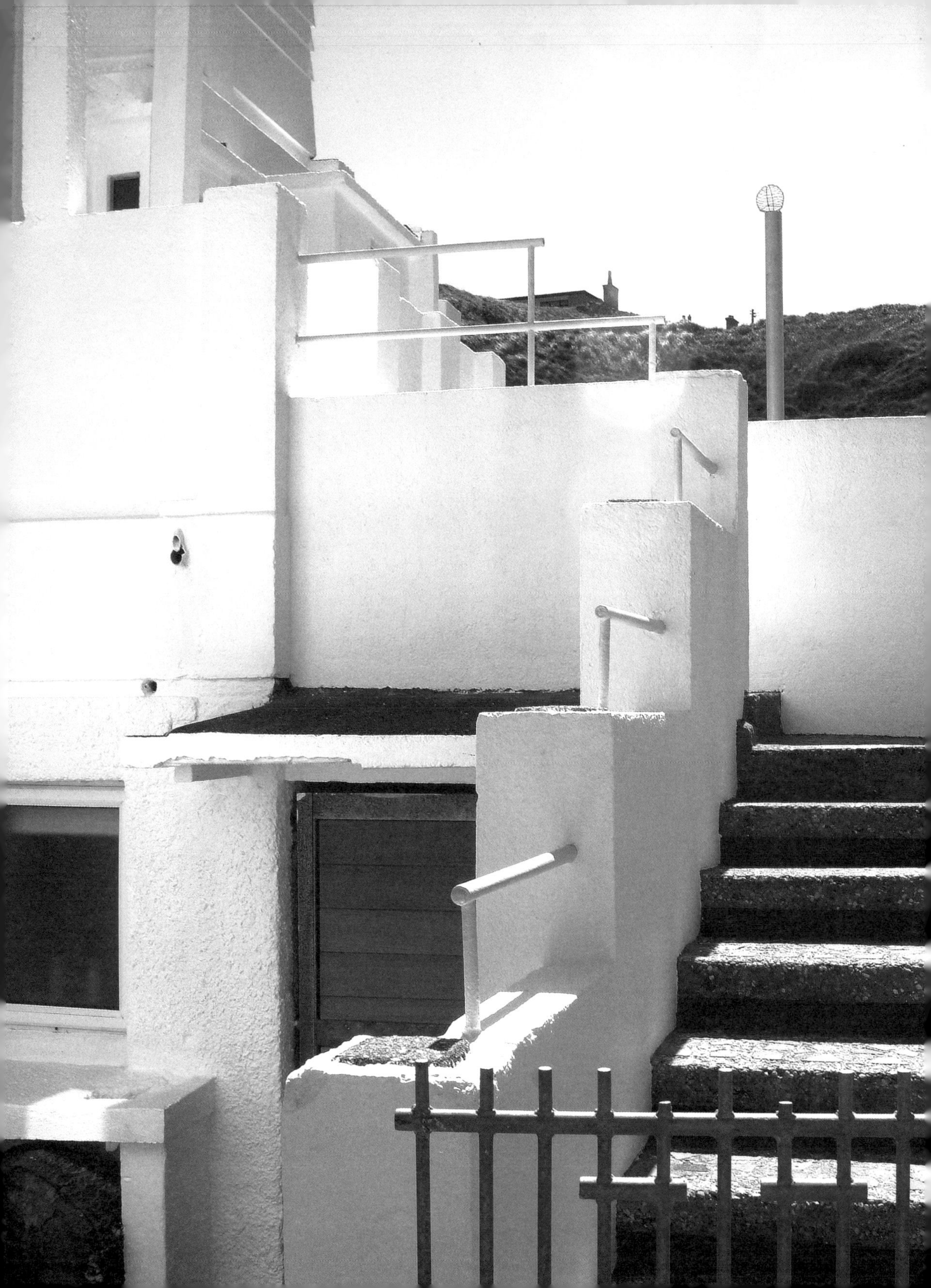

13 End piece

Not oft shall I descend these steps, which I have chiselled to the shore. For soon I shall depart for foreign lands. And if perchance there is extended consciousness, then I shall face another mystery beyond the door.[1]

A visit to Bendhu is memorable. You find yourself in the midst of an essentially eccentric house that has evolved incrementally, handcrafted in different styles and to changing programmes over seventy years – conjuring many images and associations.[2]

Almost impossible to categorise stylistically, the building is a one-off. From Newton Penprase's earliest designs for a flat roofed single-storey 'bungalow' to be built on the shoreline with streamlined features and distinctive windows of Moderne appearance, to the three-storey construction of Bendhu that evolved over forty years, to the modernisation and extension of the building in the recent period by Michael Ferguson – in all its incarnations Bendhu is strikingly different from the seaside houses nearby, with their pitched slate roofs, harled walls, sash windows, and in Penprase's day, low cost corrugated iron construction. It is perhaps at a literary and conceptual level that the ethos of Bendhu is best communicated, in words embracing both the physical essence and imaginative responses to the building. From this viewpoint, Bendhu may represent many things:

Ancient shelter
Work of naiveté
Marine refuge
Citadel withstanding north Atlantic storms
Regional variant of Modernism
Artwork in progress
Building without rules
Quest for self-knowledge
Protest about conformity
Self-build adventure
Hermitage in which Newton Penprase is still high priest
Holistic habitat

13.1

13.1–13.2
Carn Brea castle,
Redruth, Cornwall

13.2

The author's experience in researching the background to Bendhu, and the Cornish roots of Newton Penprase, may be of interest to the reader. During the course of this study I was invited to Redruth on two occasions to give a talk about Newton Penprase. Despite his influence as teacher to a generation of Ulster artists, and his legendary reputation in the north of Ireland as the builder of Bendhu, Pen remains a little-known figure in his home town, or in Cornwall generally. The mining town of Redruth has been described in the first chapter, and travelling there by train from Exeter, reading my photocopied notes, the following description caught my eye:

About a mile south-west of Redruth ... lies Carn Brea, a granite hill of great picturesque beauty ... containing many remains of supposed Druidical circles ... this hill [is considered] to have been one of the principal resorts of the Druids for the celebration of their mysterious rites ... [3]

There was something intriguing about this description that lodged in my mind, and after my lecture to a local audience at the excellent Cornish Studies Library, I explored Redruth the following day. Finding myself towards the end of the morning in the south-west edge of the town, with fields in prospect and a steep hill (or what looked like a small mountain) beckoning, I sensed this to be Carn Brea. I was later reminded that in the mining heyday in the nineteenth

END PIECE   201

13.3

Tin mines in Cornwall 1893

century there were eleven engine houses on the northern side of Carn Brea, and a plethora of mining buildings. None of this survives today, but abandoned mines survive as ruins on the south side. Carn Brea beckons, and two landmark edifices are visible from a distance surmounting the hilltop. The first, a huge monument to Lord Dunstanville, owner of land as far as the eye can see, captain of industry and mining magnate in days gone by, the memorial dating from 1836 and erected by Cornwall County Council; and the second, much older edifice of Carn Brea Castle – sometime chapel, fortification and hunting lodge, of which more later.

The ascent to the top of Carn Brea is physically demanding from the north-east, but on looking behind I was aware of a grand view unfolding. Breathless at the top, I appreciated the 270 degree panorama, described in Kelly's Directory as "a magnificent view ... extending from St Michael's Mount in the west to Devonshire in the east, and to the north and south as far as St George's and the British Channels". The summit is well named – carn – characterised as it is by huge granite boulders eroded smooth by wind and rain. From one of these groups the structure of Carn Brea castle emerges.

In climbing Carn Brea, I was retracing a journey that as a youngster Pen, his family and friends must have made.[4] At the castle I felt that the first source of Bendhu was revealed – Carn Brea with its magnificent panoramic views over Cornwall, every bit as dramatic as the panorama from Bendhu – the latter with Donegal in the west and Rathlin Island and Scotland to the north and east. The fact that Carn Brea castle is built out of the rock, the base supported on huge boulders, makes it a structure of some drama that arguably has its parallel at Ballintoy, where Bendhu is anchored to a narrow headland. The granite walls of the castle also share the sombre grey quality of Bendhu in its concrete finish, the quality envisaged by Pen, both structures having a brooding quality in changing light.

That same dourness can be seen in many other structures built for mining in the Cornish landscape. Camborne and Redruth were the twin centres of a great industry, the land between the two towns still peppered with redundant mine workings and associated structures: huge engine houses built to pump water from the mines, raise the mineral ore, and transport cages lifting men up and down mine shafts. In Penprase's youth these structures were highly visible, their tall chimneys giving out plumes of black smoke. The walls on which the wheels had bearings were heavily load bearing and constructed massively in granite, and today it is often these elements that survive in the crumbling buildings. In ruins, the mines can resemble a collection of castle towers viewed from a distance; or ruined temples in a Piranesi landscape.

Arguably the memory of these structures was powerful, whether consciously or subliminally, for Pen, when at the age of forty-seven, and after an absence from his native Cornwall of over twenty years, he came to build at Ballintoy. The memory of these Cornish industrial structures was arguably the second major influence on Penprase in his building of Bendhu.

This book has discussed how Bendhu has evolved over a time span of three quarters of a century, the house conceived and interpreted by its three owner-builders. It is a house that evokes strong responses, its enchantment often vividly expressed in words. Two testaments to Bendhu and Newton Penprase are here quoted, the first by the artist Roy Johnson, and the second by Richard Mac Cullagh:

By any standards [Bendhu] is the unique and remarkable product of a highly individualistic and creative personality .... In its construction it embodies a process which is essentially sculptural, and it is this characteristic which gives the building its character and eccentricity. It is a complex building, not only in its building method and its external appearance and in the applied ingenuity of the solitary builder to its interior, but it is also a complex building for that which it represents. To consider the creative energy of Newton Penprase, sustained, applied, and devoted to this building for forty years, is at once to consider the very basis of the creative impulse, and the drives which sustain it.[5]

This wind-walled citadel of the proud human spirit, sited 'twixt the heavens and the ocean of Ulster's storied coast, is something we cannot afford to lose. Pen, Cornishman as he was, had to create, was driven to create, something seemingly immutable. Michelangelo struck the rock and brought out Moses, Penprase struck the rock and brought out Bendhu.[6]

Though the house has been extended, modernised and refurbished, the spirit of the original builder is, arguably, not far away. This description of the Cornish architect John Campbell's holiday house that he built himself at the age of sixty-seven, as recorded by his biographer, resonates with Bendhu:

OVERLEAF
Madonna and
child, detail.
Also see A.26

The Ark was finished. It lay compactly on the ground, it was altogether clothed in bark, a true log cabin, and its windows were polished. I entered .... There was nobody in it but in the fire-place a wood fire burned brightly and a kettle was singing on the hob. In front of the hearth [his] Windsor chair was drawn up, with a book lying face downwards on the seat. ... The whole arrangement was orderly, colourful, fresh, cheerful, welcoming and homely. ... it was not the appearance of the room that really arrested me, it was the sense of presence. The builder had become incorporated in his work ... [7]

That description, in essence, might be of Bendhu, and apply to all three custodians: Newton Penprase, Richard Mac Cullagh, and Michael Ferguson, who between them have created on the north Antrim coast, perhaps unwittingly, a unique work of architecture.

ENDNOTES

1. Newton Penprase, unpublished papers.

2. Bendhu is a private house. Visitors are asked not to intrude or disturb.

3. Kelly's Directory, 1889.

4. Pen's father painted at least one watercolour view of Carn Brea castle.

5. Johnson (1977).

6. Mac Cullagh, Richard. Notes on Bendhu, unpublished, 1994.

7. Powers (1997) p 60.

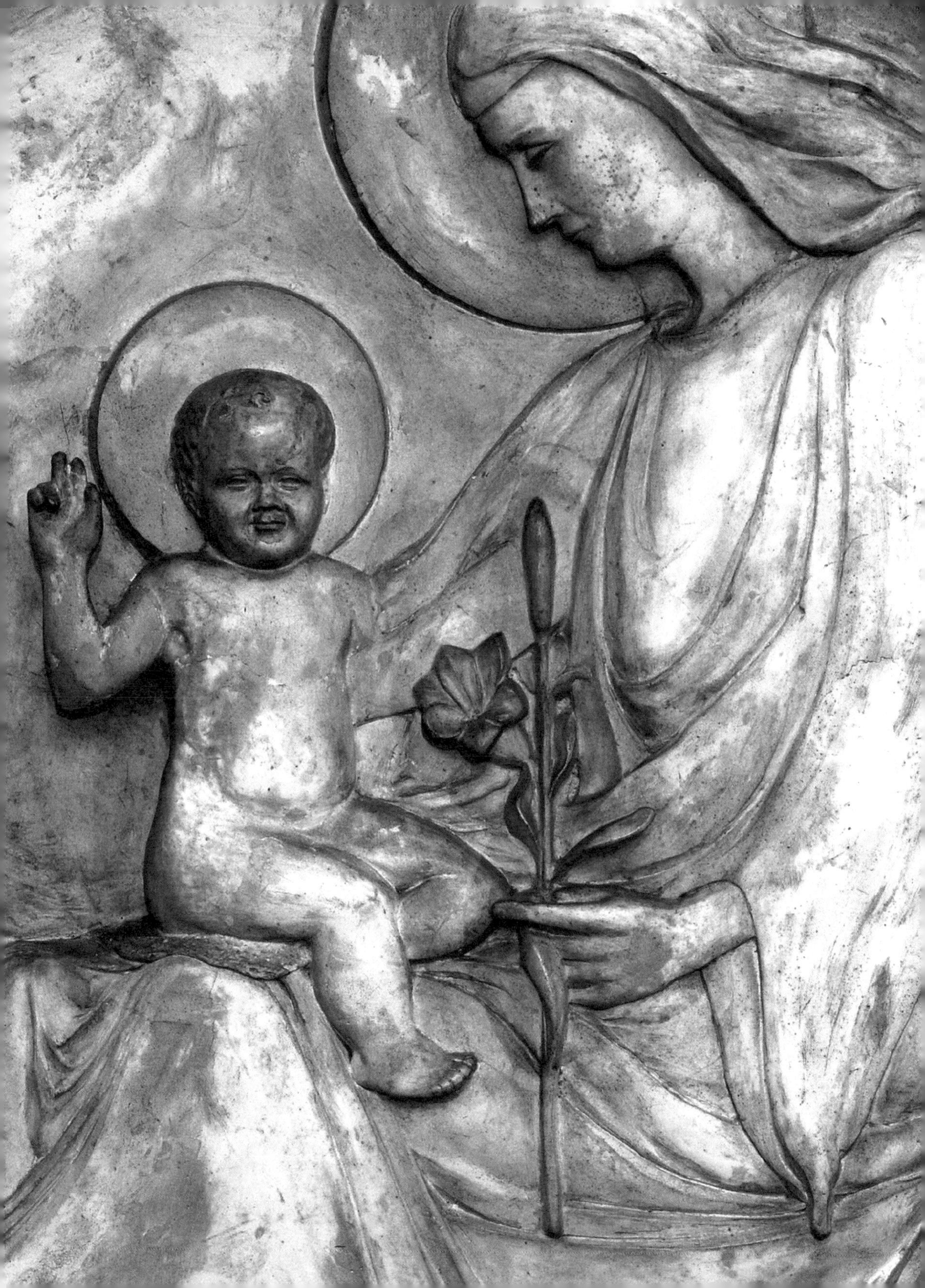

Appendices

CHRONOLOGY

REVIEW OF
ARTWORKS

TRANSACTIONS
WITH LOCAL
AUTHORITY

1 Chronology

1935

1957

1888
Newton Herbert Penprase born in Redruth, Cornwall, 24 March.

1903
Penprase enrolled in the *School of Science and Art*, Redruth.

1904-1905
9 drawings by Penprase, of wood carving and church silverwork, purchased by the Victoria & Albert Museum, London.

1911
Penprase moves to Belfast to take up teaching appointment at Belfast College of Art.

1916
Penprase marries Mildred Ethel McNeice.

1923-1924
Newton and Mildred commission a 'subsidy' house for their home in Belfast.

1934-1935
Land purchased at Ballintoy, Co Antrim. Penprase starts building a small holiday home. The authorities order work to cease because the site is too near the shoreline.

1936
Building Bendhu commences on new site.

1948-1949
Correspondence with local authority to stop work on Bendhu because of changes in plan.

1953
Penprase retires from Belfast College of Art at 65.

1963

1992

2003

1956
Local authority decides not to pursue compliance with plans.

1959
Daily Express article on Bendhu, 10 August, reports that "Mr Penprase is currently chiselling steps down the cliff face for quicker access to the beach".

1960
Penprase continues building Bendhu (or Pen's Folly, as it is often called).

1974-1976
Mildred Penpraze dies; accident at home in Grasmere Gardens forces Newton Penprase to cease building work at Bendhu; he moves to Rathmoyle Care Home, Ballycastle.

1977
Retrospective exhibition *All his own work: Newton Penprase* organised by the Arts Council of Northern Ireland; Roy Johnson curator.

1978
Newton Penprase dies in Dalriada Hospital, 9 January.

1979
Richard Mac Cullagh purchases Bendhu.

1992
Bendhu is listed by DOE as a building of special architectural or historic interest.

1994
Michael and Lorna Ferguson purchase Bendhu.

1994-2004
Renovation and extension of Bendhu by Michael Ferguson and his team.

2006
Bendhu features in *BBC-tv Coast* programme.

2009
UAHS publishes book: *Bendhu and its Builders*.

CHRONOLOGY 211

2 Review of artworks

Newton Penprase's artistic oeuvre – drawings, paintings, sculpture, designs for damask, models and trophies – was wide ranging and spanned a long career. This review of extant artworks, mostly pre-dating and independent of Bendhu, is intended to give a rounder picture of the man. It is, perforce, a tentative record, as the whereabouts of particular pieces are unknown, and some have been lost or damaged. Most of the items, though not all, were exhibited in the 1977 Arts Council of Northern Ireland exhibition *All His Own Work*, and where this is the case catalogue numbers are included that refer to that exhibition. Penprase's artworks are mainly in private collections, with the exception of items held by the Ulster Museum. It is hoped that making a record of Penprase's surviving artworks at this time is a useful step to further interest in his work, and to unearthing lost items.

SHADING FROM CAST

Detail of pencil on board
47x34cm
By Newton Penprase, 1900 age 12.
Embossed ESK
(exhibited South Kensington)
Cat.1 (exhibition: 'All his own work').

A.6

PERSPECTIVE ANALYSIS

Detail of pen and ink on board
55x77cm
Signed: Newton Herbert Penprase, 1903 age 16
Embossed ESK. Cat 2.

A.7

STUDIES OF DRAPERY

Details from collage, pen and wash on board
51x75cm
Signed by Newton Penprase 1907, age 18
ESK. Cat 11.

A.8, A.9

A.10

STILL LIFE GROUP

Detail of charcoal and pencil on board
43x71cm
By Newton Penprase, undated
ESK. Cat 12.

PLANT STUDIES

Detail of watercolour
76x55cm
Signed Newton H. Penprase, undated
ESK. Cat 13.

BIRD, FISH, ANIMAL STUDIES

Detail of watercolour
75x55cm
Signed Newton H. Penprase, undated
ESK. Cat 14.

A.11, A.12

A.13

ANTIQUE STATUE

Drawing from pencil
70x37cm
Signed Newton H. Penprase, undated
ESK. Cat 18.

A.14, A.15

FACIAL EXPRESSIONS

Two of six drawings illustrating Laughter, Rage, Remorse, Contemplation, Fear, Pain;

Pencil on white paper
54.5x35.6
By Newton Penprase
Ulster Museum collection Ref: 2686-91.
Cat 27

Martyn Anglesea writes: Both in style and subject-matter, these (6 drawings) seem to be derived from Lebrun's Traité sur les Passions, and other well-used art-students' textbooks on facial expression. The facial type suggests an interest in the works of Hogarth and William Blake (Penprase and his wife seem to have been inclined to Blake's frame of mind).[1]

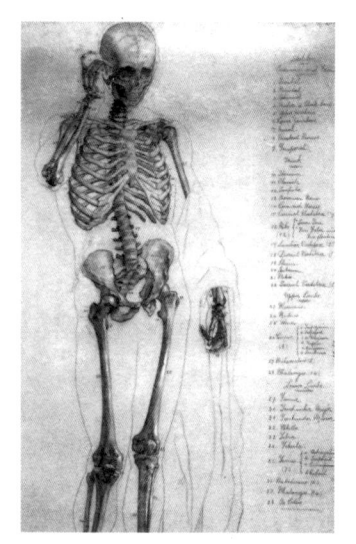

HUMAN SKELETON

Charcoal and white chalk on buff paper
74.5x40.8cm
Ulster Museum collection Ref: 2706
Cat 30.

A.16

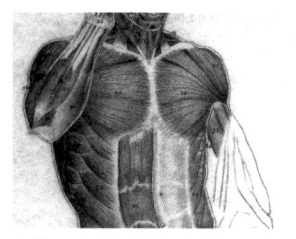

ECORCHÉ FIGURE

Detail of anatomical study in charcoal and red chalk on white paper
74.5x46.2cm
Ulster Museum collection Ref: 2707
Cat 29.

A.17

TIRED OUT

Terracotta bust
60x32x52cm
By Newton Penprase, 1914
Cat 49.

A.18

GREEK FESTIVAL

Detail for damask, white paint on buff paper,
119x131cm,
By Newton Penprase, undated
Cat 31.

DESIGN FOR LINEN DAMASK

Detail, white paint on grey paper
By Newton Penprase, undated
Cat 32 or 33.

MAQUETTE FOR MEMORIAL

Painted plaster, wood,
32x25x42cm, by Newton Penprase, 1928
Cat 51.

DESIGNS FOR A TROPHY

Copper
28x27x27cm
By Newton Penprase, undated
Cat 58.
Trophy for Ballintoy regatta
Copper
39x18x21cm
By Newton Penprase, undated
Cat 59.

A.24

MAQUETTE FOR MEMORIAL

Painted plaster, wood
32x25x42cm
By Newton Penprase, 1928
Cat 52.

A.25

MADONNA AND CHILD

Detail, plaster relief
60cm dia
By Newton Penprase, undated
Cat 57.

A.26

PORTRAIT OF A LADY

Oil on canvas
102x76cm
By Newton Penprase, 1920.

THE PILGRIMS' CHORUS - TANNHAUSER

Detail of painting
By Newton Penprase
100x85cm
Cat 38.

A visual interpretation of Wagner's music and opera, this is one of the few abstract paintings by Penprase. The work has some resemblance to pictures of the early-1930s by the Irish artist Mainie Jellett.

A.27

THE MYSTIC

Sculpture, plaster
65x39x46cm
By Newton Penprase, undated
Ulster Museum collection Ref:2672
Cat 56.

John Hewitt has commented on Penprase's as artist:

In contrast to his practical gifts and the meticulous accuracy of his drawings, many of his paintings and sculptures went far beyond the confines of observed appearance. One large canvas, for instance, its title, 'Progression'[2], was a rendering of the legendary Hercules and Hydra duel, the many-headed monster belching out, not only smoke and flame, but bats and lizards, the foreground and background rich with symbolical shapes; an unexpected amalgam of G F Watts and his Victorian rhetoric with the more recent conventions of Superman. In his sculpture the same grotesque inventiveness gave such a piece as 'The Mystic', a gaunt, emaciated mask with shut lids and a single eye staring from the middle of a high bald forehead.[3]

A.28

A.29

PROGRESS —
THE DAWN OF A NEW DAY

Oil on canvas
143x192.5cm
By Newton Penprase, undated
Ulster Museum collection, ref: 2677
Cat 48.

Penprase's narrative for this startling picture, 'Progress – the dawn of a new day' has survived:

I have represented the dawn of a new day with Hercules and the Hydra, one of the twelve labours allotted to him. The twelve, symbolic of the twelve working hours of the day, or, as some state, the twelve signs of the Zodiac, or the year. I have portrayed Hercules not as the strong muscular man as is the usual but the strong mental man overcoming the obstacles for man's advancement. He is using the shield of knowledge and has overcome one of the evil heads of the Hydra, but seven lesser evils have sprung forth, which will be dealt with in time. The Hydra is being slowly driven back into its lair. The water-fall (purity) being polluted in its course through the lair (or the pollution of purity through evil). The rising sun lights up the left of the picture, where can be seen the Egyptian obelisk, and coming forward, is the Aqueduct of the Romans, showing the great advancement of man, collectively through law and order, politically, City, Empire etc. The white swan (represents) purity of thought, more especially ... aesthetics. Towards the foreground is the cogged wheel of Leonardo da Vinci which altered the train of thought in the Middle Ages (mechanical) and on the rock(y) foreground, Newton's telescope which again gave a new outlook (mathematical) towards the Laws of Gravity. Towards the right will be seen a prehistoric animal and bird; Darwin's 'Selection of the Species', which again advanced man with further thought (Theology) etc. Passing onwards is seen the symbol of Atomic energy – aluminium in this case – thus man has again advanced.[4]

ENDNOTES

1. Ulster Museum (1986) pp 72,133.
2. Also known as 'Progression'.
3. Hewitt & Catto (1977).
4. From an undated letter from Penprase to a friend or colleague.

3 Transactions with local authority

It is part of the folklore surrounding Bendhu that Newton Penprase designed the building as he went along and frequently changed plan, to the frustration and annoyance of the authorities. His well-mannered though sometimes argumentative response to building and planning regulation produced a lively correspondence. Pen's letters were handwritten on foolscap sheets prior to typing a final version, with carbon copies kept as a record.

His correspondence with the local authority is with both Ballycastle Rural District Council and Antrim County Council. The District Council was responsible for administering the Building Bylaws of 1936, while the County Council administered the 1931 and 1944 Planning Acts of Northern Ireland, from their offices in Belfast.

Penprase wrote to the Clerk of Ballycastle District Council on 14 April 1936 [1] submitting the 1936 building plan for approval:

I am forwarding under separate cover the plans of the proposed bungalow to be built of concrete reinforced with 4" H steel girders ... I would be pleased if you will place it before your committee at its next meeting so that I may have the result of their finding the sooner. Thanking you ...

The letter is sent from Belfast, but also notes Pen's temporary address at Ballintoy, staying

A.30

A.30
Bendhu in 1949.
A similar photograph set off alarm bells with the local authority

at the Coast Guard Cottages, accommodation that overlooked the Bendhu site.

The 1936 building plan (p 52) was thus submitted to the local authority for approval on 14 April 1936. The drawing has been over-marked by council officials with Referred to [District] Council's surveyor 21/4/36, who duly approved the drawing with the proviso ... subject to approval of Co[unty] Surveyor 12/5/36. There is no record as to whether the County Council surveyor duly approved the drawing or not – but, critically, it was not refused. Undoubtedly there was some prevarication by the County Council in the matter of whether to grant approval or not.

Penprase proceeded to build the layout shown in this plan, in spirit if not in detail, but only in regard to the ground floor storey. The change of plan in the upper floors and absence of revised drawings caused consternation with the local authority over a number of years, coming to a head in the post-war period. On the 4 Nov 1948 the County Council solicitor Samuel Cumming wrote to Penprase:

I have to request you to discontinue your building operations, and to call upon you forthwith to lodge the required plans with the Planning Authority ... In the event of your failing to comply ... and proceeding with the work ... the necessary steps will be taken to compel compliance with the Regulations in force ...

By the following May a different solicitor was dealing with the matter for the County Council, Samuel Anderson of Ballymena. Pen replied to him on 23 May 1949, thanking him for a recent letter and noting that

... it contains the same request and command as did the letter sent to me by a Mr Cumming, Solicitor .... In answer to that letter I stated "That work has ceased and would not be resumed before I submitted plans and had the sanction from the proper authorities to start again." That statement has held good, no work whatsoever has been done to the building and shall not be done before I submit the plans and have news that they are accepted.

One may speculate that the authorities' keen interest in the existence or otherwise of approved drawings at this time had been sparked by Newton's constructing an additional storey (the second floor) on the north-west corner of the building facing Harbour Road, to an ever more complex design of concrete sculptural form, making the building three storeys high.

There follows correspondence regarding a recent snapshot of Bendhu (similar to A.30) on which the Planning Office had based its concerns. In his letter of 16 June 1949 the Deputy Planning Officer summarised the County's concerns to the District Council:

For some time past the County Council has been concerned regarding a house which Mr Newton H. Penprase is erecting at Ballintoy Harbour, and, on the instructions of the Council, the County Solicitor has been in communication with Mr Penprase. When the Planning Acts came into force Mr Penprase had already commenced the building of this structure and it was considered that it was exempt for that reason from Planning control.

An interesting point – the legislation referred to must be the 1931 Planning and Housing Act (Northern Ireland), that was subsequently amended by the 1944 Planning (Interim Development) Act (NI). It was not until the 1944 Act came into force that a more effective development control system was put in place. The letter continues:

The building has, however, now assumed a most peculiar shape and the County Solicitor has been instructed to take action to ensure that steps be taken to have the building completed with the plan previously approved, or, alternatively, to prevent further work being carried out which would injuriously affect the amenities of the area. In a letter dated 23rd May 1949 ... Mr Penprase [states] that the building was approved by the respective authorities and passed by them as a two-storey building [and] that in the early years of the war he had to alter the second storey for want of the necessary steel ... I enclose a snapshot of the structure which, I think, will explain the reason for our concern, and I shall be very glad if you will return this when finished with it.

The snapshot photo was the source of alarm at the County Council offices, showing as it does a stark three storey structure emerging in raw concrete, of unusual if not radical design, instead of the two storey bungalow of the 1936 building plan. On 27 June 1949 the Deputy Planning Officer wrote to the County Solicitor, Mr Samuel Anderson:

A.31
Approvals to the 1936 building plan: recommended for approval by the County Surveyor, neither formally endorsed nor refused

A.31

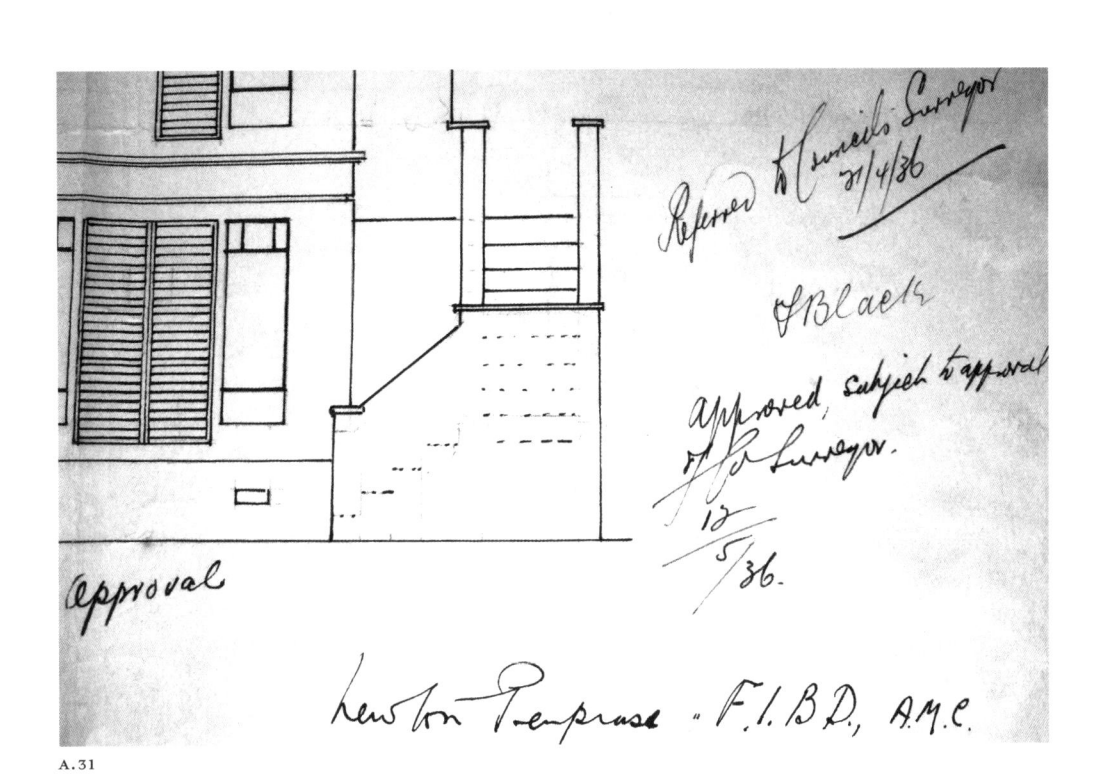

I have now been informed by the Ballycastle Rural District Council that, on the 12th May, 1936, a plan of the proposed house at Ballintoy submitted by Mr N. Penprase was approved, subject to the approval of the County Surveyor. Whether the approval of the County Surveyor was ever obtained would now be difficult to ascertain, but in any event he raised no objection to the building of the house which has been in existence now for a good many years.

This is notable for being the nearest written endorsement by an officer in Antrim County Council of the 1936 building plan, albeit by internal correspondence. The letter continued:

The Clerk to the Ballycastle Rural Council forwarded to me a copy of the original plan, of which I have made a tracing, and it would seem that Mr Penprase is departing from the design indicated in that plan. I think it would be well to write to Mr Penprase pointing this out and requesting the submission of an amended plan showing how he intends to complete the building, and informing him that if any further work is carried out without consent action will be taken by the council. He appears to change his ideas from time to time and I think determined efforts must be made to get him to adhere to a definite plan.

The following day a letter was sent to Pen by the solicitor:

I am now instructed that the Clerk of Ballycastle Rural Council has forwarded to [the County Council] a copy of the original plan of your building [from] which it would seem that you have departed from the design indicated in that plan .... In the circumstances I am directed to write and point this out to you and to request that you will now submit an amended plan showing how you intend to complete the building. I am again directed to inform you that if any further work is carried out without consent action will be taken by my Authority.

A few days later, on Monday 4 July 1949, Pen replied to the County Solicitor, responding with a degree of guile and appeal to higher purpose, noting it was the end of a busy academic year:

I received your letter as we were disposing of our Diploma Students that day. They have finished their delightful days of study and are now ready to go out into this avaricious mercenary world. "Sic Transit Gloria Mondi".[2]

With my own work I am ... two months behind. I shall [DV] be in Ballintoy on or about the 9th or 10th inst. where I shall have a few days rest before starting to make the drawings which the Authorities are so anxious to receive. This year I shall content myself by putting up at the headland some little earthen walls to act as screens from the North wind, and trap the sun from the east and south. Trusting that this will give you further assurance ...

The "little earthen walls" provoked further correspondence with the local authority as to their nature and position, and the County Surveyor, William Grigor, was asked to investigate in case they impinged on the public highway, but the walls referred to were on the garden side of the house, away from the road, on the headland overlooking the beach. On the main point of the correspondence, the furnishing of a revised plan showing how the building would be finished, Penprase appears to have won some more time. There is no evidence of

OVERLEAF
One of six drawings illustrating Rage, Remorse, Contemplation, Fear, Pain and Laughter

a new drawing being made, or correspondence either then or later regarding a new drawing. The matter went quiet for a while.

Several years pass before the next letter appears on file on a different topic when Mr Grigor was again asked to inspect the site, this time in relation to the possibility that Pen was constructing a garage on the north side of the house that would have access from the public highway. Penprase, in contrite mood, wrote to the Planning Office on the 8th September 1956:

I regret having taken the liberty of removing the road fence without permission from the highway authority. Tomorrow I shall write [to] Ballycastle ... Council for permission and explain that I have not tried to evade the Law in any manner whatsoever — I still wish to remain a true citizen. The car would be better off the road at this point [where there] is rather a sharp turn [in the road], and at certain times of the year, with a careless driver + thoughtless children, trouble could easily arise. Again, I am sorry for my action ...

Further correspondence passed between the District and County Councils and ends in 1956 with a "Note for File" made by the County Planning Officer on 7 December 1956. This records the Planning and Highways Committee decision at their meeting a few days before:

This development at Ballintoy was considered by the Planning and Highways Development Committee at its meeting on 4/12/56. It was decided that there was little point at the moment in trying to force Mr Penprase to comply with the plans, which he originally submitted to Ballycastle R.D.C. The Secretary reported that he had been through the house recently, that no part of it is finished, and he feels that Mr Penprase will never complete it. The Committee decided that in the circumstances they should do nothing in the case.

It is understood that the excavation made at the side of the house is not for the purpose of erecting a garage, but is simply to provide a space on which Mr Penprase's car is to be parked.

Peace at last! Pen was doing no harm – a view that would be endorsed by future generations. He continued working on Bendhu for another eighteen years.

ENDNOTES

1. The 14 April was the first Tuesday after the Easter weekend in 1936.

2. The Latin translates: 'Thus passes the glory of the world' – and more idiomatically suggests that worldly fame and splendour are short-lived. The phrase used to be said at papal coronations to remind the Pope that despite the trappings of office he was a mere mortal. Penprase seems to suggest that the idyllic days of college cannot last, before we encounter grim reality. I am indebted to Professor Brian Campbell for both the translation and interpretation; he has also pointed out that Penprase should have written 'mundi'.

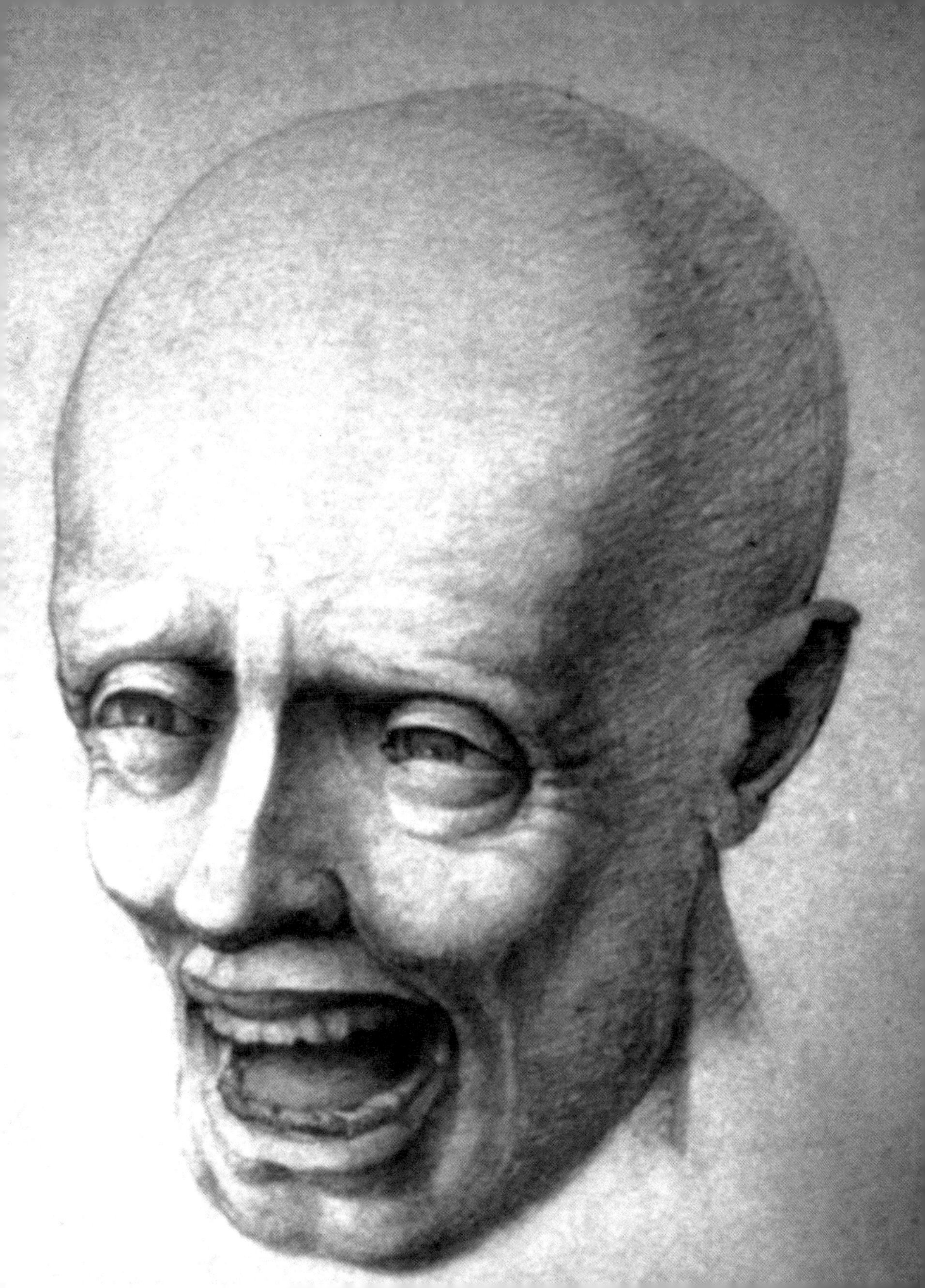

Bibliography

Picture credits

Index

Bibliography

Adam, Peter (1987) *Eileen Gray, Architect / Designer — a Biography.* London, Thames and Hudson.

Angelsea, Martyn (1981) *The Royal Ulster Academy of Arts — a centennial history.* Belfast, The Academy.

Arnold, Bruce (1991) *Maine Jellett and the Modern Movement in Ireland.* New Haven and London, Yale University Press.

Auld, John McConnell (2004) *Letters to a Causeway Coast Mill House.* Port Braddan, Con Auld.

Belfast Newsletter (1931) 26 January. pp 5, 8.

Belfast Telegraph (1978) 11 January. Obituary of Newton Penprase.

Belfast Telegraph (1993) 14 April. Article by Richard Mac Cullagh.

Belfast Telegraph (1993) 30 September. Article by Darwin Templeton.

Bell, Henry V (2006) *Diligence and Skill — 100 years of Education at Belfast Institute.* Belfast, Institute of Further and Higher Education.

Board of Education, Great Britain (1905) *National Competition: List of students awarded, with the report of the examiners on the selected works of schools of science and art classes.* London, National Art Library, Victoria & Albert Museum. p 37.

Board of Education, Great Britain (1910) *National Competition: List of students rewarded, with reports of the examiners on the selected works of schools recognised under the regulations for the technical schools, schools of art, and other forms of provision of further education in England and Wales.* London, National Art Library, Victoria & Albert Museum. p 21.

Brett, Charles E B (1996) *Buildings of County Antrim.* Belfast, Ulster Architectural Heritage Society. p 213, and colour plate XIV b.

Brooks, Linda (1996) 'White House – Architecture without an Architect' *Perspective*, Vol 4 No 5 (May / Jun) pp 42-44.

Catto, Mike *et al* (1994) 'A Normal School' *Art and Design Matters*. Belfast, University of Ulster.

Catto, Mike (2009) *A School of Design and Art for Belfast 1849- 1960*. Belfast, University of Ulster.

Cornubrian newspaper Cornwall (1906) 15 September, p 4, col. 3.

Cowser, Andrew (1995) 'Bendhu – the Modernist Masterpiece Revisited' *Perspective*, Vol 3 No 5 (May / Jun) pp 20-23.

Cowser, Andrew (1997) 'Newton Penprase and Bendhu' *Cornwall Today*, summer edition, pp 12-14.

Cowser, Andrew (2004) 'Bendhu Renaissance' *Ulster Architect* Vol 20 No 7 (September) pp 7-11.

Curtis, William (1996) *Modern Architecture since 1900*. London, Phaidon Press.

Daily Express (1959) 10 August, 'The Battleship goes up'.

Day, Angelique et al (eds) (1994) *Ordnance Survey Memoirs of Ireland, Volume twenty-four ... North Antrim Coast and Rathlin*. Belfast and Dublin, Queen's University of Belfast in association with the Royal Irish Academy.

Evans, David (1977) *An Introduction to Modern Ulster Architecture*. Belfast, Ulster Architectural Heritage Society.

Evans, David et al (2006) *Modern Ulster Architecture*. Belfast, Ulster Architectural Heritage Society.

Frampton, Kenneth (1985) *Modern Architecture: a Critical History*. London, Thames & Hudson.

Friers, Rowel (1994) *Drawn from Life: an Autobiography*. Belfast, Blackstaff Press. pp 87-88, 92-93.

Harwood, Elaine (2002) 'The Sixties, life, style, architecture', *Twentieth Century Architecture 6*. p 70.

Hewitt, John and Catto, Mike (1977) *Art in Ulster*. Belfast, Blackstaff Press.

Higgins, A M (c.1977-1980) *History of Bendhu*. Unpublished dissertation, Ulster Polytechnic.

Irish Times (1977) 3 February. Review of Newton Penprase exhibition, by Ray Rosenfield.

Johnson, Roy (1977) *All his Own Work: Newton Penprase*. Belfast, Arts Council of Northern Ireland, exhibition catalogue.

Lambton, Lucinda (1996) *A to Z of Britain*. London, Harper Collins. pp 15-16.

Lampugnani, Vittorio M (ed) (1986) *The Thames and Hudson Encyclopaedia of 20th Century Architecture*. London, Thames & Hudson.

Larmour, Paul (1973) 'Bendhu House', *Big A3 magazine*, 3, May Department of Architecture, The Queen's University of Belfast.

Larmour, Paul (1987) *Belfast – an Illustrated Architectural Guide*. Belfast, Friar's Bush Press.

Larmour, Paul (1992) *The Arts & Crafts Movement in Ireland*. Belfast, Friar's Bush Press.

Larmour, Paul (1997) 'Style Master' *Perspective: Journal of the Royal Society of Ulster Architects* Vol 5 No 6 (July / August) pp 18-31.

Le Corbusier (1927), English edition) *Towards a New Architecture*. Translated from the original *Vers une architecture*, by Frederick Etchells.

Mac Cullagh, Richard (1958) *Vikings' Wake.* London, Van Nostrand.

Mac Cullagh, Richard (1992) *The Irish Currach Folk.* Dublin, Wolfhound Press.

McIntosh, Gillian (2006) *Belfast City Hall: One Hundred Years.* Belfast, Blackstaff Press and Belfast City Council.

Maguire, William A (1991) *Caught in Time: the photographs of Alex Hogg of Belfast 1870-1939.* Belfast, Friar's Bush Press.

Moss & Hume (1986) *Shipbuilders to the World: 125 years of Harland & Wolff, Belfast 1861-1986.* Belfast, Blackstaff Press.

Overy, Paul *et al* (2000) 'Post-War Houses' *Twentieth Century Architecture 4.* pp 8-18.

Peter, C Thurson (1904) *Mate's Illustrated Redruth.* Bournemouth, Mate & Sons.

Powers, Alan (1997) *John Campbell: Rediscovery of an Arts and Crafts Architect.* London, the Prince of Wales's Institute of Architecture.

Powers, Alan (2005) *Modern: the Modern Movement in Britain.* London, Merrell.

Powers, Alan (2007) *Britain: Modern architectures in history.* London, Reaktion Books.

'Richard Mac Cullagh 1913-2000: an Appreciation' *Stranmillis Bulletin* (2000) Issue No.18.

Rudofsky, Bernard (1964) *Architecture without Architects.* London, Academy Editions.

Snoddy, Theo (2002) *Dictionary of Irish Artists: 20th Century.* Dublin, Merlin Publishing. pp 521-522.

Thompson, M Kirk (1987): *Knowledge from Naiveté: a Study and Analysis of the work of Naive Artists and Architects.* Unpublished dissertation for the Diploma of Advanced Architectural Studies, Queen's University Belfast.

Ulster Museum (1986) *A Concise Catalogue of Drawings, Paintings and Sculptures in the Ulster Museum.* Belfast, Ulster Museum. pp 72, 133.

Warncke, C (1991) *The Ideal as Art: De Stijl 1917-1931.* Cologne, Taschen.

Weston, Richard (1996) *Modernism.* London, Phaidon Press.

Yorke, Francis R S (1937) *The Modern House.* London, Architectural Press.

Picture Credits

The author and publishers wish to thank the individuals and institutions who have provided drawings and photographic material for use in this book and granted permission to reproduce them. Every effort has been made to trace and contact the copyright holders before publication but the publishers will be glad to make good any errors or omissions brought to our attention in future editions.

We are grateful to the following for permission to reproduce illustrative material:

NICHOLAS ALLEN
PP 52, 53, 142, 184, 185.

BILL BANNISTER
8.7, 8.9.

DONALD CARSTAIRS
7.6.

CORNISH STUDIES LIBRARY
Images courtesy of Cornish Studies Library, Redruth (Cornwall Council)
1.8, 1.9, 13.3.

IVAN EWART
5.4, 9.9, 11.8, 12.3, 12.13, and studio photographs for Appendix 2.

MICHAEL FERGUSON
5.2, 6.2, 9.2-9.8, 10.1, 10.3-10.5, 10.7, 10.8, C.20, 12.4-12.15, AND PP 128-129, 140-141, 199.

JOE FITZGERALD
5.6, C.16.

ROWEL FRIERS
2.4–2.6.

WILLIAM GALBRAITH
FRONT COVER, 11.1, A.30.

JOHN GILBERT
5.9, 6.3, 6.4.

IMRAY LAURIE NORIE & WILSON
5.1.

TIM KOSTER:
Instituut Collectie Nederland / Amsterdam, Rijswwiijk (ICN)
11.9.

PAUL LARMOUR
PP 174–175

ROBERT MCKINSTRY
6.5, 6.9, 12.1, 12.2, AND PP 69, 92–93.

ANTHONY CW MERRICK
6.10, 9.11, 9.12, 10.2, 12.9, C.12, C.13, C.17–C.19, AND PP 74, 87, 194–195.

MINACK THEATRE TRUST
12.11.

ORDNANCE SURVEY
Licence No. 545
5.2.

DAVID PENPRAZE & ESTATE OF NEWTON PENPRASE
1.2, 1.4, 1.5, 1.13, 3.2, 3.5–3.7, 3.9–3.12, 6.1, 6.11, 7.1, A.6–A.14, A.19–A.26, C15, AND PP 18–19, 96–97, 119, 152–153, 157, 207.

RIBA LIBRARY PHOTOGRAPHS COLLECTION
11.11.

ULSTER MUSEUM
Photographs reproduced courtesy of the Trustees of the National Museums Northern Ireland, collection Ulster Museum:
2.2, A.15–A.18, A.28, A.29, AND PP 154–155.

V&A IMAGES
(Victoria & Albert Museum, London)
1.10–1.12 AND PP 150–151.

NUALA WADE
8.1, 8.2, 8.5.

Other photographs in the book were taken by the author, Andrew Cowser

Index

Emboldened page ranges refer to chapters;

italicised page numbers refer to illustrations.

C locators refer to colour illustrations pp 149-164.

Entries refer to works of Newton Penpraze and Bendhu unless otherwise indicated.

A

Academy of Arts, Royal (London), 147
Adam, Peter, 179
"All his own Work" (exhibition), 37, 90
Allen, Fred, *18–19*
Allen, Nicholas, *143*
Anglesea, Martyn, 99
Antrim County Council, 51
Antrim, North, **38–47**
Antrim Road, no. 736, Belfast, 176
Apollo Pavilion, Co. Durham, 192, *196*, 197
Architects' Journal, 121
Ardhowen Arts Centre, Enniskillen, 147
Art and Design Matters, 25
Art Deco, 61, 80, 178, 187, 192
    furnishings, 133
    gateposts, 73
    ironmongery, 83
Art in Ulster (J. Hewitt), x, 25, 166
Art Nouveau, 77
Arts and Crafts, 80, 187, 192
Arts Council of N.I., 88, 90
Arup, Ove, 179
Ash Green, Antrim, 121

B

Ballintoy, Co. Antrim, 38, *39*, 45, *050*, 127
    Regatta, 83
Ballintoy Painting School, 84, *85*
Ballintoy Port, *51*
Ballycastle, Co. Antrim, ix
Ballycastle Council, 44, 50, 51
Bannister, William James, 113, 118
    1986 survey by, *111*, 171, 181
Beaumont, Ivor, *18–19*, 20, 22, 25, 47
Belfast Art Society, 23, 24
Belfast College of Art, **14–25**, 75–77, 90, 102
Belfast Museum and Gallery, 23
Belfast News-Letter, 22, 25

Belfast School of Art see Belfast College
  of Art
Belfast Telegraph, 98, 99, 103, 115, 118
Belfast Zoo, 177
Bendhu
  site and early design, 50–69
  1936 building plan, *52*, *184*
  construction and decorative work, 70–87
  1986 survey, *53*, *111*, 171, 181, *184*
  media coverage, 88–99
  design elements, 180–99
  owned by Richard Mac Cullagh, 102–19
  purchased and refurbished by Fergusons, 120–35
  extended, 136–47
  with Ferguson's renovations completed, C.17–C.20, *125*
  possible design influences, 166–79
  1992 historic listing, 113–14
  author's impressions, 200–207
  Ben Dhu Experience, The (Mac Cullagh), 118
Bermuda (ocean liner), 86
Big A3 Magazine, 89, 90
Blight's Row, Cornwall, 2
Bloomsbury Group, 188
Boyd, David, 176
Brett, Sir Charles, x, 115, 116, 118
Brooks, Linda, 135
Brown, Sir Percival, *88*
Bubble of Life (painting), 98
Buildings of County Antrim (Brett), x

C

Cade, Rowena, 187, *188*, 198
Camborne, Cornwall, 2, 203
Campbell, John, 204
Campbell, Noel, 121
Campbell, W.J. & Son, 37
Carn Brea Castle, *4*, 203, 206

Carn Brea, Cornwall, 3, 13, 201, 202
Carstairs, Donald, 89, 91
Casson, Sir Hugh, 135
Catto, Mike, 14, 16, 25
Cenotaph, Belfast City Hall, *33*, *35*
Chareau, Pierre, 193
Chermayeff, Serge, 172
Cheval, Ferdinand, 179
Cleaver Gardens, no. 4, 176, *177*
'Coast' television programme, 145, 147
Coastguard Cottages, Ballintoy, 50
Connell and Ward (architects), 172
Construction Employers Federation, 122
Corbusier, 168, 169, 172, 177, 179
Cornubrian newspaper, 13
Cornwall County Council, 203
Cowser, Andrew, 147
Cowser, Ben, viii, 27, 47
Craig, Dan, 118
Crow's Nest, 139, *191*
Cubism, 192
Cupples, Jeffrey, 130
Curl, James Stevens, 25
Cycle of Life (painting), 89

D

Daily Express, *54*, 63, 64, 145
Dawson, George Alexander, 39
De Stijl movement, 170, 172, 178
Dibble, James, *18–19*
Dudley Zoo, 179
Dunstanville, Lord de, 3, 202

E

E1027 house (Gray), 169
Effort Moderne Gallery, Paris, 179
Environment, Department of, 113, 123
  Historic Buildings Branch, 115
Erebus and Nox, *81*
Esler, David, 134

Euterpe (stained glass window), *C.8*
Evans, David, 115, 179

F

Ferguson, F.T. & Co., 120
Ferguson, Michael and Lorna, vii, xi, 75, 98, 117, **120–35**
  extend Bendhu, **136–47**
  impact on Bendhu design, 190–91
Fitzgerald, Joe, 68
Floral Hall, Belfast, 176–77
Foster Associates, 147
Friers, Rowel, 17, 20, 21, 25
Fry, Maxwell, 173
Fry, Roger, 188
Fullerton Arms, 39
Fullerton, Captain, 47
Fullerton, George Cecil Downing, 39–40

G

'Gallery' television programme, 95
Gaudi, Antoni, 77
Gault, Hugh, 176
Geddes, Wilhelmina, 82, 86
Geevor mine, Pendeen, 6–7
Geragh house, Dublin, 177, *178*
German Pavilion, Barcelona (Mies van der Rohe), 168, 169
Gesamtkunstwerke (Total Work of Art), 77, 178
Gilbert, John, 66, 68
Gilmore, Ken, 130
Gilmore, Raymond, 127
Girvan, Donald, 115
Glencraig Manor, Antrim, 122
Goldberg, Marie (later Penpraze) (daughter-in-law), 33, 37
Gordon Bowe, Nicola, 86
Grasmere Gardens, no. 22, Belfast, **26–37**, 47, 173

Gray, Eileen, 169
Gropius, Walter, 172

H
Hatrick, Colin, 115
Hewitt, John, x, 17, 25
Higgins, A.M., 86
Hinds, Claire (later Mac Cullagh), 103, 118
Historic Buildings (Dept. of Environment), 115, 118
Hodge, Francis, 83
Horta, Victor, 77
Housden House, London, 192, 193, 197
House Builders' Council, National, 121
Housing Acts (N.I.), 27, 120

I
International Style, 123
Ireland, Republic of, 177
Irish Currach Folk, The (MacCullagh), 105
Irish Times, 94, 99

J
John, Augustus, 172
Johnson, Philip, 123
Johnson, Roy, 83, 86, 90, 91, 204, 206

K
Kelly's Directory, 206
Knox, John, *88*

L
Lagan Vale Terracotta Works, 89
Larmour, Paul, 89, 99, 118, 135, 179
Lavery, Sir John, 24
Leger, Fernand, 172
Lisburn Technical College, 102
Lismoyne Park, no. 20, Belfast, 173,
  174–75
Loos, Adolf, 169, 170, 179
Lubetkin, Berthold, 172, 179
Luke, John, *18–19*
Lyons, Eric, 121

M
McCaw, Raymond, 130
Mac Cullagh, Claire (née Hinds), 103
Mac Cullagh, Richard, vi, xi, 98, 146, 198
  impact on Bendhu design, 188–89
  Michael Ferguson meets, 124
  ownership of Bendhu, **102–19**
  pays tribute to Newton Penprase, 204
MacCullagh, Richard P.L., vi, 109, 117
McCurdy, Daniel, 40, 44, 50, 51
McDonald, Angus, *91*
McGeagh, John, 187
McGonaghie, William George, 68
McGrath, Raymond, 172
McKinstry, Robert and Cherith, 92
Mackintosh, Charles R., 77
MacNeice, Louis, 26
McNeice, Mildred (later Penprase) (wife), 26, 37
Madonna and Child (relief), *207*
Maison de Verre, Paris, 193
Malcomson, A.P.W., 47
Manogue, Laurence, 115
Mansfield, Edward, *18–19*
Maritime panel, 70–71
Marr, Edward, *18–19*
Mendelsohn, Erich, 172
Middleton, Colin, 98
Mies van der Rohe, Ludwig, 168–69
Millfield Foundry, 86, 186
Minack Theatre, Cornwall, 187, *189*
Modern House, The (Yorke), 121, 179
Moderne style, 45, 183
Modernism, 136, 190, 192, 200
  in architecture, 166–67, 172, 193
Moneypenny, Sir Frederick, 34
Moonlight (watercolour), 89
Morton award, Sir Stanley, 135
Mount Druid dolmen, 72
Mullarkey, Tom, 147
Müller House, Prague (Loos), 170
Municipal Technical Institute, Belfast, 14, 15, *17*, 25
Murray, William, *18–19*
Mystic (sculpture), 83, 98

N
Naturalists' Field Club, Belfast, 145
Neill, Sandra and Des, 132
Neptune group, 70–71, 91
Neutra, Richard, 123
Newlyn house, 29, 37
Nicholson, Christopher, 172
Nicolson, Harold, 198
nothingtoseehere.net, 198

O
Omega Workshops, 188, 198
Overy, Paul, 198

P
Pain and Fear (drawings), 98
Pasmore, Victor, 197, 198
Penguin Pool, London Zoo, 179
Penprase, Mildred (wife), xi, 88
Penprase, Newton, vi, x, xi, *18–19*, 23
  aged 17, 3
  early years, **2–13**
  Belfast School of Art career, **14–25**
  passport photo, *036*
  construction and decoration of Bendhu, **70–87**
  in 1965, *69*

recognition and final years, **88–99**
Penprase, Richard Henry (father), 2, 5, 8, 13
Penprase, William Richard Newton (son), 37
Penpraze, David (grandson), vi, 68, *96*, 99, 198
  inherits Bendhu, 108
  installs electricity in Bendhu, 60
  on Newton Penprase's accident, 94
Penpraze, Richard (son), 26, *29*, 33, 117
  attitude towards Bendhu project, 55
  on McCurdy's initial sale of land to his father, 44, 47
Penpraze, Susan (mother), 2, 5
Pen's Den, *56–57*, 59
  described, 63
  remembered by Richard P.L. MacCullagh, 110
  remodelled, 137, 139
  and window design, 171
Peterlee, Co. Durham, 197, 198
Phoenix Rising, 70–71, *119*, *127*, 186
Pilgrim's Chorus, Tannhauser (painting), C.8
Piper, Raymond, 20, 77
Poems of Love and War (Mac Cullagh), 117
Portrait of a Lady (painting), 133
Portrait of a Miner (sculpture), 5, 6
Powers, Alan, 206
Praeger, Rosamund, 37
Prometheus ceiling, 82
Pym, Francis, 123

Q

Queen's University Belfast, 25, 89, 115, 117, 182

R

Rainey House, Portrush, 121

Rathlin Island, *40*
Rathmoyle Home, Ballycastle, 94, 95, 99
Raumplan, 170, 179
Redruth, Cornwall, **2–13**, 201, 203
Redruth School of Mines, 5, 9, 13, 90
Reverie (sculpture), 89
Rietveld, Gerrit, 171, 193
Rodia, Simon, 179
Rosenfield, Ray, 94, 96

S

Sackler Galleries, 147
Sackville-West, Vita, 198
Saltdean, England, 172, 179
Schmidt, Clarence, 179
Schröder House, Utrecht, 171, 193
Scott, Michael, 177
Scott, William, 98
Secessionist architecture, 77
Sissinghurst Castle, Kent, 198
Slade School of Art, 12
Smyth House, Portstewart, 121
Soane, John, 15
St. Ann's Hill, Chertsey, 172–73
St. Martin's Church, Camborne, 9
St. Michael's Mount, Penzance, 13
Stevenson, Samuel, 15
Stewart, Alexander, 39
Stormont, 34
Stoupe, Seamus, *18–19*
Stranmillis Bulletin, 118
Stranmillis College, 103, 108
Sun-Fish Hunt (Mac Cullagh), *104*
Sun House, Hampstead, 173

T

Taggart, Lyle, 130
Tent Green, Co. Antrim, 50
Thomas, Sir Alfred Brumwell, 33, 34

Thompson, M. Kirk, 179
Thornely, Arnold, 34
Total Work of Art (*Gesamtkunstwerke*), 77, 178
Towards a New Architecture (Corbusier), 179
Twentieth Century Argonauts, The (Mac Cullagh), 117
Twentieth Century Society, xi, 179
Tzara, Tristan, 169

U

Ulster Academy of Arts, Royal, 23, 98
Ulster Architect, 147
Ulster Architectural Heritage Society, 145
Ulster Arts Club, *88*, 89, 99, 117
Ulster College of Art and Design, 25
Ulster Museum, 83, 91, 123
Ulster Polytechnic, 25
Ulster, University of, 15, 25, 145
University College, London, 12

V

van Doesburg, Theo, 170, 171
van Eesteren, Cor, 170
Victoria & Albert Museum, 10, 13, 90
Vikings' Wake (Mac Cullogh), 104
Villa Savoie, Poissy (Corbusier), 168, 169
Voysey, Charles, 77

W

Wagner, Otto, 77
Wagner, Richard, 77
Wallis, H.C., 10
Warwick, James, 14
Watson, Tommy, 86
Weston, Richard, 179
White House, Knockagh, *121*, *122*, 123, *124*, 147

White Park Bay, 38, *39*
Whitla Hall, Queen's University, 182, *186*
Workman, Clark, 86
World War I, 24
Wright, Frank Lloyd, 121

Y
Yorke, F.R.S., 121, 179
Young and Mackenzie, architects, 36, 173

Z
Zodiac ceiling, *C.10–C.13*, 80, 91, 109